75 Years of Universal Monsters

A Complete Guide to the Appearances of
the Famous Monsters of Hollywood

John L. Flynn, Ph.D.

Galactic Books
Owings Mills, Maryland

Galactic Books
Post Office Box 1442
Owings Mills, Maryland 21117-9998

75 Years of Universal Monsters
By John L. Flynn, Ph.D.

PRINTING HISTORY
Second Edition / September 2019

Acknowledgements: Most of the photographs used in this book were issued by the original production companies at the time of the release for publicity purposes, and we make no claim as to ownership or copyright. We are simply reproducing them for the purpose that they were originally intended. Most of the photos are courtesy of Universal Pictures, and we are extremely grateful for their use.

A special, limited edition of this book was produced
for the 2006 San Diego Comic Con.

Editor: Nicholas Carraway
Design & Layout: John L. Flynn
Cover Design: John L. Flynn

Library of Congress Cataloging in Publication Data
Flynn, John L. 75 Years of Universal Monsters
1. Universal's Monsters--History and criticism. I. Horror films--History and criticism. II. Dracula, Frankenstein, Wolf Man themes, etc. III. Title.

ISBN: 0-9769400-6-X

PRINTED IN THE UNITED STATES OF AMERICA

10 9 8 7 6 5

Table of Contents

Dedication:

To the memory of
Lon Chaney, Bela Lugosi
and Boris Karloff,
the men behind the monsters.

Introduction: Of Gods & Monsters

To a new world of Gods and Monsters!
—William Hurlbut, "Bride of Frankenstein" (1935)

They were like Gods.

Count Dracula, Frankenstein's Monster, the Phantom of the Opera, the Bride of Frankenstein, the Wolf Man, the Mummy, the Invisible Man, and the Creature from the Black Lagoon formed a modern-day pantheon that ruled the mythical kingdom of Hollywood. They dwelled at Universal, their Olympian-like home nestled in the hills of northern Los Angeles. Their stories were the stuff of legend in the most successful horror films ever made. From 1931 to 1956, twenty-five golden years, these famous monsters of filmland head-lined box office marquees around the world. In the last fifty years, their influence has had a profound effect on George Lucas, Steven Spielberg, Peter Jackson, and those others who create the entertain-ment that we enjoy today. These Gods and Monsters are the immor-tals that we celebrate on this seventy-fifth anniversary of the Golden Age of the horror film.

Before the 1930s and the advent of sound, the horror genre was a loose collection of experimental films that were occasionally in-spired, like Wiene's "The Cabinet of Dr. Caligari" (1919) or Murnau's "Nosferatu" (1922), but more often than not overwrought, and relegated by critics to secondary status. With "The Hunchback of Notre Dame" (1923) and "The Phantom of the Opera" (1925), however, Universal Pictures under the leadership of Carl Laemmle seized upon a formula for success. By pairing a well-known actor, like Lon Chaney, with literary source material that had elements of the fantastic, Laemmle felt he could create a series of moderately-budgeted movies that would appeal to a broad audience. They were better known as creature-features. His idea would not only give birth to Universal's great monsters but also launch the horror genre.

The first of these films, "Dracula," debuted on February 14, 1931, and its phenomenal over-night success was a Valentine gift from moviegoers to Carl Laemmle Jr. that meant he had succeeded in his father's place. His follow-up film, "Frankenstein," premiered several months later on November 21, 1931. When that picture broke all of the previous box office records that had been set by "Dracula," Universal saw that as a mandate from the public to make more films just like them. Subsequently, the company unleashed mummies (starting with "The Mummy," 1932), invisible men (starting with "The Invisible Man," 1933), and werewolves (starting with "The Werewolf of London," 1935) to join Dracula and Frankenstein's monster in scaring up box office dollars. Other monsters soon followed as the Junior Laemmle dug deep into the vaults for other literary sarcophagi. They included the Bride of the Monster in "The Bride of Frankenstein" (1935), cursed Larry Talbot in "The Wolf Man (1941), the Opera Ghost in "The Phantom of the Opera" (1943), and the Gill-Man in "The Creature from the Black Lagoon" (1954).

Boris Karloff, Bela Lugosi, Claude Rains, John Carradine, and Lon Chaney Jr. became household names as the first horror stars, and came to represent a certain kind of motion picture that only Universal could make. Their creature-features were not only good for a first-time chill but could also be seen again and again, savored like a fine wine. Unlike most movies from the same time period, they have actually improved with age. And even the company itself, famous for its magnificent backlot, created an indelible image of what 19th century Europe should look like. Universal Europe was where the plains of Vasaria one day would become transformed into the moors of Llanwelly the next. These familiar faces and familiar places created a familiar world that made audiences feel fright at home.

When the last of Universal's monsters, the Creature from the Black Lagoon, walked among us in 1956, the horror film had run its course, and was replaced for a short time by its nearest relative, the science fiction film. Universal still continued to thrill audiences with the greatest of Alfred Hitchcock's thrillers, and even dabbled in science fiction, adding a handful of atom age monsters to its roster of creature-features with "This Island Earth" (1955), "Tarantula" (1955), and "The Deadly Mantis" (1957). But the Golden Age of Universal's great monsters had given way into legend.

For those not old enough to have seen "Dracula" or "Frankenstein" on the big screen, the first showings of these films on television helped acquaint a whole new generation with the most famous vampire, the most infamous mad scientist, and their companions. I was part of that baby-boom generation that hungered for anything and everything that celebrated the exploits of our modern-day gods. And we turned to Forry Ackerman's *Famous Monsters of Filmland* magazine (started in 1958) as our bible and source for adoration. Each issue was packed with dozens of rarely seen vintage photos and behind the scenes stories about our favorite horror films. We also bought our first 8mm movie projectors so that we could run Castle Films edited versions of the Universal classics whenever we wanted.

Audiences soon tired of Count Dracula and Frankenstein's Monster and the Wolf Man, and replaced them with Norman Bates and Michael Myers, Jason and Freddy, the Alien and the Predator. But despite the change in tastes, the legacy of Carl Laemmle Jr. and his great monsters continued to live on in other forms and other films. Steven Spielberg's shark in "Jaws" (1975), particularly in the film's memorable opening, was none other than the Creature making a return engagement. On Broadway and in the film adaptations they have subsequently inspired, both Dracula and the Phantom of the Opera have returned from the dead. The Invisible Man has "appeared" in several television shows. Frankenstein's Monster has donned a top hat and tails for an encore performance. Even the Mummy has crawled out of his sarcophagus for two additional curtain calls, in "The Mummy" (1999) and "The Mummy Returns" (2001).

In "House of Frankenstein" (1944), Professor Bruno Lampini as portrayed by George Zucco declared, "I have here a collection of the world's most astounding horrors." Of course, as a carnival barker for a most unique kind of circus, he speaks in absolute terms to attract an audience. But his words resonate to this day, and remind us that the great monsters and their legacy of great horror films are always with us…as a collection of wonderful memories and treasured shudders from a bygone era of Gods and Monsters. This book is a loving tribute to those famous monsters of Universal Pictures.

In terms of chronology, I know that Dracula, followed closely by Frankenstein's Monster, was the first. But instead I begin with Lon Chaney's Phantom of the Opera, without whom none of the other monsters would have existed. The 1925 version of "The Phantom of the Opera" established the pattern that all of the other films would eventually follow. I also conclude with chapters featuring the Creature and those other atom age monsters that make up Universal's second wave of monsters. I hope you will enjoy reading the book as much as I enjoyed writing it.

John L. Flynn, Ph.D.
February 29, 2004

1

The Phantom of the Opera

*The Opera ghost really existed. He was not, as was
long believed, a creature of the imagination of the artists, the superstition of the managers, or a product of
the absurd and impressionable brains of the young ladies of the ballet, their mothers, the box-keepers, the
cloak-room attendants or the concierge. Yes, he existed
in flesh and blood, although he assumed the complete
appearance of a real phantom.*
—Gaston Leroux, Le Fantôme de l'Opera (1911)

Mention *The Phantom of the Opera* at a dinner party or other
social gathering, and each guest will have his or her own vivid, almost visceral recollection of the tale of a disfigured musical genius
and his unrequited love for a beautiful, young singer. Someone will
undoubtedly pantomime the famous scene from the silent era film in
which Mary Philbin (as Christine Daae) sneaks up behind the Phantom, while he is playing the organ in his subterranean lair, and unmasks the great Lon Chaney, revealing his horribly disfigured face to
the audience and her. Another guest is likely to burst into song, recalling "The Music of the Night" from the Andrew Lloyd Webber
musical. Still another guest will strike the pose of Erik as the Masque
of the Red Death at the masked ball, while yet another may describe
the scene in which the Phantom cuts the cables free and sends the
magnificent chandelier crashing down upon the patrons of the Paris

Opera House. The original story contains so many richly textured scenes that each of us, at one time or another, has been seduced by the Phantom, and embraced the dark, labyrinthine world of author Gaston Leroux.

For many, the love affair with Erik—that masked "phantom" of the Paris Opera House—began in 1925, with the first of many imaginative thrillers Carl Laemmle produced for Universal Studios; for others, it was more than a decade ago when a youthful Michael Crawford emerged from behind the mirror, swept Sarah Brightman (as Christine Daae) off her feet, and carried her down into his lair below the playhouse; for recent filmgoers, it was the moment Gerard Butler took Emmy Rossum into his arms in Joel Schumacher's Hollywood spectacular. Few others have actually encountered the Phantom in print, and yet *Le Fantôme de l'Opera* has inspired more than a dozen films, two television movies, one miniseries, several stage productions, and a Tony award-winning musical--45 productions in all. However, the question of the ninety-five year-old novel's popularity provides many elusive answers. Why would the tragic tale of a disfigured composer and his love for a young opera singer—a story clearly rooted in the annals of Victorian melodrama—continue to remain such a favorite subject for adaptation?

Perhaps the reason for its longevity and prolificacy has to do with a message that is universal: the beauty or darkness of the human soul should not be measured by outward appearances or deformities. Or perhaps it has something to do with myth and our collective unconscious. Though the original classic by Frenchman Monsieur Gaston Leroux is a fairly recent entry (published in 1911), the origins of the Phantom's story may be traced directly back to much earlier forms in legend and folklore. Or perhaps it has more to do with our love of creative individualists who, though they are often portrayed as villains, reflect our inner desire to rebel against conformity. Whichever the case, we have embraced the Phantom of the Opera and allowed his deeply rooted, mythic tale to be a ubiquitous part of our popular culture. The purpose of this book is to expose the various guises of the Phantom and to discover why its nearly one-hundred year-old story continues to entertain us.

Part horror story, part historical romance, and part detective thriller, the story of the masked musical genius who lives beneath the Paris Opera House is certainly a familiar one to millions of readers and moviegoers. But in all fairness to Gaston Leroux's classic tale, the terms "horror" story or "monster" story are largely inappropriate. "Horror," by definition, suggests an intense, painful feeling of revulsion or loathing, and "monster" conjures images of an offensive grotesque

who commits perverse acts of random violence. These terms might more amply describe the bestselling potboilers of Stephen King or Dean Koontz, or the splatter films of Herschel Gordon Lewis or Tobe Hooper, but certain not the work of Monsieur Leroux or his greatest creation, the Opera Ghost.

Alone, misunderstood, shunned by those who see him, Erik the Phantom is certainly no monster; his acts of violence are committed solely for the woman he loves and to protect his world of anonymity. In fact, this much more contemporary version of the "Beauty and the Beast" fable rightly belongs in a class by itself or, at the very least, with the select group of imaginative, Victorian masterpieces that include *Dracula, The Strange Case of Dr. Jekyll and Mr. Hyde,* and *The Adventures of Sherlock Holmes.*

Because *The Phantom of the Opera* draws from such a rich literary heritage, questions about the nature of beauty and ugliness, good and evil, creativity and conformity elevate most of our recollections of the book or its many other incarnations above the commonplace. Joseph Campbell, in his treatise on the power of myth in literature [*The Hero With a Thousand Faces*], recognized that man chose certain archetypes and symbols to deal with those questions. Clearly, several archetypal or symbolic characters from the last two hundred years have provided the mythopoetic basis (and are forerunners) of Leroux's doomed, musical genius. Aylmer, the alchemist in Hawthorne's "The Birthmark," is the archetype for the first mad scientist and a symbol for those misguided individuals who equate beauty with goodness and ugliness with evil. Shocked by his wife's "visible mark of earthly imperfection"—a symbol in his mind of mankind's fallen nature—he takes drastic steps to remove the ugliness. Tragically, he fails to recognize that her beauty extends beyond the physical plane, and his experiments contribute only to her death. The Beast, in the classic children's fable, is visually repulsive; he is described as a creature "so frightful to look upon that men would faint in fear." But inwardly, his soul reflects kindness, gentility, and unselfish devotion to his beloved. By sharp contrast, Beauty's two sisters who are very pretty have cold hearts and cruel dispositions. In fact, when Beauty agrees to live with the Beast in order to spare her father's life, they berate and torment her with the knowledge that they have married handsome, clever husbands. Befittingly, Beauty's love breaks the old curse and transforms the Beast into a handsome prince, reminding all of us "a true heart is better than either good looks or clever brains."

Erik the Phantom believes that old French fable and goes to great lengths to insure that he will live "happily ever after" with the woman of his dreams. Unfortunately, his idealistic, fairy-tale vision of love is out of place in the real world. No matter how kind, gentle, and well intentioned the great composer and musical tutor may be, he fails to consider Christine's feelings. Later, distraught over her decision to love another man, the Phantom abandons all traditional avenues of courtship to pursue his own maniacal desires for her. Erik is, after all, a product of his own environment; his "birthmark" represents an outward manifestation of evil to all those who behold him, and he becomes the monster that they all believe him to be. Abducting the young opera singer, he demands that she remain in his labyrinthine world below the Paris Opera House as his wife in exchange for her lover's life. Christine accepts his unholy bargain and, in doing so, transforms Erik. Although he does not change into a "handsome prince," he begins to understand the real meaning of love. Still outwardly hideous, Erik reveals the true beauty of his soul by allowing the woman he loves to go off with his rival.

Thematically, the Phantom story also concerns the struggle of the individual to express creativity in a world that rejects his passion for life. Those roots of nonconformity lie not only in the "Beauty and the Beast" fable and the classic novel by Gaston Leroux, but also in older, literary conventions and attitudes from Greco-Roman mythology and

medieval folklore. Both the legend of Orpheus and the story of Phineus are parables of human presumption—about artists who struggle against the will of god for the love of a woman—that predate the Phantom story by some five thousand years. Orpheus, the Thracian poet whose music moved even inanimate objects, descends into the subterranean regions of Hades (and crosses the Stygian river) to parlay with the devil for the release of his wife at the cost of great suffering and eternal damnation. When he returns without her, infuriated Thracian citizens tear him to pieces. Phineus (Caliban in some traditions) loses his betrothed Andromeda to the handsome Perseus because he cannot invoke the muse of lyric poetry (Euterpe) to save her from the sea monster. Both acts challenge the natural order of things, and both individuals suffer similar punishment from the gods for their arrogance. Similarly, the medieval story of Dr. Faustus (or "Faust")—which is often fused (or confused) with Leroux's novel in cinematic traditions—portrays a man who is willing to sell his soul to the devil in exchange for the answers to the mysteries of the universe. "Faust", like Orpheus and Phineus, defies the gods (or, in this case, a Judeo-

Christian god), and only the love of Helen (the woman "whose face launched a thousand ships") can save him from eternal damnation. These familiar stories of struggling, passionate artists and their demonic pacts contribute much to our understanding of the circumstances behind Erik's tragic tale.

Like its mythological, legendary, or literary precursors, the theatrical translations of the last ninety years have relied heavily upon many of the same traditions and themes for inspiration. This continued use of common elements, familiar archetypes, and set symbols has certainly not diminished the audience's enduring affection for Leroux's story; but, rather, it has enriched the material with a variety of ingenious and imaginative narrative approaches. After all, how many times can the same story be told if the focal point remains unchanged? Much can be learned about the Phantom, his personality traits, and origins by considering each adaptation as a separate facet or interpretation.

For example, in the 1925 version starring the great Lon Chaney, the Phantom is an escapee from Devil's Island who has been tortured in the dungeons below the playhouse. His motives for revenge and notoriety overshadow all other *rationale de compri*. Both the 1943 and the 1962 versions portray the Phantom as a wholly sympathetic character whose face has been scarred by acid thrown by a rival composer. While he secretly desires to have his musical talents recognized by the owners of the theatre, he works selflessly (behind the scenes) so that the young diva can ascend to greater glory. In 1974's "Phantom of the Paradise," Brian DePalma's satiric rock opera that fuses the legends of "Faust" and the Phantom, Winslow Leach (as the titular character) must contend not

only with exploitative record promoters but also demonic pacts. The Phantom in Andrew Lloyd Webber's Tony award-winning musical and subsequent film is part Valentino and part mad, musical genius. Charming, confident, and seductive, Erik proves more than a match for the lovesick Raoul and nearly succeeds in winning Christine with his "music of the night." His incarnation in the 1989 version (with Robert Englund as the Phantom) is a cold-blooded assassin who dispatches street ruffians, like a Victorian "caped crusader." When Erik fails to win Christine's hand in his own era, he time travels into the present in order to try again. Other Phantoms have included a blood-sucking vampire (in a 1963 film), a disfigured actor haunting a movie studio (in 1974), a classically trained conductor (in 1983), an impresario whose terrible secret is guarded by his father (in 1990), and a young man raised and protected by intelligent rats (in 1998).

And even though the Phantom has worn the same guise (with subtle variations) for eighty years, the face behind the mask has provided audiences with a diversity of characterizations. Lon Chaney, the legendary "man of a thousand faces," evokes pity and fear with a repulsive, macabre, and entirely believable makeover (which the actor alone devised). In fact, the unmasking of Chaney's Phantom by Mary Philbin—considered one of the great moments of the silent cinema—caused many moviegoers in 1925 to faint at the horrible

sight. Claude Rains, a soft-spoken and distinguished British actor, brought much pathos to the role as a shy, middle-aged Phantom. A fellow countryman of Rains, Herbert Lom gave the Phantom a distinctly British flavor with his Shakespearean training and gentlemanly reserve. More recently, however, Michael Crawford's youthful exuberance and romantic charms have added much to his interpretation, while Robert Englund's Erik walks the psychological tightrope between manic-depression and ultra violence. Gerard Butler, Maximilian Schell, Charles Dance, Jack Cassidy, Julian Sands, and others have also contributed their own special acting talents to create other interesting portraits of the Opera Ghost. The greatest of them all was Lon Chaney.

However, with the exception of the 1925 version and the Andrew Lloyd Webber musical, most adaptations have strayed far from the original story as authored by Gaston Leroux. Erik was born with a physical deformity, much like the Elephant Man, and developed a highly intelligent, resourceful, and creative personality in order to compete with "normal" men. Filmmakers have chosen instead to portray the Phantom as a normal man who has suffered an unjust yet accidental disfigurement. Thus, his obsession with Christine and his desire for anonymity could be simplified into a single motive—revenge. The Phantom of the novel was also a master mason and architect who contracted for work on the Paris Opera House and built his world of mazes, trap doors, and secret chambers. Most cinematic and theatrical adaptations, which have focused on the more horrific aspects, have completely failed to explain how Erik became custodian of such a wondrous lair. Leroux's Phantom was also a master of disguise and did travel beyond his sanctuary into the streets of Paris. Only one version (made in 1989) has permitted him to venture out beyond the cellars of the playhouse. Other attempts in the last few years to return the romance and mystery of the original story have proven to be less than successful. Regrettably, the definitive version of *The Phantom of the Opera* has yet to be made; perhaps, it never will be. Perhaps the definitive version is the one that we create in our own minds each time we read Gaston Leroux's words and imagine, just for a moment, that we are the Phantom or Christine alone in the darkest recesses of the Paris Opera House.

Who Was That Masked Man?

In *The Phantom of the Opera*, Gaston Leroux chose to protect the identity of the "Opera Ghost" by referring to him simply as Erik or "the Phantom." Not once does Leroux identify his family name. Though we are given a few details about his background, most of his personal history remains forever cloaked in secrecy. Recent historians and biographers have debated whether his last name was "Destler" or "Claudin" or "Carrier" or "Petrie" based upon obscure records unearthed during a recent excavation of the original site of the Paris Opera House. They have also argued about his birthdate in 1830 or 1831 and whether he came from a working class or aristocratic family. Years of exhaustive research have produced precious little information beyond the material the journalist and news correspondent left us...

Erik was born in September 1830 or 1831 (??) in a small village not far from Rouen, France. His father was a master mason and builder, and his mother was the town's washerwoman. His earliest memory had been of a mask being placed over his head in the cradle to hide his horrific features. As a young boy, his fellow schoolmates tormented Erik because of his facial disfigurement. He ran away from home at the age of thirteen, when the horror and embarrassment of his deformity threatened the very livelihood of his parents. For several years, he appeared in fairs and carnivals as the "living corpse," and traversed the whole of Europe, moving from fair to fair, befriending the other sideshow "freaks." When a greedy showman at the fair of Nijini-Novgorod refused to pay his standard fee, Erik strangled him in his sleep and became a fugitive from justice.

In 1849, he found refuge among the Gypsies, and completed his strange education as an artist, magician, ventriloquist, stage performer, mind reader, and musician. He already sang as nobody on this earth had ever sung before, and soon became one of the Gypsies top performers. In order to protect his identity, Erik assumed a number of elaborate disguises but later relied solely on a mask he fashioned from leather and canvas to hide the look of his "death's head." Word of his astounding acts of ventriloquism and prestidigitation traveled with the caravans returning to Asia, and Erik's reputation quickly reached the attention of the little sultana—the favorite of the Shah-in-Shah of Persia—at the stately palace of Mazenderan.

The daroga of Mazenderan brought Erik to Persia in 1853 to entertain the little sultana, and for several months the Shah extended him every courtesy and luxury imaginable. Unfortunately, Erik had never known such pleasure, and was soon guilty of excesses beyond measure, for he did not know the difference between good and evil. His Majesty recognized his weakness for the good life, and exploited his talents by involving him in a number of political assassinations. Erik was, at first, appalled by the murder of the Emir of Afghanistan and other enemies of the Persian Empire, but in no time at all his diabolical inventiveness proved to be the scourge of the Shah's secret police. Similarly, he had very original ideas about architecture— no doubt learned from his father and the years he spent as a magician—and offered to create a palace for the sovereign so ingenious that "His Majesty would be able to move about in it unseen and to disappear" without detection at will. The Shah ordered him to begin construction on a new palace, but shortly before its completion in the winter of 1856, he decided that Erik and all his laborers should be put to death in order to protect the secrets of his new home. The execution of this abominable decree fell upon the shoulders of the daroga of Mazenderan, who had originally brought Erik to Persia. The daroga felt responsible for him and engineered a way in which he might escape. He then produced a corpse, half-eaten by birds that was found on the shore of the Caspian Sea, to prove that the French architect was indeed dead.

Just as before, Erik was forced to run for his life and sought refuge in Asia Minor, then finally Constantinople where he entered the service of the Sultan. Because of his propensity for disguise, he was employed first as a double for the Sultan. He would appear, dressed like the Commander of the Faithful and resembling him in all respects, at various locations around the country, while the Sultan conducted his affairs or slept. Later, he utilized his talents as a master builder to construct a mighty fortress with trap doors, secret passageways, and hidden chambers for the Sultan. But again, Erik had to flee Con- stantinople for the same reasons that he had left Persia; he knew far too much about the fortress and was now a huge liability.

Tired of his adventurous, formidable and monstrous life, Erik returned to France and sought the simple life of a builder/architect. Like any other contractor, he built "ordinary houses with ordinary bricks." When planning began on the famous Paris Opera House in December of 1860, his construction company tendered a bid for part of the foundation. His estimate was accepted, and he started work on the cellars of the enormous playhouse in the summer of 1861. One day, while reviewing the architectural plans of Charles Garnier (the 35-year old designer), his "artistic, fantastic, wizard nature" took over. Erik dreamed of creating a "dwelling unknown to the rest of the world, where he could hide from men's eyes for all time." It was at that moment he decided to make his dream a reality. Calling upon the talents he had used in the service of the Shah and the Sultan, Erik produced a dark, labyrinthine world of his own below the Paris Opera House—a honeycomb of passages and chambers which linked the mysterious subterranean lake to the theatre above. At night, while dreaming of his new home, he began composing an opera, entitled *Don Juan Triumphant*.

The Ministry of Fine Arts dedicated the state-funded building on January 5, 1875, with an elaborate masked ball, and M. Debienne and M. Poligny took over as the first managers of the Opera House. Not long after, Erik began his career as "creative consultant" (as well as "opera ghost"), demanding an allowance of 20,000 francs a month and a permanent box (Box Five) at his disposal for every performance. Fearful of the consequences, Debienne and Poligny reluctantly agreed to his terms.

Five years later, M. Richard and M. Moncharmin replaced the original managers of the playhouse, but refused to honor the terms of Erik's arrangement, dismissing it as superstitious hokum. Several unexplained deaths and the shattering of the Opera House's famous chandelier quickly persuaded them that the Phantom was real. Although authorities attributed the tragedies to the madness of the "opera ghost," the Vicomte de Chagny knew the awful truth. Jealous of Erik's affection for his fiancée Christine Daae, Raoul enlisted the aid of his brother and a Persian (the former daroga of Mazenderan) to hunt down and destroy "the phantom of the Paris Opera House."

Several months passed while Erik continued to tutor the young opera singer and completed work on his opera *Don Juan Triumphant.* Unfortunately, his hopes of having it produced were dashed by the intrusion of Raoul and the Persian into his secret lair. Erik was driven away (to his death?) before he could enjoy his final triumph. Thirty years later, excavators uncovered the remains of "The Phantom of the Opera." His skeleton was found lying near the little well, where Erik had first held Christine fainting into his trembling arms, on the night when he carried her down to the cellars far below the famous playhouse.

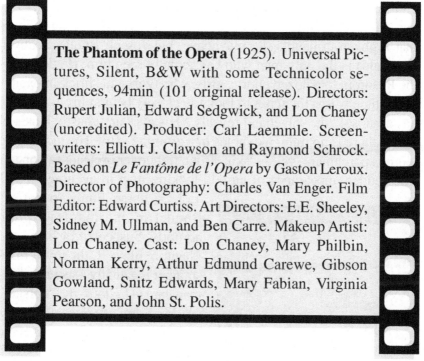

The Phantom of the Opera (1925). Universal Pictures, Silent, B&W with some Technicolor sequences, 94min (101 original release). Directors: Rupert Julian, Edward Sedgwick, and Lon Chaney (uncredited). Producer: Carl Laemmle. Screenwriters: Elliott J. Clawson and Raymond Schrock. Based on *Le Fantôme de l'Opera* by Gaston Leroux. Director of Photography: Charles Van Enger. Film Editor: Edward Curtiss. Art Directors: E.E. Sheeley, Sidney M. Ullman, and Ben Carre. Makeup Artist: Lon Chaney. Cast: Lon Chaney, Mary Philbin, Norman Kerry, Arthur Edmund Carewe, Gibson Gowland, Snitz Edwards, Mary Fabian, Virginia Pearson, and John St. Polis.

Lon Chaney at the Masked Ball

The 1925 version of "The Phantom of the Opera" was (and remains to this day) the best of the cinematic translations of Gaston Leroux's classic 1911 novel. Fraught with production delays, creative disputes, and infighting, the silent picture still managed to transcend its troubled origins to become the biggest box office feature of the year. The film also broke new thematic ground which would have a long-range influence on Universal's horror series. By making the villain a sympathetic character (who functions as both protagonist and antagonist), the adaptation demonstrates considerable insight: Erik the Phantom becomes a monster only after the society which views ugliness as evil has rejected him. But the real strength of the production lies with the incredible performance of Lon Chaney, "the man of a thousand faces." Even though the film may appear "dated," "hokey," "overly melodramatic," or "an antique for collector's only" as some contemporary critics have contended in their recent reviews, Chaney still thrills as the mysterious masked Phantom.

The Screen Story

In the opening reels of the silent film, the presence of an opera ghost is established by inexplicable shadows on the wall or mysterious silhouettes glimpsed for a second in stairwells. Everyone believes that a phantom haunts the playhouse, but Joseph Buquet (Gibson Gowland) is the only man who has actually seen him. He describes the Phantom to a dozen chorus girls, who twirl and shriek in excitement, then warns them not to look too closely behind his mask. "He has no nose!" the stagehand reveals. "His eyes are ghastly beads in which there is no light, like holes in a grinning skull. His face is like leprous parchment, yellow skin strung tight over protruding bones." The sudden appearance of an odd-looking man in evening clothes

and an astrakhan cap causes Buquet to end his description abruptly. Suspected of being the Phantom himself, the mysterious stranger is actually a secret policeman named Ledoux-the "Persian" (Arthur Edmund Carewe). He has been hunting "The Phantom of the Opera" for more than ten years, but is no closer now than when he first started. As Ledoux slips gingerly into the shadows, the chorus girls scurry back to their dressing-rooms in terror.

The Paris Opera House, sanctuary for song lovers, rose nobly over medieval torture chambers and hidden dungeons. Melody floats through its long hallways and dark corridors, even to the executive offices where a strange deal is being closed. Once they have sealed the contract for the sale of the playhouse, Monsieurs Debienne and Poligny warn the new owners about the Phantom. They must abide by the original agreement with the Opera Ghost, or they will face terrors beyond their imagination. Monsieurs Richard and Moncharmin believe that the warning is part of an elaborate practical joke (probably perpetrated by their predecessors), and choose to ignore Debienne and Poligny. No sooner have the former managers departed, however, then Carlotta's mother (Virginia Pearson) appears with a letter from the Phantom. The letter demands that Christine sing the role of Marguerite in "Faust" on Wednesday night, or a major disaster will occur. Outraged, Carlotta's mother insists that her daughter will sing; but when Wednesday night arrives, Carlotta (Mary Fabian) is strangely ill, and Christine Daae (Mary Philbin) has taken her place.

Part of the audience, on Wednesday night, Philippe De Chagny (John Sainpolla) questions his younger brother Raoul (Norman Kerry) about Miss Daae. "I hear a lot of rumors, Raoul. Be careful," he warns him, but the Vicomte is so madly in love with Christine that he ignores his brother's warnings. He hurries backstage, at the conclusion of the performance, and takes the young singer into his arms. Their romantic scene is cut short, when Raoul's sweet words turn to talk of marriage and family. Christine reminds him that she will never leave the opera, and that he must forget about their love. Feeling rejected, Raoul de Chagny leaves her dressing room, and pauses momentarily in the corridor outside. Meanwhile, from hidden places beyond the walls a melodious voice, like the voice of an angel, reminds Christine that he alone has placed the world at her feet. (Raoul listens from the other side of the door with suspicion.) The Phantom promises that all Paris will one day worship her, but the young singer must first forget all worldly pleasures and concentrate on her music. Christine agrees, then insists that "the angel of music" should come to her soon in human form.

A few days later, the new managers receive the first of many notes from the "Phantom" (signed simply O.G., for Opera Ghost). His instructions are very clear: Christine Daae is to be given the lead in their new production, and his box seat is to remain open; otherwise, they face the wrath of the Phantom. Annoyed, they defy his requests and sell box five for all the remaining performances. They then attempt to calm Carlotta and her mother who believe that Christine's friends (notably Philippe and Raoul) are plotting against the diva. Richard and Moncharmin assure them that the new production will feature Carlotta, not Christine. However, when the directors of the Paris Opera House disobey his orders to let the young singer appear on stage, the Phantom becomes angry. Watching from the catwalks high above the stage, he realizes that they must all be taught a lesson in terror. "Behold! She is singing to bring down the chandelier," the Phantom shouts aloud, then sends the giant crystalline chandelier crashing into the audience.

Following the great tragedy, which injures a dozen audience members, the Phantom emerges from the mirror in Christine's dressing room. Dressed in a black cloak and white mask, he quickly hypnotizes the young singer, then directs her through the labyrinth of catacombs and across an underground lake to his hidden lair. Once there, he confesses his love for Christine (which has been aroused by her purity), and warns that she must never attempt to look behind the mask. The Phantom then sits at an organ and plays "Don Juan Triumphant," his own composition, requesting that she accompany him. She refuses, recognizing him as the dreaded opera ghost. He professes to be neither an angel, nor a demon, but simply Erik. "Man's hatred made me the Phantom," he tells her, "but your love redeems me." Overwhelmed by his passion, and finally unable to resist the temptation to see her tutor's face, Christine tears the mask away to reveal the Phantom of the Opera's unholy visage.

"Feast your eyes, glut your soul, on my accursed ugliness!" the Phantom exclaims madly, forcing her to look at him squarely in the face. The young singer fights his grasp and begs for her freedom in the name of love. He reluctantly agrees to let her return to the playhouse, but then reminds Christine that she is forever bound to him. She acknowledges his terms, and promises him that she will never see Raoul again.

One night each year all Paris mingled at the merry, mad Bal Masque de l'Opera. Party goers revel in all manner of costume, while Raoul searches the crowd for his beloved Christine. In the midst of the revelry strode a fearsome figure in crimson cloak and scarlet skull

-Edgar Allan Poe's "Red Death" in primitive, two-tone Technicolor - the Phantom. Everyone stands aside in horror, as he attempts to walk among them and rebuke their merriment. But his grand entrance is foiled by the embrace of the two young lovers. When Erik does finally spot his rival -the Vicomte -and Christine at the top of the steps, he is much too late to prevent them from escaping safely into the darkness.

High above the Paris Opera House, the singer confesses her fear of the Phantom, proclaiming that "he's a monster" and begging Raoul to take her away. The two lovers resolve their petty differences and decide to flee to England after tomorrow night's performance. Unbeknownst to them, the Phantom is perched on a statue of Apollo, high above their heads, and has been listening to every word of the young woman's betrayal. Enraged by what he has heard, Erik curses them both, and tries to prevent the lovers from leaving the roof. When Raoul and Christine attempt to circumvent his wishes, the mysterious Persian intervenes, directing them to an alternate escape route. Further enraged, the Phantom returns to the masked ball to proclaim his superiority over all he surveys, then disappears through a convenient trapdoor.

At nine o'clock the following evening, Raoul arrives with a carriage that will take his beloved to safety immediately after the performance. However, the Phantom has other plans for Christine. Subsequent to poisoning several backstage workers and strangling Joseph Buquet, Erik again abducts the young singer in the midst of her final curtain call. Powerless to stop him, Raoul watches the events unfold before his very eyes in horror, then races backstage moments too late. The Phan-

tom has made a clean getaway with Christine! Ledoux, the mysterious Persian, emerges from the shadows and reveals to the Vicomte that he has been pursuing Erik for over ten years now. He knows how the man operates, and will take Raoul to the singer if he promises to follow his instructions. The young aristocrat agrees, and the two men quickly descend into the cellars below through the mirror in Miss Daae's dressing-room. All the while, they hold their arms up to the level of their eyes, as a precaution against the deadly Punjab lasso the Phantom uses to kill his victims.

Descending into the darkness, they encounter many wild and strange happenings. The two men eventually reach what they think is Erik's lair, and lower themselves inadvertently into a torture chamber, which has no visible means of escape. Meanwhile, in his subterranean lair, the Phantom curses Christine for having betrayed him. All he wanted was to live a normal life with her as his wife. But she wants no part of his nightmare! Angered, Erik forces the young singer to choose between a wedding mass or a requiem, life with him or the death of her lover. "If you turn the scorpion, you have said 'yes' and spared de Chagny," he instructs her to choose between one of two ornamental boxes. "Turn the grasshopper, and the Opera House is blown to a thousand bits!" The Phantom races off to deal with another intruder, leaving Christine alone to deal with her dilemma. (Philippe has not only stumbled into the dark, labyrinthine world below the playhouse, looking for his brother, but also become the madman's next victim. Little does Erik realize, when he is drowning the Comte de Chagny, that hundreds of townspeople have also followed the trail to his hidden lair.)

Raoul and the Persian suffer through endless tortures at the hand of the Phantom, until Christine turns the scorpion, flooding their room. Provided that he will save them from drowning, she promises to do anything Erik asks. The Phantom agrees to her bargain, and reluctantly pulls the two men to safety.

When a second series of alarms announce the arrival of more intruders, Erik wrests Christine from the arms of her lover and races off in Raoul's carriage. Pursued by the torch-bearing mob, the Phantom recklessly drives his coach through the Parisian streets. The vehicle finally overturns, and he is forced to flee on foot without his beloved Christine. Eventually, they surround him near the Cathedral of Notre Dame, and move in for the kill. Trapped, cornered, with nowhere left to run, Erik tries to hold them at bay with a magician's trick, but they are not amused. The crowd grabs the Phantom, beats him severely, then throws his limp, nearly-dead body into the Seine river to drown. Finis.

Production Notes

Delighted with the returns from "The Hunchback of Notre Dame" (1923), the first of Universal's new horror series, Carl Laemmle looked around for another property to send before the cameras. He remembered that he had met Gaston Leroux the previous summer (while vacationing in Paris) and had enjoyed reading the copy of *Le Fantôme de l'Opera* he was given by the author. Although he found the 1911 novel to be overly melodramatic, the story of a masked, disfigured composer haunting the Paris Opera House was exactly the kind of high-concept drama that interested Laemmle. Several problems (to which the studio chief often referred to as "opportunities") immediately presented themselves: How could they film scenes in-and-around the Opera House setting? Who would direct the picture? And, more importantly, who would play the lead role of Erik the Phantom?

In those days, since most studios actually found it cheaper to construct replicas of existing places (rather than shoot on location), the film mogul decided to build a magnificent set of the playhouse (one that would rival the Notre Dame set). Construction of the mammoth structure was begun in April 1924 on Stage 28 at Universal Studios, and was completed a few days before actual filming began late that summer. Ben Carre was called in to design the sets, and although he had worked at the Paris Opera House, he had already been living in California for some time doing sets. Because the auditorium set would have five tiers of box seats and hold hundreds of extras, a steel framework (imbedded in the concrete foundations) was used in place of the customary wooden planking. The skeleton was later reinforced with corrugated iron. Carl Laemmle's decision to build the Opera House proved to be such a sound one that the huge indoor set has never been struck. In fact, the auditorium has appeared over the years in several other features, including the 1943 version of "The Phantom of the Opera," "A Double Life" (1948), "Torn Curtain" (1966), and "The Sting" (1973). Today, the only part of the set sill standing is Ben Carre's Opera House, though the only parts left completely untouched are the boxes and stage sides.

The Phantom's dark, labyrinthine world below the playhouse was actually built under the floor of Stage 28 in a huge water tank. Other sets, notably the Grand Foyer (with the double staircase) and the roof (with the huge statue of Apollo), were built in full scale just adajacent to the playhouse. Laemmle's first major concerns about the production were resolved by set designer Charles D. Hall and the uncredited Ben Carre, but the issue of a director and a star remained irresolute.

Carl Laemmle's first choice as a director was Wallace Worsley, the man responsible for the successful "Hunchback of Notre Dame." But Worsley was reluctant to work for the studio chief again (after all the problematic interference he had endured while filming the 1923 silent), and declined numerous monetary incentives. Laemmle's next selection was Rupert Julian, a former actor from New Zealand who had distinguished himself as a director by salvaging Erich Von Stroheim's "The Merry-Go-Round" for Irving Thalberg. After turning two low-budget thrillers, "Love and Glory" (1923) and "Hell's Highroad" (1924), into moderate successes, the hot, young director was signed contractually in an exclusive agreement with Universal Pictures. Carl Laemmle was not bothered by Julian's reputation as an arrogant auteur, and eagerly handed him the studio's biggest project. He would soon regret that decision, but at the time the aging film mogul was concerned with only one problem: How could he acquire the services of the legendary "man of a thousand faces" from his arch-enemy at M-G-M?

Lon Chaney, a legend in the silent film era, was known as "the man of a thousand faces" for good reason. Having played a gallery of tortured grotesques, from Fagin in "Oliver Twist" (1922) to Quasimodo in "The Hunchback of Notre Dame" (1923) for a pittance at Universal, Chaney had been lured away by a better salary offer at Metro-Goldwyn-Mayer. Thus, when his former studio began preproduction on "The Phantom of the Opera," Hollywood's boy wonder was contractually bound to a rival company. Carl Laemmle remained undaunted. The Universal studio chief was so convinced that Chaney was the only actor who could play the title role that he actually called Louis B. Mayer, the president of M-G-M, to discuss how he might arrange to have Lon "loaned" back to Universal for one final film. After several weeks of secret negotiations with Mayer and associate Irving Thalberg, Laemmle secured his former contract player for a role that would become legendary. Chaney was delighted to find himself back at his old studio with a much higher salary, and literally transformed himself into the character of Erik the Phantom.

Ten weeks into the shoot, however, Laemmle came to regret his decision to team Chaney with Julian. Friction between his perfectionist star and the arrogant auteur had brought the production to a standstill. Portions of the film shot in a primitive red-and-blue

Technicolor process had been scrapped by Julian, restored by Chaney, then scrapped again and rescheduled for shooting by Julian. An entire sequence, with Lon Chaney as Erik drowning in his forgotten, underground lake, was filmed in eight different ways by Julian and then discarded. Mob scenes with several thousand extras storming the Phantom's lair were filmed by both Julian, then scrapped. The concept of a dark, romantic triangle between Erik, Christine, and Raoul was changed by Julian (in direct opposition to Chaney) in order to expand the role of Norman Kerry as the young aristocrat. To further complicate matters, Lon Chaney's father had become seriously ill and was dying during the production, but because of Julian's rigorous shooting schedule, the great actor was refused time off to attend the sickbed. (Between takes, Chaney spent time on the phone, checking on his father's condition.)

When Carl Laemmle learned of all these difficulties, he screened a rough cut of the film (late in 1924) and was disappointed by what he saw. He fired Julian, gave the company a few days leave, then hired Edward Sedgewick to replace the New Zealander as director. Sedgewick had directed mostly routine action films, from "Live Wires" (1921) and "The First Degree" (1923) to "Two-Fisted Jones" (1925), and was the ideal choice to shoot the chase scenes at the climax of the film. But his limited range as a director allowed perfectionist Chaney to take over, directing whole sequences of the silent film himself.

Several sequences were shot in various color processes for the top general release prints. Technicolor was used for scenes from "Faust" and the Bal Masque scene; Prizmacolor sequences were shot for the "Soldier's Night" introduction, and Handschiegel (a process that uses stamps to hand-color prints) for the Phantom's notes and red cape on the rooftop. Regrettably, only the Technicolor Bal Masque sequence is known to survive (and appears as an IB print in the 1929 re-release). Just prior to Christmas 1924, production on "The Phantom of the Opera" wrapped on Stage 28 at Universal Studios, Hollywood.

The Film's Release and Critical Reaction

Following the Los Angeles previews in January 1925, Sedgewick was asked to add a number of comedy sequences, featuring Chester Conklin as a superstitious stagehand, in order to lessen the tension of the film. Further editing with the addition of new title cards was hastily undertaken weeks before the premiere to make the storyline more coherent. Finally, nearly a year after the production had begun, "The Phantom of the Opera" debuted in San Francisco on April 26, 1925, and made box office history. Considering the production delays, the creative differences, the hirings and firings, and the massive re-editing involved in trying to save the picture, the film turned out reasonably well.

Surprisingly faithful to its 1911 source, "The Phantom of the Opera" embraces many of the elements which made the book so memorable, including the masked ball, the chandelier disaster, Christine's journey to the Phantom's subterranean hideaway, and the famous unmasking. Gounod's "Faust," which also figured in the original novel, has been retained to suggest Erik's pact with dark, preternatural forces, and the inclusion of the mysterious Persian (identified as "Ledoux") draws attention to the Phantom's bloody past. The only major sequence that has been omitted from the film is the young singer's visit to her father's grave. Otherwise, the events of the book, from the opening scene with the ballet girls to Christine's deadly

choice (between a scorpion and a grasshopper), have been beautifully rendered on film. The two-strip Technicolor sequence, in which Erik appears as Edgar Allan Poe's "Red Death" at the Masked Ball, is matched only by the unmasking scene as the best in the silent picture. When the Phantom makes his majestic entry down the grand staircase of the Opera, the dancing revelers part in horror (like the Red Sea before Moses). Costumed all in red, he is the living embodiment of death, and any who remain in his way fall victim as his prey. Regrettably, Erik's demise - so poetically realized in Leroux's narrative - has been exchanged for a routine chase and summary execution by the French mob.

Most of the acting is consistent with the given limitations of the silent cinema. Mary Philbin, a twenty-one year-old beauty queen, tries her best to add complexity to the role of Christine Daae but is ultimately handcuffed by the melodramatic direction of Rupert Julian. Norman Kerry is stiff and useless as the hero, and Arthur Edmund Carew turns in an effective yet underscored performance as Ledoux. As for the Phantom, Lon Chaney is arrogant, self-assured, mad, passionate, and darkly sinister in a role that he was born to play.

Unlike Gaston Leroux's mad musical genius who chose to hide his birth-defect from polite, French society, however, Chaney's Phantom was an escapee from Devil's Island. Confined during the Commune in the dungeon and torture chambers below the playhouse, he chose to remain. When the film opens, ten years later, he is still living there, out of sight, haunting the Paris Opera House. Although numerous references link the Phantom to his Middle-Eastern origins, no explanation is ever offered as to how Erik managed to furnish such a wondrous lair. His motivation (for saving Raoul and Ledoux) offers similar confusion. After saving the two men from drowning, he again kidnaps Christine and races from the playhouse in a stolen carriage. If (all along) he had intended to spirit the young singer away, why rescue the very men who might later track him to the four corners of the world? His actions make little sense for a man who has spent years developing a superior intellect in order to compete with normal men. But these inconsistencies, after all, are minor when you consider the film as a whole and recognize the outstanding central performance of Chaney as the living embodiment of Leroux's Opera Ghost.

Contrary to popular opinion at the time, Chaney's makeover as Erik the Phantom was not based on a mask or layers of face putty, but his own skill as a makeup artist. "There are tricks in my peculiar trade that I don't care to divulge any more than a magician would give away his art," Lon confided in an interview conducted a few months before his death. "In 'The Phantom of the Opera' people exclaimed at my weird makeup. I achieved the death's head of that role without wearing a mask. It was use of paint in the right shades and the right places - not the obvious parts of the face - which gave the illusion of horror."

Lon Chaney used not only grease paint to create the suggestion of a living skull but also special devices which altered the appearance of his face. First, he attached a strip of fish skin (a thin, translucent material) to his nostrils with spirit gum, pulled it back until he got the tilt he wanted, then attached the other end of the fish skin under his bald cap. For some shots, he inserted a small wire into his nose, which would spread his nostrils wide and tilt the tip upward and back to give a skeletal effect. According to cameraman Charles Van Enger, the wire cut into his nose and caused a good deal of bleeding. Then, he used prongs attached to protruding false teeth to draw his mouth back at the corners to achieve the skull-like grin. He glued his ears back. Drops in his eyes produced the bloodshot, pop-eyed look. Next, he placed circular disks of cotton and collodion in his mouth to accentuate his cheekbones, and finally, on the top of his head, he secured a domed wig of skin, stranded with lank hair. The result - which typically took several hours to achieve - was one of the greatest contributions to the silent cinema. The sight was said to have caused some

patrons at the premiere to have fainted.

Although Lon Chaney's makeup merely hints at the hideous description of the Phantom from Leroux's original novel, it is certainly very effective. Prior to the film's release, not one photograph of Chaney's Phantom was issued to the press. Thus, when Erik's face is eventually revealed, late in the film, it was a terrifying surprise for audience members. The classic sequence of shots - regarded, by many, as the best montage ever devised in the history of the cinema -reveals his horrible visage not once but twice. By careful placement of his camera and the two lead characters, Julian doubles the shock value. For the first shock, though she cannot see his face, Christine removes his mask for the audience. Then, for the second shock, the Phantom turns to face her, and we see the horror reflected in her eyes. "Feast your eyes, glut your soul, on my accursed ugliness!" he exclaims to the young singer, but his message is really meant for the audience in what remains the best unmasking sequence in horror movies.

Critic Roberta O'Toole admitted: "I shrieked right out loud in the theatre and buried my head unashamedly on my husband's chest when Mary Philbin slipped the mask off Chaney as he sat playing the organ." The revelation sent shudders through most audience members, and caused many women to faint and grown men to cry in terror. So awful was the sight, many theatre managers (upon the advice of studio publicists) purchased additional stocks of smelling salts in advance to revive their nervous patrons. O'Toole, who was one of the few critics to write favorably about the movie when it first debuted, proclaimed that "his outraged visage was horror incarnate: bulging, blooshot eyes fatigued with violet semicircles beneath them; the grotesquely exaggerated mounds of cheekbones; the looked-up, flaring, porcine nostrils; the rotted, jagged teeth, like the rim of an enameled tin can top opened with a ragged knife; the scraggly strands of dead gray hair hanging like soggy serpentine from the incredible pyramid of a head. Chaney's Phantom is truly the master of all he surveys!"

Lon Chaney – The Master of a Thousand Faces

Even though many of her contemporaries did not share Roberta O'Toole's enthusiasm for the motion picture, "The Phantom of the Opera" soon became an unqualified success. Audiences were compelled by Chaney's performance, and returned again and again to be frightened by his Phantom. Each decade would have its stock menace, an expert in contortion and make-up, who became the cinema's resident monster and mad psychotic. In the Thirties and Forties, it was Boris Karloff; in the Fifties Vincent Price; in the Sixties Christopher Lee, and in the Eighties Robert Englund; but Chaney dominated the Twenties with a series of brilliant characterizations of legless freaks, twisted hunchbacks, and demented composers. "Don't step on IT! It may be Lon Chaney" was the catch phrase and slogan which identified the actor at the height of his career. Chaney, in real life, was a rather ordinary-looking, slightly middle-aged man, with horn-rimmed glasses and a face that made him look more like a business manager than an actor. He spent more than ten years of his life altering that image (by twisting his body or distorting his face), and established the fashion for movie monsters to come. His roles became so legendary that everyone in the industry began calling him "the man of a thousand faces."

Alonzo Chaney was born April Fool's Day of 1883 in Colorado Springs. Because both of his parents were deaf mutes, he developed skillful mine in learning to communicate with them. He dropped out of school at age 12 to care for his sick mother, and worked many odd jobs before joining his brother's traveling theatrical troope. Lon Chaney began his career as a stage actor (in 1901), by playing a variety of roles from the hero to the villain to the spear carrier. "It was purely by chance," he dismissed his inate ability to undergo fearsome physical deformation.

"All during that time, the thing that interested me most was makeup, but not merely grease-paint and putty noses but mental makeup as well. If I played the role of an old man, I tried to crawl into the old man's mind. .." His first screen appearance was twelve years later in "Poor Jake's Demise" (1913). Executives at Universal Pictures (notably Carl Laemmle) saw great potential in Chaney's work and signed him to an exclusive contract for $5 a day. "The False Faces" (1919) was one of his earlier make-up jobs and virtually launched his film career. He continued to playa variety of roles which required the use of grotesque makeup or physical transformation, including Fagin in "Oliver Twist" (1922), Quasimodo in "The Hunchback of Notre Dame" (1923), and Erik, the disfigured composer, in "The Phantom of the Opera" (1925).

Lon Chaney followed his role in that silent classic by playing a fictitious vampire in Tod Browning's "London After Midnight" (1927). Universal tried several times to convince rival Louis B. Mayer (at M-G-M) to loan Chaney again for a film titled "The Return of the Phantom" (of the Opera), but the aging mogul refused. Instead Lon made "The Bugle Sounds" (1927), "Laugh, Clown, Laugh" (1928), and "West of Zanzibar" (1928). Carl Laemmle Jr. did finally manage to acquire him for the role of Dracula at Universal, but Chaney became suddenly ill and died of throat cancer on August 26, 1930, having spoken only once on the sound screen. (In fact, he spoke in four different voices, as a sideshow ventriloquist, in the talkie remake of "The Unholy Three", 1930.) Although only a handful of his 150 movie roles have survived to this day, Chaney is considered one of the great stars of the silent screen. And with his passing, the silent era came to a close, heralding a new epoch of sound motion pictures.

The 1929 Re-Issue

Two years after "The Phantom of the Opera" was released, Warner Brothers introduced the first "talkie" with "The Jazz Singer" and revolutionized the motion picture industry. Carl Laemmle and his corporate executives at Universal recognized that the silent picture was doomed by the new technology of sound and examined their existing roster of films in an effort to determine which ones might benefit from a sound track. Not surprisingly, they selected one the studio's most successful and influential films, "The Phantom of the Opera."

Whole dialogue sequences, featuring opera singer Mary Fabian (singing the role of Carlotta) and Norman Kerry, were written by Frank McCormack and shot by Ernest Laemmle. In the re-edited version, Virginia Pearson, who had played Carlotta in the silent 1925 version, is credited and referred to as "Carlotta's Mother" instead. Several sections, notably those featuring Chester Conklin, were dropped, while singing voices were recorded to highlight the various scenes from "Faust." Music and other sound effects were added to the silent sections, and Lon Chaney's Phantom was dubbed by a contract player. For the sound edition, Lon Chaney was not available, and contractually, Universal Pictures was not allowed to have mouth synchronization of the Phantom. However, they cleverly wrote third-person lines to be dubbed over shots of the Phantom's shadow. The voice to these lines was unaccredited, but probably belonged to that of

Universal regular Phillips Smalley. Nearly, forty percent of the film was re-shot in synchronous sound, and the rest had music or sound effects added.

"The Phantom of the Opera" was re-released in sound in 1929 using Vitaphone/Western Electric sounds disks. While less than a third of the motion picture had actual dialogue and singing, the re-release advertised "Talking! Singing! Dancing! Sound Effects! Music! Color!" And the first translation of Leroux's work enjoyed another brief moment in the spotlight before "Dracula" (1931), "Frankenstein" (1931), and their progeny established a brand new tradition for horror movies.

Finis

Slightly more than fifteen years after the film's debut, on December 11, 1940, Lon Chaney Junior attended a ceremony which honored his late father. Having just completed work on his first horror movie entitled "Man Made Monster" for Universal, young Chaney was following in his father's footsteps. On the great set of the Paris Opera House, five survivors of the original crew acknowledged him as Lon's successor and unveiled a plaque to his father, which read: "Dedicated to the memory of Lon Chaney, for whose picture 'The Phantom of the Opera' this stage was erected in 1924." Even though Lon Chaney and his illustrious son are no longer with us, the legacy of the Phantom lives on. That plaque and the original sound stage still exists today, a popular stop on the famous Universal Studios Tour. And, if tour-goers listen closely, they can still hear the familiar chords of Bach's "Tocatta & Fugue in D Minor" echoing from the dark cellars of that familiar playhouse.

The silent version of "The Phantom of the Opera" is available on DVD and video-cassette from a variety of sources. The videodisc version differs slightly from the others in that it offers both the 1925 original and the 1929 partial-talkie as well as marvelous behind-the-scenes material. The print restored by the Kino company is a 1929 re-release version that was re-edited, eliminating some scenes and inserting new material shot after the 1925 version was finished. This version also contains an original score composed by Gabriel Thibaudoux, and includes an operatic solo by soprano Claudine Cote. Kenneth Brownilow finished a complete restoration of the 1925 original edit in 1996 with an original score by BBC composer Carl Davis, but this film has only been shown twice in live performances and is not available commercially or on video. Another full restoration was completed by Richard Lloyd in 1999, with the transfer from D1 supervised by Kevin Phelan (Digital Film at The Moving Picture Company). The film is also available as a computer colorized version.

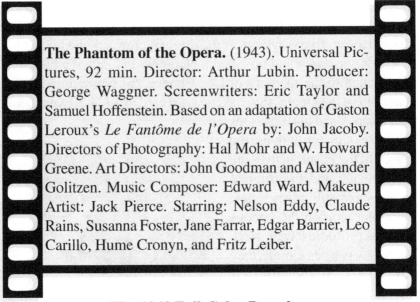

The Phantom of the Opera. (1943). Universal Pictures, 92 min. Director: Arthur Lubin. Producer: George Waggner. Screenwriters: Eric Taylor and Samuel Hoffenstein. Based on an adaptation of Gaston Leroux's *Le Fantôme de l'Opera* by: John Jacoby. Directors of Photography: Hal Mohr and W. Howard Greene. Art Directors: John Goodman and Alexander Golitzen. Music Composer: Edward Ward. Makeup Artist: Jack Pierce. Starring: Nelson Eddy, Claude Rains, Susanna Foster, Jane Farrar, Edgar Barrier, Leo Carillo, Hume Cronyn, and Fritz Leiber.

The 1943 Full-Color Remake

The 1943 rendering of "The Phantom of the Opera," the most extravagant production of its time and the first sound version, is also the least satisfying in terms of cinema and cinematic adaptation. Produced at a cost of $ 1.75 million, the motion picture boasts lavish costumes, elaborate set designs, and operatic sequences recorded (for the first time) with pristine clarity. But the real menace, so chillingly portrayed by Lon Chaney in the 1925 silent and driving force of the film's action, is conspicuously absent. In fact, when Universal Pictures revised most of the story's mythic elements and erotic horror in favor of a standard Forties musical, the central character of the Phantom was reduced to secondary importance. Whereas Gaston Leroux's story requires a strong figure to terrorize the Paris Opera House as well as compete for the attention of the young singer, the Phantom in this motion picture appears simply as an afterthought. Tragically, this flawed cinematic monstrosity, directed by Arthur Lubin, is more opera than opera ghost.

The Screen Story

The film opens predictably as the orchestra of the Paris Opera House begins playing the overture to Friedrich Von Flotow's "Martha." Erique Claudin (Claude Rains), one of the many violinists, appears very adept at his craft but continues to miss key transitions in the music. After twenty years of service to the orchestra, his fingers have grown weak, and he can no longer maintain pace with the hectic demands of the composition. None of the audience members seem to notice the discord in the violin section, and readily applaud as the curtain rises and the colonial drama begins. The camera travels up and juxtaposes the famous chandelier with the opera, then pulls back to reveal a distinguished-looking police man. Inspector Raoul Daubert of the Surete (Edgar Barrier) has come to watch girlfriend Christine Du Bois (Susanna Foster) perform as part of the chorus. His rival Anatole Garron (Nelson Eddy), a baritone in the opera, looks at him disdainfully. He, too, is in love with Christine, and would like to see the inspector disappear. Unfortunately (for him), when the opera ends, Chris-

tine races to Raoul's side, and misses her final curtain call.

The very next day, both Christine and Erique Claudin are sum-moned to the director's office. He reminds the young soprano that she must choose between two different lifestyles, one devoted to music, or one devoted to a husband and family. He does not want to see her years of singing wasted. As she exists, Erique is called. The two pass each other in the hall, and Claudin - enchanted by her beauty and talent - tells Christine that he is her eternal servant. Moments later, the middle-aged violinist is then discharged from the orchestra because the director realizes Claudin can no longer perform. Alone and discouraged, he returns to an empty household. Erique Claudin is broke and can no longer pay his landlady. For the last three years, he has been secretly paying Signor Ferretti (Leo Carrillo), a great music professor, to give her music lessons; but now the money has run out. Christine is totally unaware of Claudin's patronage or undy-ing devotion, and he has nothing else to show for his twenty years of service except an unpublished concerto that he's written.

With the hopes of selling his manuscript, Erique Claudin sends it to Pleyel and Desjardins, then impatiently barges into the music publisher's office, demanding that he be given a few moments time. Pleyel (Miles Mander) is more interested in playing with his female assistant than looking at his work and tries to dismiss the distraught musician. At about the same time, Franz Litz (played by science fic-tion great Fritz Leiber's grandfather) sits down at a piano in the next room and plays a few notes (at the insistance of a junior patner). Hearing his composition played in the adjacent room and believing that it has been stolen, Claudin attacks and strangles Pleyel. He be-comes hideously disfigured when a tray of acid is hurled in his face by the publisher's female assistant, and runs into the night, a broken man. The police are called, but Erique manages to elude them, escap-ing into a convenient sewer hole located beneath a stationary car-riage. He follows the sewer tunnels into the dark, labyrinthine world below the Paris Opera House.

Several weeks later, the managers of the theatre notice that food, costumes, and other items are mysteriously vanishing. Several back-stage sightings of a masked figure in a dark cloak are reported, but no one seems to have gotten a very good look at him. They believe the mysterious figure is the Opera ghost.

"Amour Gloire," a fictitious opera utilizing themes from Chopin, opens the new season, and members of the rich, upper class crowd into the theatre. As Christine completes final preparation in her dressing room before going onstage, she is told by a disembodied voice that tonight all the world would know her voice. She tries to locate the source of the prophecy, but finds no one. During the performance, the Phantom gingerly slips poison into the resident diva's glass, and Christine is called to take her place when Laurence Biancaroll (Jane Farrar) can no longer continue. The young understudy triumphs in the lead role, and further enchants her two suitors with her angelic, charismatic voice. Below the opera house, Claudin listens to Christine's glorious performance and weeps with happiness.

The resident diva recovers from the poison, and accuses Christine and Anatole of attempted murder. Inspector Daubert dismisses the charges, claiming that someone else is responsible. He begins to piece together parts of the puzzle, and determines that Erique Claudin has been haunting the opera house on account of his dismissal from the orchestra. When a letter arrives demanding that the young singer be given the lead role in a concerto written by the deceased composer, Raoul arranges a trap to capture the murderer. He then places several of his men in the choral section of the new production. Dressed as one of the many costumed police officers, the Phantom easily infiltrates the troupe and starts searching for Christine. She has retired to her dressing room, at the insistance of Raoul, and does not plan to sing Claudin's concerto. Inspector Daubert and the managers have duped him, by assigning the lead role to Biancaroll. Angered, he cuts the chain that suspends the chandelier over the auditorium, and sends it crashing down. In the chaos following its lethal decent, Erique abducts Christine from backstage, taking her down through the long corridors to his underground lair. Once there, he begins playing his concerto. He insists that the young soprano sing along, and she does so unwillingly. Her voice echoes through the dark tunnels, and provides Raoul and Anatole with a direction to her whereabouts. The two men quickly follow in pursuit, the inspector from the Surete armed with his service revolver.

Meanwhile, Christine has managed to get closer and closer to Claudin. She finally snatches the Phantom's mask and reveals the disfigured face of the middle-aged violinist. At that very moment, her two suitors burst in and rescue her from his evil clutches. A shot is fired, and Erique Claudin is buried in a rockslide triggered by the sound. Raoul and Anatole rush the young singer to safety (in the nick of time). The final image of his mask and violin reminds the audience of the Phantom's unhappy demise. Later, in a needless postscript, both the baritone and the inspector arrive at Christine's dressing room door for dinner after her triumph on the stage. She dismisses them both in order to face her public, and the two bachelors decide to have dinner together.

Production Notes

The fact that "The Phantom of the Opera" (1943) is more of a musical spectacular than a bizarre thriller may reflect the cautious time in which the motion picture was made. The innovative richness of the Twenties and Thirties had been followed by a period of disintegration and decline wherein the horror film descended to its lowest level. The old Hollywood, which had produced such cinematic gems as Lon Chaney's "The Phantom of the Opera" (1925), Bela Lugosi's "Dracula" (1931), and Boris Karloff's "Frankenstein" (1931), had passed away into legend, and what remained was an industry in which the values and foundations of the past had been muted and corrupted into something that was largely unrecognizable. Carl Laemmle Jr. was dead, and his eagerness to experiment with bold, original ideas and had been replaced by an attitude of conservatism as well as a general lack of vision. Wild-eyed auteurs, like Tod Browning and James Whale, were supplanted by business-suited executives with accounting ledgers and corporate mentalities. Productions became a matter of dollars and cents rather than imaginative creativity.

As a result, the new bosses of Universal Pictures, convinced that they knew what audiences really wanted, teamed the famous monsters of filmland with silly comics or simply turned to the safety of remaking past motion picture hits. They reasoned that members of the public, who had suffered through the ravages of the Depression and the climate of fear precipitated by the Second World War, would buy tickets to laugh at the likes of Abbott & Costello or be wowed by the latest advances in Technicolor and sound. The 1943 version of "The Phantom of the Opera" was conceived by that corporate mentality, rather than inspired by a creative director or producer who had a new vision of the Gaston Leroux classic.

Insult was added to injury when horror films came under attack for decency in the early Forties. During World War Two, horror films were banned in England, parts of Europe and North Africa because individual governments thought these motion pictures had a negative effect on morale. Soon after the war, stricter regulations dealing with theme and content were initiated throughout the world; in particular, the United Kingdom established the British Board of Film Censors. That organization became the watchdog of the Eastern Hemisphere, creating the first rating system for movies. A "U"-rating meant that a film was suitable for general audiences (today, the equivalent of a "G" rating.) An "A"-rating meant that the film was mature and suggested parental guidance (much like the "PG," or "PG-13" rating). The kiss of death for most movies, in that era of repression, was the "H"-rating, which meant that the film was graphic in its portrayal of horror (equivalent to an "R" or "X"-rating, today). The Motion Picture Association of America (MPAA) followed the lead of the United Kingdom.

Many horror films, except for the light, comic spoofs, were classified under that rating system and came under the attack of religious and civic groups. That threat translated to fewer markets and even

less take at the box office. Studio executives became very cautious with the type of product they created, and may have insisted that a remake of "The Phantom of the Opera" focus more on opera than horror. Thus, the darker, expressionistic vision of the first motion picture was exchanged for a bright, Technicolor extravaganza. Featuring lavish costumes, elaborate set designs, and musical sequences that would be staged with a large cast of operatic singers, the production resembled a Busby Berkley spectacular, rather than a typical horror film. Universal Studios, which had distinguished itself in the past with low-budget horror films, Sherlock Holmes thrillers, and Abbott & Costello comedies, now looked at competing with the A-quality pictures of M-G-M, Paramount, and Warner Brothers.

Originally, the film had been intended as a vehicle for the popular singing actress Deana Durbin in the role of Christine, with Broderick Crawford cast as the Phantom. But the United States entry into World War Two in December 1941 meant that most leading men (Crawford included) would be drafted into military service. The celebrated but portly British actor Charles Laughton was the next choice of studio executives. A few years earlier, he had scored big with the remake of "The Hunchback of Notre Dame" (1940), and was renowned for his distinguished elocution. However, the project fell apart less than six weeks later due to production delays, salary negotiations, and numerous script revisions.

By 1943, Universal Pictures had again altered the focus of the motion picture. Deana Durbin and Charles Laughton were out, and the role of Anatole Garron was rewritten and enlarged to accommodate the baritone sensation Nelson Eddy (recently split from his "singing sweetheart" Jeanette MacDonald). He was to be paired with the newly discovered Susanna Foster, who had made her film debut in "The Great Victor Herbert" in 1940 at the age of fifteen. Producer George Waggner had hoped their teaming would create a new screen partnership, that Eddy and Foster would become "America's (new) singing sweethearts," but he failed to consider the vast discrepancy in their ages. Other production changes were likewise unexceptional and not fully thought out. Arthur Lubin, known primarily for his lackluster Abbott & Costello comedies, had replaced both Henry Koster and William Diertele as director, and contract player Claude Rains was cast in the secondary but pivotal role of the Phantom.

Claude Rains, a soft-spoken and distinguished British actor, was certainly no stranger to imaginative thrillers. Ten years before, he "appeared" in his first film as doomed scientist Jack Giffin, "The Invisible Man" (1933). Although audience members don't see him until the final seconds of the movie, Rains made a lasting impression in James Whale's brilliant adaptation of the H.G. Wells novel. He went onto play King John, opposite Errol Flynn and Basil Rathbone in "The Adventures of Robin Hood" (1938), and pivotal roles in "Mr. Smith Goes to Washington" (1939), "The Sea Hawk" (1940), and "Here Comes Mr. Jordan" (1941). Ironically, though he lost the role of the wolf man to Lon Chaney Jr., his portrayal of the sympathetic violinist in "The Phantom of the Opera" opened the door to numerous other opportunities. His breakthrough came as Inspector Louis Renault in what many consider to be the greatest motion picture ever made, "Casablanca" (1942). As the scheming, cynical director of police, Rains managed to upstage both Bogart and Bergman in a number of key scenes. That fine performance led to fifty other screen appearances in films as diverse as "Mr. Skeffington" (1944), "Notorious" (1946), "The Lost World" (1960), and "Lawrence of Arabia" (1962). His thirty-five year career ended with a small cameo in George

Stevens' "The Greatest Story Ever Told" (1965); he died two years later. Though hardly one of the highpoints of his career, Rains essays a brief yet capable turn as the Phantom.

Unlike Gaston Leroux's mad musical genius, however, the second authorized version of *The Phantom of the Opera* (to reach the silver screen) is portrayed as a pathetic, old man whose musical abilities are fading. Whereas Lon Chaney's Erik was an escapee from Devil's Island who had been confined in the torture chamber below the theatre, Erique Claudin is an ordinary man whose life is suddenly changed by an unfortunate series of events. When he fears his musical concerto has been stolen and he wrongly strangles the unsympathetic publisher, a tray of acid is thrown into his face. Only then, does Claudin (as the Phantom) begin his journey toward madness, which climaxes with him dropping a chandelier on innocent bystanders. Soon after, he spirits the young singer away to his underground lair and declares his undying affection, like a lovesick teen, even though he is old enough to be her father. He even resembles Christine's father (from the book), more so than the Phantom. The original script revealed Claudin to be Christine's father, who abandoned her and her mother in order to pursue a musical career. When this was excised from the final film, it left Claudin's obsession with Christine unexplained and just a bit creepy.

The Frenchman's creation was born with his physical deformity, and developed his keen, highly resourceful personality in order to survive. His madness was the result of years of isolation and loneliness as well as the scorn of a society that viewed ugliness as evil. He tutors Christine because his soul is filled with music, and falls in love with her voice. Their two characters may appear to be superficially alike, but they are, in fact, two completely different, diametrically opposed individuals.

Besides the transmutation of the story's central figure, screenwriters Eric Taylor and Samuel Hoffenstein (working from an adaptation by John Jacoby) have greatly altered or discarded elements of Leroux's bizarre thriller to favor their musical monstrosity. Names have been inexplicably changed, and characters - not the least of whom is the Phantom - have been totally rewritten. Raoul, for example, is now a policeman, instead of an aristocrat; the Persian, Joseph Buquet, Madame Giry and her daughter have all been dropped, and baritone

Anatole Garron has taken their place at center stage. While his appearance may provide a romantic tension (which should rightly belong to the Phantom) between Raoul and Christine, none of the other deletions make sense. Gounod's "Faust," utilized in the original novel to suggest a demonic pact, has been replaced with Flotow's "Martha" and two bogus operas comprised of themes from Chopin and Tchaikowsky. While the music is very beautiful (including a new composition by Edward Ward), the pieces contribute very little thematically to the film. Because the war in Europe made it so difficult to track down who had who had the rights to most operas (coupled with the studios reluctance to pay the re-quired royalties) all the op-eras performed in the film were ei-ther in the pub-lic domain or were based on classical mu-sic that was in the public do-main. The film makers were able to slip in a reference to the opera Faust (which fea-tured heavily in the original novel) by hav-ing Christine appear in the Marguerite costume as she comes off stage at the end of the film. Other elements, including the famous masked ball, Christine's nightly visit to her father's grave, and the lover's rendezvous on the roof of the Paris Opera House, and the torture chamber, are also curiously missing. Instead Taylor and Hoffenstein "treat" the audience to one fully-blown operatic sequence after another.

Director Arthur Lubin tries his best to make these disparate elements come together into a cohesive narrative; unfortunately, lacking the skill of an auteur like Browning or Whale, his cinematic approach to the material is rather a conventional one. He seems comfortable staging the large, lavish production numbers, but when it comes to creating an atmosphere of terror and menace, he is com-

pletely out of his depth. The Phantom's haunting of the Paris Opera House, which was filmed in the auditorium and stage set built for the 1925 version, is never fully explored by Lubin. Similarly, Christine's journey to Erique's underground lair lacks any tension or suspense. (She might as well be walking around a lake at night.) Even the revelation of the Phantom's face, which was one of the high points of the first film, is rather unspectacular.

Part of the blame for the failure of this important sequence belongs to the makeup supervisor. Jack Pierce, the artist who had made Boris Karloff into both the Mummy and the Frankenstein monster, had turned Bela Lugosi into the Transylvanian Count, and had transformed Lon Chaney Jr. into the wolf man, worked hard to achieve something special for Claude Rains other than the much celebrated death's head Chaney had created for the first film. Regrettably, when the mask is finally snatched from his face by Christine, there is nothing the least bit frightening about his face. He appears to have a simple birth mark or unpleasant skin ailment. Having served the industry for more than twenty-two years, Pierce had been responsible for a number of innovations in his particular field. But, with all the new advances in plastic and foam rubber, Pierce was unwilling to change and found his services no longer needed at Universal Pictures. He worked on his last monster film, "House of Dracula" (1945), two years later, and quietly retired in 1946. (Ironically, Pierce's designs for the Frankenstein monster would become the standard for the next thirty years.)

The Release and Aftermath

"The Phantom of the Opera," Universal's most expensive endeavor up to that time (costing a total of $1.75 million), was an enormous box office success when it was first released on August 27, 1943, and spawned a semi-sequel (entitled "The Climax") which premiered the following year. Although critics were quick to find fault with the production, particularly in light of the wonderful 1925 version, the film went onto win two Academy Awards from the Academy of Motion Picture Arts and Sciences for Best Art Direction (Alexander Golitzen and John Goodman) and Best Cinematography (W. Howard Greene and Hal Mohr) at the ceremony in 1944. Today, when viewed in retrospect on videocassette or DVD, the 1943 version clearly reveals its age. More opera than opera ghost, the film represents the weakest retelling of Gaston Leroux's familiar tale.

The Climax. (1944). Universal Pictures, 86min. Director and Producer: George Waggner. Screenwriters: Curt Siodmak and Lynn Starling. Based on a play by: Edward Locke. Directors of Photography: Hal Mohr and W. Howard Greene. Music Composer: Edward Ward. Cast: Boris Karloff, Susanna Foster, Turhan Bey, Gale Sondergaard, June Vincent, Thomas Gomez, and Scotty Beckett.

The 1944 Sequel—"The Climax"

The box-office success of "The Phantom of the Opera" (1943) generated this semi-sequel, which is really little more than a remake with Boris Karloff in the pivotal role of the "phantom" of the Paris Opera House. Filmed on the same Academy Award-winning sets, utilizing the same lavish costumes and production team, and featuring the same leading lady, "The Climax" (1944) virtually repeats the condition of conflict in the earlier movie. Karloff (in his first color film) plays a mild-mannered, retiring physician Dr. Hohner of the Vienna Royal Theatre who, unbeknownst to anyone, had strangled his mistress ten years before and lives with her embalmed corpse in the dark, labyrinthine world below. Apparently, she (June Vincent) was a famous opera singer, and when she refused to give up her career for a normal family life with him, he jealously murdered her. When he hears the voice of a young music student (Susanna Foster), the good doctor is convinced that his dead mistress has been reincarnated, and he has the opportunity to win her love again. His plans, which include terrorizing the opera house, go awry, thanks to the intervention of a fellow student who loves her (Turhan Bey), and Karloff dies in a familiar conflagration that also consumes the body of his first love. Extremely predictable, particularly if you've just seen the 1943 version, the film is distinguished only by the presence of Karloff in one of his many roles as a sympathetic mad doctor.

In 2004, Andrew Lloyd Webber brought his stage musical to the big screen under the direction of Joel Schumacher with Gerard Butler in the role of the Phantom. Even though it was not produced by Universal, audiences still thrilled to the return of one of its favorite monsters in a lavish production that rivals the 1943 film.

2

Dracula

*There are such beings as vampires, some of us have
evidence that they exist. Even had we not the proof of
our own unhappy experience, the teachings and the
records of the past give proof enough for sane peoples.*
                                    —*Bram Stoker, Dracula (1897)*

For over a hundred years, the vampire has freely stalked movie
theatres and preyed upon the willing patrons of over three hundred
and fifty films. Though his origins may have been lost in the cave
etchings of primeval mythology, obscured by the superstitions of folklore, or exploited by the "penny-dreadfuls" of Victorian melodrama,
the vampire has remained a popular subject for motion pictures and
television. The novel *Dracula*, for example, has been adapted for the
silver screen more times than any other book and has inspired countless imitations, sequels, parodies, and spoofs! The words "vampire"
and "Dracula" have become synonymous with sexual seduction,
power, and domination, and are an integral part of our daily vocabu-
lary. And with a handful of new movies released each year, the vampire film continues to be a lively and prominent form of entertainment. Perhaps the reason for its longevity and prolificacy has to do
with a message that is universal; or perhaps it has something to do
with myth and our collective unconscious. In either case, many media students, film critics, historians, and filmgoers contend that the
vampire film has been largely responsible for popularizing the horror
genre. This seems like an enormous claim, but there may be some

validity to that contention, considering its humble beginnings and progenitors as well as its world wide acclaim.

An Icon of Popular Culture

The image of Bela Lugosi as Dracula is one that has instant recognition throughout most of the world in both print and media forms, and it is an icon which we become familiar with from the time we are old enough to color in a coloring book, watch a television show, or read. Almost any first or second grade child (as well as many preschoolers) can identify the vampiric characters of Count "Count" from "Sesame Street," Count Duckula from the noted British cartoon series (of the same name), or Count Chocula from their favorite General Mills cereal. As they grow older and become consumers, adolescents (as well as many adults) are attracted to print advertisements and radio/television commercials which feature Count Dracula as a spokesman for products as diverse as men's toiletries (from Gillette Industries) to sugarless gum (Trident) to copper-top batteries (Duracell). The product line doesn't stop there either; over the years, the vampire image has been associated with mouthwash, cat food, alcohol, fruit juice, pizza, security systems, sunglasses and two dozen other items. During the Halloween season, the product line nearly doubles with the large variety of greeting cards, party favors, candy, centerpieces, napkins, and paper plates that feature Count Dracula or some other noted vampire (Vampirella, Vampira, Elvira - to name a few). Children of all ages dress in the traditional black cape and fangs and gain instant identification of character, while celebrating the curious holiday of demons, witches, and other creatures of the night. Throughout the rest of the year, contributors to more than a dozen

scholarly journals regularly discuss the psychological, sociological, anthropological, and literary merits of the most famous creature who never lived. It is quite obvious that the vampire image has had a major impact on so many levels of contemporary society, as with the diverse cultures of the past.

Superstitions, myths, and legends about the vampire can be found with divergent variations in almost every culture in the world. Most of the stories date back thousands of years and have been handed down orally from generation to generation. The single element, which seems to unite even the most diverse tradition, is the belief that the vampire is a dead person who returns from the grave to suck the life (ie: blood) from living persons. This conception of the vampire, known as nosferatu (the "undead"), is probably the most common among mid-European, Slavonic peoples, particularly in the Balkan countries, and in Hungary, Bohemia, Moravia, and Silesia. [Notation: Besides stories in folklore, actual documentation of historical vampires dates from the late Seventeenth Century.] In White Russia and parts of the Ukraine, the vampire is also identified as a wizard, or sorceror, who seeks to destroy the living. In Greece, the broncolaia or bourkabakos - a curious crossing of the vampire and werewolf legends - steals the heart of the living during certain lunar phases. The traditions are not, however, exclusively European. The Polynesians' *tii,* the Malayans' *hantu penyardin*, and the Karens' *kephn* are vampires who not only devour blood but also human souls. They appear as dog-headed, water demons from the sea. In Africa, the vampire is a demonic servant who steals the souls of the unfaithful. Many obvious ties link this tradition to zombie and voodoo worship. In China, vampires are mischievous shape-changers who, much like the jinn, attack babies and other helpless individuals. The United States, Britain, and other English-speaking countries have no established traditions of their own (beyond certain legends of the Native American Indian) and have borrowed many of the familiar precepts from their European forebears. But regardless of the origins or their diversity, the various beliefs all suggest that there is much more to the vampire myth than simply superstition.

Thematically, the modern vampire story deals with the disturbing survival of romantic ideals (represented by the vampire) in an era of industrialism or scientific rationalism (contemporary society). That presupposition - while it may have taken on different forms in the last

hundred years - lies at the very core of the vampire film. Magic and any force of the supernatural no longer has a place in a world where Edison's lightbulb has replaced the gas lamp, yet the vampire does attempt to survive, challenging the new order with his antiquated methods. Those roots of discontentment lie not only in the classic stories of *Carmilla* by Sheridan Le Fanu, *The Vampyre* by John Polidori, and Dracula, to which many vampire films owe as source materials, but also in older, literary conventions and attitudes from Judeo-Christian mythology and the Medieval morality play. Both the legend of Lilith and the story of Satan are parables of human presumption - about man (or demi-god) playing God - that predate the Dracula story by some five thousand years. Lilith, the first wife to Adam according to *The Talmud* and other Semitic writings, refused to concede to her husband's superiority and was damned to walk the earth in search of human blood—forever. Satan, the most beautiful angel in Judeo-Christian mythology, tried to become like God at the cost of great suffering and eternal damnation. Both acts challenge the natural order of things, and both individuals suffer similar punishment for their arrogance. Similarly, the medieval story of Dr. Faustus (though not strictly a vampire tale) portrays a man who is willing to sell his soul to the Devil for an eternal life of pleasure. Faust, like Lilith and Satan, openly defies God and must be destroyed in order to preserve the spiritual foundations of the Judeo-Christian faith. And this common theme is also central to our understanding of the vampire mythos.

Carmilla, the seductive beauty of Joseph Sheridan Le Fanu's novella (of the same name), is the archetype for the first female vampire and a symbol of sexual deviancy (inherent in many vampire stories). When her carriage is overturned in a highway accident, Carmilla is taken to a wealthy, Austrian estate. There, she meets and eventually seduces Laura, the innocent daughter of the household. What she fails to realize is that the Lesbian relationship calls attention to herself and reveals the ages-old vampire Mircalla, Countess Karnstein. Lord Ruthven, the first great fictional vampire from John Polidori's *The Vampyre*, dresses, speaks, and in general performs like a nobleman; but there is a dark, mysterious (even dangerous) side to his nature that his traveling companion Aubrey eventually notices. Ruthven represents beauty and power, which are both seductive, as well as a tragic side, which echoes Satan's sentiments in Milton's epic poem: "Better to rule in Hell than serve in Heaven." Unfortunately, Aubrey fails to recognize his friend as evil until it is too late: the vampire has already seduced and destroyed his innocent sister.

Count Dracula is the quintessential vampire and symbol of romanticism, immortality, sexuality, aggression, and power. Having dominated his Transylvanian homeland for centuries, he moves into Carfax Abbey and instantly attempts to impose his own values and way of life upon the citizenry of England. At first, he is welcomed into the finest homes and quickly establishes himself as a visiting nobleman and a man of great importance. His old-world charms and mysterious sexual allure causes heart flutters in Mina Murray, Lucy Westenra, and other women he encounters. However, the charm and sexual allure are merely illusionary. Dracula intends to feed upon his female conquests, and in order to fully satisfy his needs, he must dominate them completely—both body and soul. Unfortunately for Dracula, his control becomes unraveled with the appearance of a man of science. Dr. Abraham Van Helsing recognizes Dracula

for what he is, and soon his first victim Lucy is staked, his servant Renfield imprisoned, and Mina placed under protective care. The vampire is forced to flee to his homeland to re-establish his world and power base. Bram Stoker's novel brilliantly explores that unknown territory of the soul where love, imagination, and mutual satisfaction become sex, fantasy, dominance, submission, and degradation of spirit — all of which are central to our understanding of the vampire mythos.

Literary scholar James Twitchell, in his landmark article "The Vampire Myth," wrote that Dracula (along with his counterpart Frankenstein) was the most important archetype from Victorian literature and that his presence - in our popular culture - was significant. Besides being "the stranger in a strange land," the outsider, Dracula is a constant reminder of the many, old-world traditions that never quite made the transition to contemporary society. He is the romantic hero, like many of us, lost in an unfamiliar world of micro chips and computer technology. Whereas we might stumble around in ignorance or allow ourselves to be intimidated, Dracula refuses to acknowledge such reproaches, surviving at all costs. He also represents the symbol of eternal life; like Peter Pan, the boy who refused to grow up, Dracula remains unchanged in a changing society with no conscience or remorse for his actions. He knows only that he wants and satisfies those desires without any consideration for the consequences. He is the embodiment of evil without guilt, power without restraint, and sexuality without conscience. And, in essence, we secretly admire his ability to resolve or ignore problems with which we ourselves have difficulty in dealing.

Similarly, the act of blood ingestion works on many different levels. The most obvious reason is for food and nourishment. Traditional Christian mythology views blood as the lifeforce which Jesus Christ sacrificed in order to grant his followers eternal life. Since the vampire myth is a perversion of that belief, Dracula drinks the blood of the living as a short-cut to immortality. Less obvious reasons concern sexual deviance and the need for power or dominance over another. Dracula has total control over Lucy Westenra and Renfield through his manipulation of blood; for Lucy, the control is somewhat sexual, and for his servant, a bizarre sadomasochism. They can be free only after his control is broken. Finally, at the heart of the vampire myth is the desire for reunion with deceased loved ones. How many of us would leap at the opportunity to see our long-dead mother, father, or spouse? When Lucy appears from the grave, her fiance Arthur Holmwood is relieved to discover that she is not dead; but he soon realizes that she is part of the "undead" and must be destroyed in order to free her soul. Romanticism, power, sexuality, and visions of immortality - all key elements of the vampire myth - have provided endless fascination for the general public.

Like many mythological or literary stories, the vampire film relies heavily upon a set of traditions which have been handed down from generation to generation. For example, vampires are creatures of the night, afraid of the purifying rays of the sun; they must sleep in the earth of their native land, and they must drink the blood of willing victims in order to survive. They fear the Cross (of Jesus), or other holy implements, and can be destroyed by a stake through the heart. Like the morality play, which shares much of its ritual nature, plots of most vampire films deal with the struggle of ideals, good versus evil,

in terms which provide katharsis (which means "cleansing" in Aristotlean tragedy) and good entertainment. Countless times, characters, like David Gray, Dr. Van Helsing, and Carl Kolchak, have ventured forth, into darkness, or hell, as a symbol of good to defeat Dracula, Carmilla, Count Yorga, or other symbols of evil. The story is a most familiar one, and each time it is replayed, audiences thrill to the ageless conflict.

The continued use of these common elements, set symbols, and ageless traditions has not diminished the interest, nor hampered the development, of the vampire film; but, rather, it has provided an arena for ingenuity and imagination to examine old themes and to explore new ones. Early in its history, the vampire film became not only a contemporary morality play but also a social and aesthetic reflection of its popular culture. And we can learn much about the attitudes of the period in which each film was made. For example, in "Nosferatu" (1922), "Dracula" (1931), and other early films, the nocturnal blood lust equated to a necrophilic passion, in which a demon, or vampire, preyed at night upon sleeping innocence. Prior to World War II, America pictured itself as a sleeping innocent, being preyed upon by the pestilence of poverty, injustice, and war. During the fifties and sixties, in films like "The Horror of Dracula" (1958), "The Vampire Lovers" (1970), and others, the vampire was still cloaked in ritual and superstition, but had taken on an air of sadism and erotic sensationalism, much in keeping with our changing attitudes toward free love, drugs, campus revolt, the generation gap, and Vietnam. For the seventies and eighties, in an age which had rejected most religious and supernatural beliefs in favor of science and technology, the vampire was no longer simply a night stalker; in films, like "Martin" (1978), "The Keep" (1983), and "Lifeforce: The Space Vampires" (1985), he had become a maniacal psychotic, looking to drain not only blood but also the entire soul from its victims.

By implication then, the vampire film is a subject of established ritual and shifting and variable emphasis. It is also a unique art form which has contributed much to the evolution of the modern "horror" film.

But in all fairness to the form the words "horror" and "monster" - when used in conjunction with "film" - are really misnomers, and largely inappropriate to our study of the vampire mythos. "Horror," by definition, suggests an intense, painful feeling of revulsion or loathing, and "monster' conjures images of an offensive grotesque who commits perverse acts of random violence. These terms might more amply describe the splatter films of Herschel Gordon Lewis or the highly successful "Friday the 13th" film series (in which a maniac in a hockey mask indiscriminately murders teenagers) - but certainly not any in the scope of this study. Vampire films transcend those common labels; they belong to the cinefantastique, or the cinema of the fantastic, which combines the literature of imagination with the mystique of motion picture technology.

Bram Stoker and the Original Novel

Bram Stoker was born near Dublin, Ireland, in 1847, and graduated from Trinity College with honors in mathematics. In 1872, Stoker published his first melodrama, *The Crystal Cup*, a dream fantasy. While working as a clerk in Dublin Castle he wrote *Duties of Clerks of Petty Sessions in Ireland*, although it was not published until 1879. He married Florence Balcome, a former girlfriend of Oscar Wilde, in 1878. He and his new bride moved to London shortly thereafter. With the help of Henry Irving, he became the business manager of Irving's Lyceum Theatre – a post which he had for 27 years. His collaboration with Irving allowed him access to London's high society, and soon he was hobnobbing with the elite members of society, including James McNeil Whistler and Sir Arthur Conan Doyle, the creator of Sherlock Holmes. Stoker also made several trips abroad with Irving, and during one of these trips to Eastern Europe, heard the name Vlad Dracula associated with stories about vampires.

During the next eight years, Stoker spent his free time researching European folklore. He also began creating characters based upon those patrons that he met and entertained at the Lyceum Theatre. Henry Irving became the real-life inspiration for the character of Dracula. His dramatic presence and his gentlemanly mannerisms were perfect for the part of Stoker's villain. He also read extensively, including Emily Gerard's 1885 essay "Transylvania Superstitions," Sheridan

Le Fanu's 1871 *Carmilla*, and John Polidori's *The Vampyre*.

The Dead Un-Dead was Stoker's original title for *Dracula*, and the titular character was going to be Count Vampyre. He later changed the title to *The Un-Dead*, and finally *Dracula*, when he decided that his vampire would be based upon the historic figure known as Prince Vlad Dracula (also known as Vlad the Impaler). He also borrowed the literary style of his novel from one of the most popular novels of the nineteenth century, *The Woman in White* (1860). *The Woman in White* was an epistolary novel, written as a collection of diary and journal entries. The style was considered old fashioned by the time of *Dracula*'s publication in 1897, but its collection of telegrams, letters from characters, and diary entries adds a certain level of realism that makes the average reader think the story is true.

The story begins when Jonathan Harker, a real estate broker, is invited to Count Dracula's crumbling castle in Transylvania to discuss Dracula's purchase of Carfax Abbey in Whitby, England. Harker soon finds himself trapped by Dracula and his three vampire wives, but he does manage to escape with his life. Later, the story picks up when a Russian ship runs aground during a fierce tempest off the shores of Whitby. All the passengers and crew are found dead. A huge wolf is seen running from the ship, and we later learn that Dracula has come ashore in animal form.

Soon, Dracula is romancing Harker's devoted fiancée, Wilhelmina (Mina) Murray, and her friend, Lucy Westenra. He is also menacing Renfield, a patient at a local asylum run by Dr. John Seward. Renfield consumes insects, spiders, birds, and other creatures in order to absorb their "life force," in much the same way that Count Dracula is forced to drink blood from the living.

When Lucy becomes ill, Seward calls upon the assistance of Professor Abraham Van Helsing from Amsterdam. Van Helsing has seen the marks of the vampire before, and without revealing his suspicions, he attempts to use blood transfusions to cure her. Lucy eventually dies, and comes back as a beautiful lady, stalking little children at night. The good professor confides in Seward and two of Lucy's suitors, Arthur Holmwood and Quincy Morris, explaining his fear that Lucy has become a vampire. Together, they put a stake in her heart and cut her head off. They then turn their attention to dealing with Dracula himself.

Dracula learns of their plot against him, and takes his revenge by biting Mina three times and feeding her his blood. This creates a bond between them that not even Harker can break. Later, Dracula flees back to his castle in Transylvania, followed closely by Van Helsing's coalition. They manage to track him down just before sunset, and kill him by "shearing through his kneck" and stabbing him in the heart with a Bowie knife. Dracula crumbles to dust, and his spell on Mina is lifted.

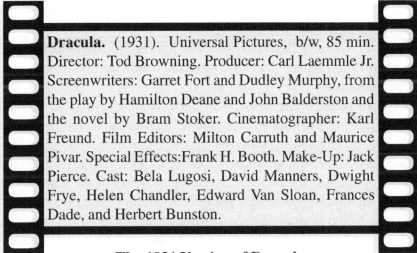

Dracula. (1931). Universal Pictures, b/w, 85 min. Director: Tod Browning. Producer: Carl Laemmle Jr. Screenwriters: Garret Fort and Dudley Murphy, from the play by Hamilton Deane and John Balderston and the novel by Bram Stoker. Cinematographer: Karl Freund. Film Editors: Milton Carruth and Maurice Pivar. Special Effects:Frank H. Booth. Make-Up: Jack Pierce. Cast: Bela Lugosi, David Manners, Dwight Frye, Helen Chandler, Edward Van Sloan, Frances Dade, and Herbert Bunston.

The 1931 Version of Dracula

The early 1930s saw the development of the second great horror school in America and the production of the first sound classics of the genre. Following the immediate and enormous success of "Dracula" and "Frankenstein" in 1931, Universal Pictures launched several highly profitable series, including the "Dracula" film cycle as well as numerous others.

One of the most enduring and influential genre films of the period was Universal's 1931 version of "Dracula." In the wake of the immense commercial and unexpected success of the stage play on Broadway, Carl Laemmle, Jr. acquired the film rights in 1930 from Bram Stoker's estate. He had already initiated several other genre productions, including an adaptation of Edgar Allan Poe's "Murders in the Rue Morgue," but he decided that the vampire classic, which had already been filmed by Murnau as "Nosferatu" (1922), would be the first in a series of high quality, moderately budgeted horror films. Junior Laemmle further announced that the team that had made the very successful "London After Midnight," Tod Browning and Lon Chaney, would direct and star respectively in his feature. Unfortunately, Chaney had become ill (and later died from throat cancer), and many of the studio's top executives urged Laemmle to begin production as soon as possible to capitalize on the hot word-of-mouth publicity from the play. The part of Dracula was then offered to Bela Lugosi, the actor who had originated the role on the Broadway stage.

Born Bela Ferenc Blasko in Lugos, Hungary, in 1882, he had starred in several European films, including Murnau's "Janus-Faced" (1920), and had also appeared as Ariztid Olt in numerous stage productions prior to immigrating to America. Lugosi was the ideal choice for many silent films as the suave European lover or the smooth European villain and was cast to type in "The Silent Command" (1923), "The Rejected Woman" (1924), "Renegades" (1930), and "Oh, For a Man" (1930). His chilling stage presence and Hungarian accent instantly established him in the stage role of the Transylvanian Count and brought him to the attention of Carl Laemmle, Jr. Ironically, his accent became a handicap in later films as sound revolutionized the cinema, and he became typecast in many inferior horror films. Lugosi was often paired with Boris Karloff, another alumnus of Universal Pictures. Disappointed in the direction his career was going, he turned to drugs and died in 1956. (Two biographies, *The Count* by Arthur

Lennig, and *Lugosi: The Man Behind the Cape* by Robert Cremer, recount the life and films of Bela Lugosi in much greater detail than this book.) No one will dispute the contribution he made to the genre, starring in over fifty horror and science-fiction films, but he will always be remembered as Count Dracula.

Tod Browning had worked with Lugosi once before, on "The Thirteenth Chair" (1929) when he cast him in the role of Inspector Delzante, and he was familiar with his accomplishments on stage. Using Garrett Fort's screenplay (based on the original play by Hamilton Deane and John Balderston), Browning wanted to avoid the melodrama of Murnau's "Nosferatu" and went back to Stoker's original conception. This decision would sometimes mean the development of the plot was far too literal. Dracula would be played as a Transylvania nobleman (instead of the embodiment of plague and pestilence) who travels to London to satisfy his vampiric craving for blood. He would be dressed in the finest suits (updating the time to the present) and, like a wealthy aristocrat, would attend the symphony, opera, and exclusive dinner parties. And only after the stroke of midnight would his Count become a night stalker. Browning was able to achieve this through Lugosi's presence and the memorable photography of Karl Freund, which is hypnotic and chilling.

The film story of "Dracula" is much the same as Stoker's novel and the play by Hamilton Deane and John Balderston, and this might account for the film's stagy quality. Little has been changed, except the combining of the roles of Harker and Renfield. When the film opens, Renfield, portrayed by Dwight Frye, has traveled into the Carpathians to discuss several rental properties in England with a mysterious count. He refuses to heed the warnings of the local townspeople, and shortly after his arrival at the Count's castle, he falls under the spell of Dracula (Lugosi).

Later, after a short sea journey to Whitby in which the vampire destroys all but the captain of the ship, Dracula emerges as the new resident of Carfax Abbey. Count Dracula quickly becomes the toast of London by posing as a wealthy displaced aristocrat. He attends the theater, recitals, and other local cultural events. He is also a frequent guest of Dr. Jack Seward (Herbert Bunston) and is introduced to many women there, including Lucy Weston (Frances Dade) and Mina Seward (Helen Chandler), who all find him quite charming. After sucking her blood and turning young Lucy into a vampire, Dracula turns his attention to her friend Mina.

When Mina becomes ill, Dr. Abraham Van Helsing (Edward Van Sloan) is called in to help. The learned professor believes that she is suffering from the bite of a vampire, and that to cure her, they must take steps to find and destroy the evil creature. Dr. Seward and Jonathan Harker (David Manners) are skeptical but follow his instructions. Van Helsing soon unmasks Dracula as a vampire by accidentally discovering that the Count casts no reflection in the mirror lid of his cigarette case. The two adversaries recognize each other for the first time. Outnumbered and with his identity exposed, Dracula attempts to make off with Mina, but he is too late. Van Helsing traps the vampire in his Hampstead cellar and drives a wooden stake through his heart.

Although the film was highly regarded in its time and is viewed today as a classic, it must be pointed out that the pacing is very slow and pedantic and the horror is kept to a minimum. Contemporary audiences, who are used to the graphic violence of the "Nightmare on Elm Street" films, will find this material pretty tame. Much of the action of the film takes place offscreen, leaving things to the imagination. Even the climax, which is glimpsed in silhouette, is handled so that Dracula's

death is merely suggested and not shown. Perhaps this is a fault of the Deane-Balderston play rather than the film, but it is nevertheless a major blunder because it robs the audience of the much needed catharsis. Tod Browning also insisted on having the period transposed to present (rather than Victorian) London, and this too is a mistake. The story works best by contrasting the repressed sexual urges of Victorian morality with Dracula's irresistible sexuality. However, Browning avoids this question entirely and in doing so takes away much of the vampire's

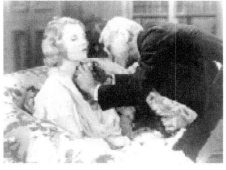

potency. Perhaps his reasoning was to minimize any controversy, but unfortunately it achieves the opposite effect by removing one of the central conflicts in the novel.

"Dracula" premiered on Friday, February 14, 1931, and in spite of its many flaws, was a major box-office success for Carl Laemmle and Universal Pictures. The motion picture grossed over $25 million from its original $441,984 investment in its initial release. During the next dozen years, the character of Dracula would appear in five more films, only one of which was a direct sequel, "Dracula's Daughter" (1936). Lugosi became an overnight success and played Dracula, or a relative vampire, six more times until his death in 1956. Although he became typecast as a heavy in a series of inferior horror movies, Lugosi remarked a few years before his death that he "wanted the public to scream with terror, as on a rollercoaster. I might have grown angry with the vampire putting me forever in the evil mold, but it was a living-or-a dying in its own way." Tod Browning went on making horror films for another ten years, including "Mark of the Vampire" (1935) with Lugosi, but he was never able to recapture the success of "London After Midnight" (1927) or "Dracula."

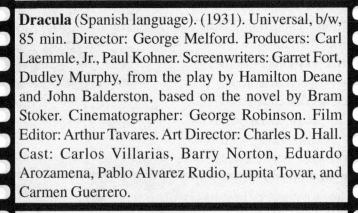

Dracula (Spanish language). (1931). Universal, b/w, 85 min. Director: George Melford. Producers: Carl Laemmle, Jr., Paul Kohner. Screenwriters: Garret Fort, Dudley Murphy, from the play by Hamilton Deane and John Balderston, based on the novel by Bram Stoker. Cinematographer: George Robinson. Film Editor: Arthur Tavares. Art Director: Charles D. Hall. Cast: Carlos Villarias, Barry Norton, Eduardo Arozamena, Pablo Alvarez Rudio, Lupita Tovar, and Carmen Guerrero.

The Spanish Language Version

Filmed back-to-back with the Tod Browning version, using the same sets and whole scenes, the Spanish-language "Dracula" was also an enormous success critically and financially. Universal Pictures and Junior Laemmle wisely recognized that half their revenues came from foreign countries, many of which were Latin. Since dubbing was years away, they decided to produce a simultaneous foreign-language version at an extremely low cost ($70,000 total). Principal photography was shot at night on the Universal lot by George Melford, cin-

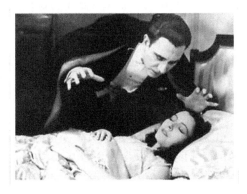

ematographer George Robinson, and a crew of Mexican actors and technicians after the American crew had gone home, and other scenes were lifted in tact from the negative print.

Carlos Villarias essayed the Lugosi role as Dracula; Barry Norton appeared as "Juan" Harker; Eduardo Arozamena as Dr. Van Helsing; and Pablo Alvarez Rudio as "Rendfield" (not Renfield). Noted actress Lupita Tovar played Eva (not Mina), and Carmen Guerrero completed the cast as Lucia (not Lucy). Ironically, Melford's version was completed first and released in Mexico weeks before the Browning picture. Critics were very enthusiastic about the foreign-language film (more so than the earlier Spanish language adaptation of Rupert Julian's "The Cat Creeps"), and "Dracula" played for many years in Spanish-speaking countries.

Numerous differences exist between the Browning and Melford versions, but the most striking difference is the lack of a flat stage play in the foreign-language film. George Melford apparently studied Browning's version shot for shot on a moviola and chose to revise certain scenes, creating more of an atmospheric chiller like "Nosferatu" (1922) than a filmed play. Personal tastes differ, and ultimately the audience must decide which is the better version.

The box office success of "Dracula" in 1931, and its subsequent reissues in 1933 and 1934, caused Carl Laemmle Jr. and other executives at Universal Pictures to ponder a sequel, but they all realized that it would be at least four years before the principals, Browning and Lugosi, would be available again. Lugosi had suddenly become a hot property (in spite of losing the role of the Frankenstein monster to Karloff) and would make seven genre films during the four-year period, including "The Murders in the Rue Morgue" (1931), "White Zombie" (1932), "Chandu the Magician" (1932), "Island of Lost Souls" (1933), and "The Black Cat" (1934, with Karloff). Browning was also in demand, directing "The Iron Man" (1931), "Freaks" (1932), and the aforementioned "Mark of the Vampire" He had also worked out an exclusive contract with M-G-M, and his availability was in question. And besides, there was the problem of the film's ending. Dracula dies at the end of the movie, and there was no contingency plan to bring the most popular character of the film back to life. Undaunted, Laemmle announced preproduction of "The Bride of Dracula" (later changed to "Dracula's Daughter" to avoid conflict with Universal's "Bride of Frankenstein," 1935), and commissioned Garret Fort to begin work on a sequel.

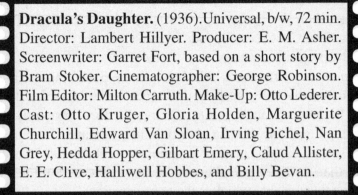

Dracula's Daughter. (1936).Universal, b/w, 72 min. Director: Lambert Hillyer. Producer: E. M. Asher. Screenwriter: Garret Fort, based on a short story by Bram Stoker. Cinematographer: George Robinson. Film Editor: Milton Carruth. Make-Up: Otto Lederer. Cast: Otto Kruger, Gloria Holden, Marguerite Churchill, Edward Van Sloan, Irving Pichel, Nan Grey, Hedda Hopper, Gilbart Emery, Calud Allister, E. E. Clive, Halliwell Hobbes, and Billy Bevan.

Dracula's Children of the Night

"Dracula's Daughter" (1936), the first of many sequels that would be made from the Bram Stoker classic, was actually based on a leftover chapter from *Dracula* entitled "Dracula's Guest." The movie bears little resemblance to its source material but does pick up (right as Browning left it) with Van Helsing (Edward Van Sloan) being charged with Dracula's murder. Apparently no one believes the good doctor has really disposed of a vampire. The daughter of Dracula, Countess Marya Zaleska (Gloria Holden), travels to London to burn her father's body and avenge herself on Van Helsing and the others. Bloodless corpses start piling up, and the Countess seeks the aide of psychiatrist Jeffrey Garth (Otto Kruger) to free her from the legacy of the Dracula family's curse.

From there, the sequel develops into a complex Sherlock Holmes mystery, with the chief of police, Van Helsing, and others in pursuit of another vampire.

Gloria Holden played the titular character with a chilling vitality that the publicists proclaimed: "More sensational than her unforgettable father!" But other than her superb characterization and Edward Van Sloan's reprise of the famous vampire hunter, the film was largely for-

gettable, a mere answer to a Trivial Pursuit question. The direction by Lambert Hillyer was uninspired, and the photography of George Robinson was purely pedestrian. One wonders what Tod Browning would have done with the material. However, the film made money and inspired Laemmle to produce a second sequel, featuring Lon Chaney Jr. as Dracula's son.

Son of Dracula. (1942). Universal, b/w, 79 min. Director: Robert Siodmak. Producer: Ford Beebe. Writers: Eric Taylor and Curt Siodmak. Based upon characters from *Dracula* as written by Bram Stoker. Cinematographer: George Robinson. Film Editor: Saul Goodkind. Make-Up: Jack Pierce. Cast: Lon Chaney, Jr., Louise Albritton, Frank Carven, J. Edward Bromberg, Robert Paige, Samuel Hinds, and Evelyn Ankers.

"Son of Dracula" (1942) was a further digression in the series of "Dracula" sequels. Budgeted at nearly twice what the original had cost, this film was proof of the old axiom that "bigger isn't necessarily better." Carl Laemmle, Jr., had become ill, and a group of executives had taken control of (what would become) Universal Studios. By the end of the 1930s, box-office returns on horror films had begun to dry up, but the 1938 re-release of "Dracula" and "Frankenstein" on a double bill demonstrated to the businessmen, who were now in charge, that there was still a market for those types of films. The decision was made to introduce another vampire sibling, and production was begun on the "biggest and most exciting" monster movie yet. In fact, the studio's original intention was to make the film in color, but tests proved that the vampire's makeup would not hold up under the intensity of the hot light. Unfortunately, the film was strictly a formula piece generated by a committee, and the use of color would not have been able to raise it above mediocrity.

A mysterious stranger, named Count Alucard (Dracula spelled backwards), travels to the United States and takes up residence at a Southern plantation. He soon becomes entranced with Southern belle Katherine Caldwell (played by Louise Albritton) and draws her hypnotically into his world of vampirism. Their relationship becomes strangely erotic as she gladly embraces the world of the "undead" to share immortality with him. He desires her position of power and wealth and hopes to use it to gain world domination. Fortunately, several locals, including her ex-boyfriend Frank Stanley (Robert Paige), who are familiar with the extermination of vampires rescue the girl and destroy the mysterious Count.

"Son of Dracula" featured a few nice moments, including a visit to the swamp-dwelling abode of Queen Zimba, and some good trick photography in which the Count disappears in puffs of smoke. But the casting is all wrong. Lon Chaney, Jr., who was far too soft-spoken and physically huge, is totally unbelievable as a vampire, in spite of the great makeup by Pierce. He is simply not suave or menacing enough, and should have continued to play werewolves, as in "The Wolf Man" (1941), instead. Also, the title cheats. Count Alucard isn't

House of Dracula (1945). Universal, b/w, 71 min. Director: Erle C. Kenton. Producer: Paul Malvern. Writer: Edward T. Lowe. Cinematographer: George Robinson. Film Editor: Russell Schoengarth. Make-Up: Jack Pierce. Cast: Lon Chaney, Jr., Martha Driscoll, John Carradine, Lionel Atwill, Onslow Stevens, Jane Addams, and Glenn Strange.

the son of Dracula but the old Count himself. The Universal series of "Dracula" films would continue into the forties, but they would never again regain the allure or the respect of the originals. "House of Frankenstein" (1944) (See Chapter Three) was the next in the series, followed by "House of Dracula" (1945).

Dracula Team-Ups with the Other Monsters

Regrettably, "House of Dracula" was a further descent of Universal's "Dracula" figure into mediocrity. The businessmen who were now running Universal Studios were only interested in the bottom line, which meant producing a product as quickly and cheaply as possible for the movie-going public. They did not seem to care whether their product was any good, or not. So, when Erle C. Kenton and Edward T. Lowe were hired to produce a sequel to "House of Frankenstein" (1944), they did the best they could within the limitations of the front office. At least, the concept was an interesting one: By attempting to discover a scientific explanation for vampirism and lycanthropy, Lowe ventures into new, uncharted territory. Unfortunately, his script mishandles every possible avenue with unintentionally humorous dialogue and clichéd characters. It is difficult to sit through the film straight-faced, particularly with Kenton's uninspired direction compounding the problem.

Clearly played for laughs rather than chills, the story opens bizarrely with Carradine's Dracula (actually Baron Latos) arriving at the cliff-top home of a mad scientist in search of a cure. Dr. Edelman (Onslow Stevens) is sympathetic to the vampire's plight and believes that he can find "an antibody that will consume the parasites of vampirism to affect a complete cure." In the midst of their conversation, Chaney's Wolf Man, Lawrence Talbot, shows up

looking for a cure. The doctor accepts him as a patient, working under the dubious assumption that Talbot's problem is due to pressure on the brain and that a softening drug will cure him. (The film makes it quite clear that the executives at Universal Pictures had taken the same soft-

ening drug prior to approving this effort.) Meanwhile, Edelman's hunchback nurse is growing special flowers in a foggy dungeon with the hopes they will revive the Frankenstein monster (Glenn Strange). The film reaches a shattering climax when the mad doctor becomes infected with the vampire's blood and goes on a rampage, releasing the Frankenstein monster. Villagers of Vasaria, led by Lionel Atwill's Inspector Holtz (whose character was wonderfully spoofed by Kenneth Mars in Mel Brooks' "Young Frankenstein," 1974), fight him back with torches and burn the house to the ground. Only Lawrence Talbot survives the conflagration and discovers, much to his amazement, that he is forever cured as the Wolf Man (that is, until the next movie).

"House of Dracula" has only two saving graces that have kept the film from obscurity-Jack B. Pierce and John Carradine. Pierce, who had created the makeup for most of Universal's monsters, including the Wolf Man, the Mummy, Dracula, and the Frankenstein monster, worked on his last monster in this movie. Having served the industry for more than twenty-two years, he had been responsible for a number of innovations in makeup. But with all the new advances in plastic and foam rubber, Pierce was unwilling to change and found his services no longer needed at Universal Pictures. (Ironically, Pierce's designs for the Frankenstein monster would become the standard for the next thirty years.)

Carradine, on the other hand, was very much in demand. Born Richmond Reed Carradine in 1906, he has been featured or starred in over 230 films since his debut in "Tolable David" (1930) and holds the Guinness record for the most screen credits. This gaunt character actor, who had scored critical praise in such films as "Stagecoach" (1939) and "The Grapes of Wrath" (1940), made a big impression as Dracula to the American public. His two performances as the Transylvanian Count first in "House of Frankenstein" and then later in "House of Dracula" established him as Lugosi's successor to the role. Until his death in 1988, he had played

Dracula, or a relative vampire, nine times on screen, with occasional stage and television performances. When the suits decided to pair the Universal monsters with two comedians in "Abbott and Costello Meet Frankenstein" (1948) (See Chapter Three), he was, fortunately, touring with his one-man Shakespeare readings and was unavailable. Instead executives at Universal cast Lugosi, despite his drug habit, in that horrible film.

Dracula (1979). Universal Pictures, 112 min. Director: John Badham. Pr, Walter Mirisch, Marvin Mirisch, Tom Pevsner. Screenwriter: W.D. Richter, based on the novel by Bram Stoker and the stage play by Hamilton Deane and John Balderston. Cinematographer: Gilbert Taylor. Film Editor: John Bloom. Special Effects: Roy Arbogast. Production Designer: Peter Murton. Cast: Frank Langella, Laurence Olivier, Kate Nelligan, Donald Pleasence, Trevor Eve, Jan Francis, Janine Duvitski, and Tony Haygarth.

Resurrecting Dracula

Universal resurrected the character of Dracula in John Badham's stylish and atmospheric 1979 remake of Bram Stoker's classic. Frank Langella who had played the role of Dracula on the Broadway stage portrays the Count as a sexy matinee idol that causes women to swoon rather than cringe in terror. His portrayal of Dracula as a handsome aristocrat was very distinctive from that of Bela Lugosi's menacing foreigner, but even more to the point, with one turn of his cape, he managed to erase the innate horror or perversity that Christopher Lee had radiated in the Hammer Films. For nearly twenty years, Lee had made the character of Dracula his in a series of memorable movies from Hammer Films. So Langella was forced to bring something very new to the part. He resembles a latter-day Valentino and brings a romantic

elegance to the role that had never been imagined. And what remains of "Dracula" is a lush, campy, romantic version of a once great horror fantasy.

The story begins after Harker's journey to Transylvania with Dracula's arrival on the doomed clipper ship. When the ship is wrecked off the coast of England, near Whitby, the only survivor is Count Dracula who has arrived with large amounts of Transylvanian soil. The Count soon takes up residence at Carfax Abbey, employs the aid of the local strong man, Milo Renfield (Tony Haygarth), and becomes the talk of polite English society. He makes friends with Dr Seward (Donald Pleasence) who runs the local asylum and with his daughter Lucy (Kate Nelligan), her friend Mina Van Helsing (Jan Francis), and with Jonathan Harker (Trever Eve), Lucy's solicitor fiancé who has arranged for the sale of Carfax Abbey to Dracula.

After midnight, however, his sexual and vampiric needs are satisfied as he seduces both Lucy and Mina. When Mina dies from loss of blood, her father Dr. Abraham Van Helsing (Lawrence Olivier) suspects that she has been killed by a vampire. Both he and Dr. Seward learn of Dracula's evil and chase him from his home. Count Dracula flees England on another clipper ship with Lucy, and Van Helsing follows in a smaller, faster ship. In the dramatic climax, the evil

Count impales Van Helsing to the wall (with the doctor's wooden stake), and he himself is impaled on a large winch hook. Then, with Van Helsing's last dying effort, Dracula is literally run up a flagpole to expire in the sun. But the Count doesn't die; instead he changes into a bat, and flies away, suggesting a sequel.

"Dracula" was very successful in its initial release, and the motion picture made a star of Frank Langella. He had played the role of the Transylvanian count at the Martin Beck Theatre in New York City from October 13, 1977 through October 1978 (when future Sherlock Holmes Jeremy Brett took over). The Broadway stage production was produced by Elizabeth Ireland McCann, John Wulp, Victor Lurie, Nelle Nugent, and Max Weitzenhoffer. With over four hundred performances on stage before a live audience, Langella made the character something special. No one before or since has mastered his hypnotic trance, his hand movements, or the way in which he handles his long cape like it was an extension of his body. Women still faint and men tremble because of his memorable performance.

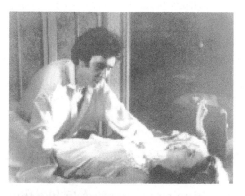

The direction by John Badham is first rate, as are the updated special effects by Roy Arbogast and Maurice Binder. The film spawned a host of imitators, and in the twenty-five years since its release, other lesser versions of the story have brought Dracula back from the grave time and again, but none have ever re-captured the true spirit of Universal's vampire.

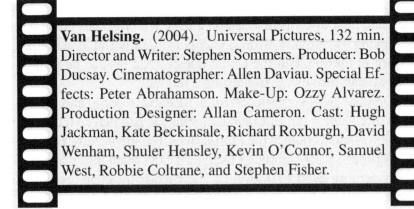

Van Helsing. (2004). Universal Pictures, 132 min. Director and Writer: Stephen Sommers. Producer: Bob Ducsay. Cinematographer: Allen Daviau. Special Effects: Peter Abrahamson. Make-Up: Ozzy Alvarez. Production Designer: Allan Cameron. Cast: Hugh Jackman, Kate Beckinsale, Richard Roxburgh, David Wenham, Shuler Hensley, Kevin O'Connor, Samuel West, Robbie Coltrane, and Stephen Fisher.

In 2004, Stephen Sommers tried to do for Dracula, Frankenstein and the Wolf Man what he had already done for the Mummy in "The Mummy" (1999). By focusing on the notorious monster hunter, Sommers adds yet another twist to Universal's famous stable of monsters. His "Van Helsing" is an over-the-top thrill-ride that is equal parts pastiche and parody. After a suspense-filled opening, in which Dr. Gabriel Van Helsing (Hugh Jackman) eliminates the threat of Mr. Hyde (Robbie Coltrane), he is ordered to stop Count Dracula (Richard Roxburgh) from using Dr. Frankenstein's research to animate a new monster (Shuler Hensley) and the Wolf Man (Will Kemp) for some sinister purpose. A Q-like figure named Carl (David Wenham) arms him with several high-tech devices, including a gatling-gun that fires wooden stakes. He arrives in Transylvania, and allies himself with the ravishing Anna (Kate Beckinsale), a member of a family committed to ridding the world of evil. Together they set off to eliminate the famous monsters of filmland one at a time.

Jackman who had played the man-beast Wolverine in the "X-Men" films remakes stuffy old Dr. Van Helsing into a dashing superhero, and Beckinsale, who headlined the "Underworld" films as a werewolf-hunting vampire, is gorgeous as ever as Anna. Universal's Monsters, of course, represent the reason why we plunked down ten bucks to see the movie, and they don't disappoint. Roxburgh makes a formidable Count Dracula, along with Hensley and Kemp in their roles, respectively. However, Kevin O'Connor steals the show as the Dwight Frye-inspired Igor. All in all, "Van Helsing" is at times scary, exciting, and fun.

3
Frankenstein

I shall not be supposed as according the remotest degree of serious faith to such an imagination; yet, assuming it as the basis of a work of fancy, I have not considered myself as merely weaving a series of supernatural terrors. The event on which the interest of the story depends is exempt from the disadvantages of a mere tale of spectres or enchantment. It was recommended by the novelty of the situations which it develops; and, however possible as a physical fact, affords a point of view to the imagination for the delineating of human passions more comprehensive and commanding than any which the ordinary relations of existing events can yield.
—*Mary Shelley, Preface to Frankenstein (1818)*

Hollywood first discovered Mary Shelley's "enfant terrible" - that hulking, metaphorical creation of Dr. Frankenstein - in 1910, with a small innovative film from Thomas Edison's motion picture company, but its love affair reached mythic proportions in 1931 when Colin Clive as Henry Frankenstein gave birth to his monster (played by then unknown Boris Karloff) and the American horror film in "Frankenstein." That most famous adaptation of the story not only spawned several sequels but also created a whole cottage industry. In fact, the novel *Frankenstein, or The Modern Prometheus* has been freely adapted for the silver screen more than a dozen times and has inspired countless sequels, parodies, and spoofs! The terms "Frankenstein" (the name of the creator often wrongly associated with the monster) and "mad scientist" have become synonymous with rampant technology and science out of control. But at the central core of the story is a parable that is universal: man's meddling in the natural order of things can (and often does) bring about his own destruction. And though the original classic by Mary Wollstonecraft Shelley is a

fairly recent entry (published in 1818) - and certainly nowhere as old as its vampire counterpart - the origins of the Frankenstein mythos can be traced directly back to much earlier forms in folklore.

Thematically, the Frankenstein mythos concerns a pattern of heretical beliefs, which are often suggested symbolically or metaphorically in film, that question man's place in the cosmos. Those presuppositions - while they may have taken on different forms in various movies - have changed very little in the last seventy five years (or several thousand, for that matter). Their roots lie not only in the scientific romances of Nathaniel Hawthorne, H.G. Wells, and the novel *Frankenstein*, to which many motion pictures owe as source materials, but also in older, literary conventions and attitudes from Greco-Roman mythology and medieval folklore. Both the legend of Prometheus and the story of Pygmalion are parables of human presumption - about man playing god - that predate the Frankenstein story by some five thousand years. Prometheus steals fire from Mount Olympus for man at the cost of great suffering and eternal damnation. Pygmalion, the lonely king of Cyprus, creates a statue of the perfect woman - Galatea - and imbues it with life, openly defying an edict from the gods. Both acts challenge the natural order of things, and both individuals suffer similar punishment from the gods for their arrogance. Similarly, the medieval story of Dr. Faustus (or Faust) portrays a man who is willing to sell his soul to the Devil in exchange for answers to the mysteries of the universe. Faust, like Prometheus and Pygmalion, defies the gods (or, in this case, a Judeo-Christian god) and must be destroyed because "there are things that man is not meant to know." And it is this common theme that is central to our understanding of the Frankenstein mythos.

Because it also draws from such a rich literary heritage, questions about the nature of beauty and ugliness, good and evil, science and faith can also be found in most, well-written Frankenstein films.

Clearly, the scientific romances of the last two hundred years have provided a wealth of mythopoetic characters that are no more than archetypes or symbols for a much larger concern. Aylmer, the alchemist in Hawthorne's "The Birthmark," is the archetype for the first mad scientist and a symbol in a simple parable that examines the nature of beauty and ugliness. Shocked by his wife's "visible mark of earthly imperfection" - a symbol in his mind of mankind's fallen nature - he takes drastic steps to remove the ugliness. What he fails to realize is that the blemish actually enhances her beauty, and his experiments only contribute to her death. Jack Griffin, the scientist with lofty ideals in Wells' *The Invisible Man*, represents both a savior and a demon as the forces of good and evil (in symbolic form) struggle for control of his soul. Driven mad by the side effects of the invisibility serum that he invents and imbibes, he becomes the scourge of the countryside. His benevolent dreams for mankind turn evil, and he, too, must be punished for meddling in the natural order of the universe.

Dr. Victor Frankenstein is the quintessential mad scientist and symbol for scientific rationalism, which, more often than not, goes wrong. No matter how objective and well-intentioned the great doctor may be, he still tends to produce a monster. Distraught over his brother's death (and thoughts of his own mortality), Frankenstein abandons his traditional Christian beliefs in favor of a new religion — known as science. He is, perhaps, too logical and rational to believe in the mysticism of Christ and the Resurrection, and prefers the simplicity of "truth" and "beauty" in the cold equations of science. Ignoring the warnings of his wife-to-be Elizabeth, Frankenstein assembles body parts from dead corpses and "creates" his own Adam. Unfortunately, his "creation" is far from the perfect man that he envisioned, and he rejects it. The "creature" - which is really not a monster at all but a beautiful innocent - runs into the wilderness and befriends a blind woodsman (who cannot tell the difference between beauty and ugliness). There, the creature learns about the fallen, imperfect nature of man by reading Milton's *Paradise Lost* and realizes that he must confront his master. Meanwhile, Dr. Frankenstein, constantly haunted by memories of the past, has been unable to start his life anew and settle down with Elizabeth. Despite his earlier rejection of the monster, he finds himself inexorably tied to his creation; but when he finally accepts responsibility for his actions it is too late. The creature has become the demon that everyone thinks he is and turns upon the man who created him. The science, in which Dr. Franken-stein "worshipped" and sought salvation, had ironically become the instrument of his own destruction, and it is specifically this theme that has imbued much of the cinema's fear and nervousness about technology.

The continued use of these common elements, archetypes, and symbols has not diminished the interest (or hampered the develop-ment) of the Frankenstein film; but, rather, provided an arena for ingenuity and imagination to examine how the old themes impact on contemporary problems. Early in its history, the Frankenstein film became not only a cautionary tale about technology out of control but also a social and aesthetic reflection of its popular culture. And we can learn much about the attitudes of the period in which each film was made. For example, in "The Cabinet of Dr. Caligari" (1919), "Metropolis" (1926), and "Frankenstein" (1931) and other early mo-tion pictures, science and philosophy were portrayed as evil mono-liths that threatened to take over the world. Prior to the turn of the century, Darwin, Nietzsche, Freud, and other learned men had rocked the moral and religious foundation of society with their provocative theories, and were threatening to change the status quo as their theo-ries swept throughout the world.

In the forties, in films like "Dr. Cyclops" (1940), "The Mad Doc-tor of Market Street" (1942), "Dr. Renault's Secret" (1942), and oth-ers, the mad scientist had a distinctive German flavor and represented the godless fascists who were terrorizing the world with their V-2 rockets and death camps. During the fifties, in films like "Tarantula" (1955), "The Incredible Shrinking Man" (1957), "The Deadly Man-tis" (1957) and others, Frankenstein's creature was no longer depicted as a mindless innocent but a monstrous behemoth usually created by the accidental detonation of an atomic bomb (another symbol of sci-ence out of control). For the sixties, seventies, and eighties, in an epoch which had rejected most religious and supernatural beliefs in favor of science and technology, cautionary films, like "Alphaville" (1965), "2001: A Space Odyssey" (1968), "Colossus: The Forbin Project" (1970), "Westworld" (1973), and others, portrayed Frankenstein's monster as a metaphorical symbol for the computer age, and warned us that we soon might become slaves to the technol-ogy that he had created.

Mary Shelley and Frankenstein

Mary Shelley is considered by many as the mother of modern science fiction. Her pioneering efforts to provide a scientific explanation for what might have been perceived as a conventional Gothic tale created the whole new branch of "speculative fiction." Ever since she first penned *Frankenstein* in 1818, the idea of bestowing human life upon the lifeless has fascinated science fiction writers. H(erbert) G(eorge) Wells, also recognized as one of the genre's founding fathers, created two scientists (Jack Griffith and Dr. Moreau) who were not satisfied with the natural order of the universe and decided to meddle in things man was not meant to know. Maurice Renard's *Les Mains d'Orlac*, in which the hands of a murderer are transplanted onto a pianist, was a similar indictment of science and scientific experimentation gone wrong. The robots in Karel Capek's *R.U.R. (Rossum's Universal Robots*, 1921) are, in essence, lifeless metal hulks brought to life with the spark of electricity. H(oward) P(hillips) Lovecraft's protagonist in *Herbert West—Reanimator* (1939) devotes his lifework to the reanimation of the dead. Robert Silverberg's Nebula Award-winning novella "Born With the Dead" describes a future time when the dead are "rekindled" to live again. And countless other tales of mad doctors and their unnatural experiments have dominated literature and film for nearly two hundred years. Thanks to an inspir-

ing and unconventional English novelist, the way in which modern audiences look at discoveries and inventions, metaphysics, religion and science, good and evil, life and death has forever changed.

Mary Wollstonecraft Godwin was born in a small English hamlet in August 1797 to William Godwin and Mary Wollstonecraft. Her father was a noted philosopher and novelist, and her mother was an outspoken feminist, intellectual and educator. When her beautiful mother died ten days after her birth from a severe hemorrhage and an ague, Mary and her three year-old sister Fanny were left to the impractical Godwin for care. Her father later remarried, and Mary gained a half sister, Claire Clairmont. At age 16, Mary Godwin was introduced to a young poet named Percy Bysshe Shelley, who was not only considerably older than she but also married to another woman. Later, when Shelley began calling on her, he and William Godwin became very friendly. Their friendship cost Shelley a considerable fortune, as Godwin was always asking for money. Percy Shelley finally grew tired of her father's demands, and eloped with Mary, aged seventeen, to the Continent in 1814.

The next year Mary Godwin bore Shelley a son, who died only a few days later. She recorded in her journal of March 15, 1815: "Dream that my little baby came to life again; that it had only been cold, and that we had rubbed it before the fire, and it had lived." Mary had many other nightmares about her son's premature death, and wished somehow to bring him back to life. She again became pregnant, and gave birth to a second son, William, in January of 1816, who also died in childhood. Of her three children by Shelley, only one of them, Percy Florence, managed to survive beyond childhood. The deaths of her children were very hard on Mary, and contributed much to her depressive, melancholy outlook on life. Like most intellectuals, she had trouble accepting the finality of death, and turned to science and the works of Erasmus Darwin for answers.

In the summer of 1816, while vacationing along the shores of Lake Geneva, Switzerland, Mary, her half sister Claire and Percy Shelley met Lord Byron, his traveling companion Dr. John Polidori and "Monk" Lewis. Byron had exiled himself from England forever, and had taken up permanent residence at the Villa Diodati, where John Milton (author of *Paradise Lost*) had once stayed. For several

nights, the group read Goethe's *Faust*, translating from German, aloud, and discussed De Sade, Darwin, vampires and the supernatural. Polidori supplied the company with most of the reading material, although it was actually Shelley who introduced Byron to Darwin's notions about evolution. They eventually became bored, like most idle rich, and decided to have a writing competition - to create the best ghost story - in order to stem their boredom. One night, just prior to her nineteenth birthday, Mary had a dream of a hideous phantasm stirring to life, and started her gothic tale: "It was on a dreary night of November . . ."

Shelley later persuaded her to lengthen the story by including several chapters as a framing device for the actual creation of the monster. *Frankenstein, or The Modern Prometheus* was completed within a year, and first published in 1818, when Mary was only twenty years old. (John Polidori wrote *The Vampyre*, which later inspired Bram Stoker's *Dracula* as well as many modern vampire tales; Byron first penned lines to Manfred and the science fictional poem "Darkness," and Shelley began work on his epic work *Prometheus Bound*.)

In December 1816, after Shelley's first wife, Harriet, had drowned herself in the Serpentine River, Mary and Percy were finally married. They continued to live and work in Switzerland. Less than six years later, Percy Bysshe Shelley drowned accidentally in 1822. Mary was devastated by her husband's death but lived on to write other novels, including the popular science fiction work, *The Last Man* (published in 1826). She died at the age of fifty-three in 1851, the year of the Great Exhibition, and was buried in a churchyard in Bournemouth.

Several motion pictures have attempted to capture that "haunted summer" of 1816 on film, and have succeeded or failed to different degrees. James Whale bookends the main action of "The Bride of Frankenstein" (1935) with a prologue based on the Preface to the 1818 edition of *Frankenstein* in which Mary Wollstonecraft Shelley (played by Elsa Lanchester) explained how she came to write such a bizarre tale. Fifty-six years later, Ken Russell would build his hallucinatory "Gothic" (1987) around those very same historical events, with Natasha Richardson (daughter of the late Tony Richardson and Vanessa Redgrave) playing Mary Shelley. "Haunted Summer" (1988) is set in the summer of 1816, and features similar events, starting with the fabled meeting of Lord Byron and Percy Shelley and leading to that fateful night when Mary Godwin and John Polidori wrote their classics. And finally, "Frankenstein Unbound" (1990) postulates the theory that Dr. Frankenstein (played by Raoul Julia) was a real person who crossed paths with Mary Godwin (Bidget Fonda) and Percy Shelley (Michael Hutchence, lead singer of the rock group INXS).

The Original Novel

Frankenstein, or The Modern Prometheus was published in 1818, and has remained continuously in print for nearly two hundred years. Fans of the various motion pictures, dating back to 1910, might be surprised to learn how much different that novel is from what has been produced for film or television. To modern readers, Mary Shelley's methods of narration may seen somewhat clumsy and confusing, but the epistolary style, made famous by Richardson, was very popular. Indeed, the collection of letters, journals and other documentation from various sources added a certain verisimilitude to the story for early nineteenth century readers. (The epistolary style remained popular throughout the 1800's, and was later adopted by Bram Stoker for his telling of Count Dracula's tragic story.)

The novel opens with a letter from a ship's captain to his sister in England. During a hazardous voyage to the North Pole, Captain Walton has made the acquaintance of a young Swiss scientist, named Dr. Victor Frankenstein. At first, the captain believes him to be mad, because he keeps raving about a monstrous creature that he must destroy; but much later, he accepts Frankenstein's story as fact and listens with much astonishment. Apparently, and this is when the narrative shifts to Victor's manuscript, the mad doctor began his career by studying the work of infamous alchemists, like Cornelius Agrippa, Paracelsus, and Albertus Magnus, in an attempt to find a connection between life and death.

Growing impatient with his limited successes, Victor Frankenstein went to the university to consult with two old professors, Dr. Kempe and Dr. Waldman. Both Kempe, a professor of natural philosophy, and Waldman, a professor of chemistry, discount the work of the ancient alchemists, and convince Frankenstein that the modern scientific method will lead him to ultimate success. The young Swiss scientist then becomes obsessed with the notion that the spark of life may be a "spark" in some literal sense. He hopes to create life itself by galvanizing dead matter, and to this end, makes a composite body from human remains. The spirit of scientific research, however, remains subordinate to his morbid obsession with death. Even while the modern Prometheus declares that "life and death appeared to me ideal bounds, which I should first break through, and pour a torrent of light into our dark world," his mind was already slipping into the shadowlands beyond the reach of others.

His creation is grotesque but mechanically sound, and when he imbues it with life "the hideous phantasm of a man stretched out, and then, on the working of some powerful engine, show signs of life, and stir with an uneasy, half vital motion." Overcome by horror at what he has wrought, Victor rejects his creature by running away. A whole summer passes before he meets it again, and during that time, his younger brother William is murdered (by the creature) and an innocent woman named Justine is hanged for the murder.

The creature returns to Frankenstein, and reveals how it has been persecuted, because of its ugliness, and hunted down by others. Initially innocent but soon distorted by hatred and bigotry, the creature has learned to become a monster. It has also learned about man's nature, by reading the story of Adam in Milton's *Paradise Lost*, and beseeches its creator to make a female companion. At first, Victor

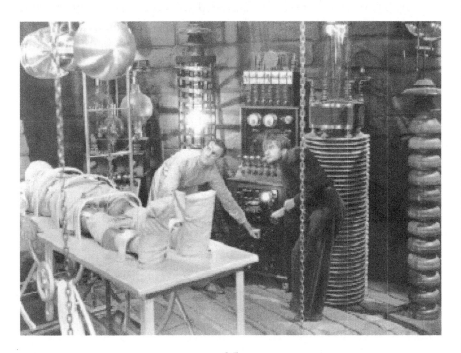

agrees, and begins work on the second creature in a new laboratory in the Orkneys. But with his work almost complete, the mad doctor pauses, considering the "race of devils" that might result in their union, and destroys the woman. When the monster discovers that it has again been betrayed by its creator, it threatens "I shall be with you on your wedding night" and then disappears. That threat ultimately leads to the death of Elizabeth, Victor Frankenstein's new bride.

The rest of the tale is about flight and pursuit, death and retribution. Victor pursues the creature to the North Pole, aboard Captain Walton's ship. When the ship is caught amid mist and ice in the polar regions, the mad doctor sets off on foot. His last words to the ship's captain reveal his feeble, anguished state: "Farewell, Walton! Seek happiness in tranquility, and avoid ambition, even if it be only the apparently innocent one of distinguishing yourself in science and discoveries. Yet why do I say this? I have myself been blasted in these hopes, yet another may succeed." Frankenstein later dies aboard the ship, and Walton writes that he found the creature leaning over the body of its master, weaping and recalling words from Milton: "Evil thenceforth became my good! The fallen angel becomes a malignant devil . . ."

Dr. Victor Frankenstein had indeed solved the riddle of life and death, but like so many tragic heroes before him, the answers to the universal mysteries that confront man, have only brought him only torment and death.

The creature in *Frankenstein, or The Modern Prometheus* is no simple monster. When it is first awakened, the creature is innocent, not knowing the difference between right and wrong. It is, in a sense, a tabula rasa - a blank slate - upon which the good and evil man does to it is ultimately written. There is great sorrow in the creature as it reads Byron Goethe's *The Sorrows of Werther* and John Milton's *Paradise Lost*. It identifies most with Adam, the first man, because it feels lost, alone, and utterly companionless. The creature's pitiful life also roughly parallels that of the Biblical figure, with the vital exception of the missing Eve; it is first created, then brought to self awareness of the world in which it lives, and finally cast out of Paradise through Victor's rejection. The creature continually refers to itself in Miltonian terms, alternating between "Adam," "fallen angel" and "malignant devil." Like Adam, it curses the day that it was created, echoing lines from the earliest chapters of *Paradise Lost:* "Did I request thee, Maker, from my clay to mould me Man? Did I solicit thee from darkness to promote me?"

Besides Goethe and Milton, the creature also steals a copy of Frankenstein's journal. Once it has read the mad doctor's words, it understands the horror and torment of its creator; it also feels sympathy for the man that rejected it, and realizes that he is the greater criminal for trying to do things which only God can do. In many ways, it reasons far better than Frankenstein! Bereft of traditional notions of good and evil, the creature soon learns hatred, bigotry and murder from those who seek to destroy it. When it finally confronts Frankenstein, the monster decries: "Remember, that I am thy creature; I ought to be thy Adam; but I am rather the fallen angel, whom thou drivest from joy for no misdeed. Every where I see bliss, from which I along am irrevocably excluded. I was benevolent and good; misery made me a fiend." By chapter sixteen of the novel, the creature is frequently referred to as "the fiend," but it is really Frankenstein who is the fiend. He seems much more cruel and brutal than his creature because of the way he mistreats his creation. The mad doctor sees a reflection of his own diseased soul in that of the creature.

"You must create a female for me with whom I can live in the interchange of those sympathies necessary for my being. This you alone can do, and I demand it of you as a right which you must not refuse to concede," the creature demands of its creator. It wishes to escape from this world and return to the natural life, with "the vast wilds of South America" as its Eden. The creature desires to play out Milton's *Paradise Lost*, with special emphasis on a mate and a garden of pleasure. For all of its pains and sorrows, it asks very little of its creator, and it is no wonder that Dr. Frankenstein's refusal to complete work on an "Eve" turns the creature into a savage monster. Only then does it turn on its master. By destroying Elizabeth, the creature seeks only to even the score.

The terrible paradox in Mary Shelley's work is that the "monster" is more human than its master. The creature, before it is enraged by the local villagers and Victor Frankenstein, is naive and gentle. Almost benevolent in nature, though monstrous in shape and form, the creature protects the blind man in the forest from harm. When it realizes that the food it has been stealing to eat has been draining the villagers' stores, it immediately stops, then brings cut wood as compensation. Frankenstein is just the opposite; he uses all those people around him, including Henry Clerval, Elizabeth, the professors at the university, Captain Walton, and even the creature, to further distinguish himself in science. He wants to be the one to "pour a torrent of light into our dark world." Like Goethe's Faust and Milton's Satan, Frankenstein has endeavored to gain the whole world and, in the process, lost his soul.

Towards the close of the novel, the struggle between Victor and the fiend, which embodied in his creature is in fact an outward manifestation of Frankenstein's diseased soul, reaches its tragic climax when, on the night following his wedding ceremony, he finds Elizabeth dead. Frankenstein despairs: "The apple was already eaten, and the angel's arm bared to drive me from all hope." He can no longer ask God for forgiveness, and he accepts the fate that he is doomed: "Like the archangel who aspired to omnipotence, I am chained in an eternal hell." The mad doctor dies soon after, and it is only his creature that shows him any compassion or depth of feeling. Captain Walton discovers the creature weeping over its master's body. It can offer Frankenstein no absolution from his blasphemy or promise of salvation in the hereafter, only sorrow and pity—human emotions

which the creature has learned from an inhuman world.

The durability of the Frankenstein story lies not simply in foreshadowing our anxieties about scientific progress but in this simple exchange between creator and created, and is essential to any study of the cinematic mythos of Mary Shelley's tale. The creature is not always a menace, and sometimes embodies many admirable qualities that its human counterparts lack.

"Frankenstein" (1931)

During the 1930's, the second great horror school developed and flourished in the United States with the introduction of the first "sound" classics of the genre. The tremendous success of Universal Pictures' "Dracula" in 1931 launched several highly-profitable series, including eight films in the "Frankenstein" cycle, six films in "The Invisible Man" cycle, and a handful of other motion pictures which dealt with the familiar theme of science (or technology) out of control. Carl Laemmle (at Universal) lured some of the finest talents of the silent period from Germany and France, and built a strong industry upon the cinematic traditions of Europe that audiences had found so remarkable. Outside the United States, the horror tradition all but died out, leaving very few exceptions, as European filmmakers flocked to the safety of America. Their work is still highly regarded today.

These milestones of the horror genre also helped create a certain degree of respectibility in the Thirties before the genre plummeted to its lowest depths in the Forties with a series of ripoffs and spinoffs. During the early part of the decade, the ravages of the Depression (in this country) and the talk of war in Europe caused many people to seek out the simple, escapist fare of fantasy films. But the motion pictures were so much more than that, as many of the Frankenstein films proved to audiences to be a popular indictment of America's financial institutions and Nazi Germany's totalitarian regime. The monolith of our economic systems - a Frankenstein monster created by wealthy industrialists - had collapsed under its own weight, leaving millions literally destitute. The mad doctor was one (or more) of those industrialists, and the fact that his monster had turned on him provided something of a catharsis for weary populations. Later in the decade, the doctor assumed a distinctive German flavor and related directly to the godless fascists who were trying to perfect a master race. Audiences couldn't get enough of these pictures, and the studios cranked them out in large numbers. This gave rise to low-budget, second features - known as "B"-movies - that were generally not very good and largely exploitative. By the end of the period, the horror genre in the United States had run its course, deteriorating into a slap-dash of sequels, parodies, and monster team-ups. Most filmmakers had forgotten how to make a simple creature feature.

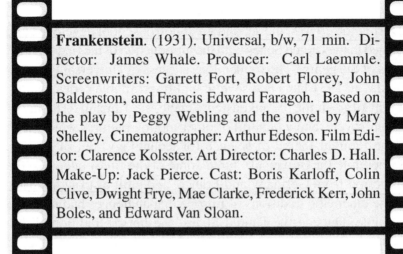

Frankenstein. (1931). Universal, b/w, 71 min. Director: James Whale. Producer: Carl Laemmle. Screenwriters: Garrett Fort, Robert Florey, John Balderston, and Francis Edward Faragoh. Based on the play by Peggy Webling and the novel by Mary Shelley. Cinematographer: Arthur Edeson. Film Editor: Clarence Kolsster. Art Director: Charles D. Hall. Make-Up: Jack Pierce. Cast: Boris Karloff, Colin Clive, Dwight Frye, Mae Clarke, Frederick Kerr, John Boles, and Edward Van Sloan.

"Frankenstein" (1931) is probably one of the most celebrated and influential motion pictures ever made, and easily stands the ultimate test of time. In the wake of the immense commercial and unexpected success of "Dracula" (1931), Carl Laemmle looked around desperately for another horror property. Hollywood, in those days, expected every success to have a successor. He had several projects to choose from, including "Dr. Jekyll and Mr. Hyde" (a version of which was already in production at Paramount), "The Hound of the Baskervilles" (which was being made at Gaumont), and "The Murders in the Rue Morgue." But he decided on Mary Shelley's classic, which had already been filmed three times (in 1910, 1915, and 1920) and had inspired a hit play. Junior Laemmle further announced that French auteur Robert Florey would direct the feature, and that Bela Lugosi, Leslie Howard, and Bette Davis would star (respectively as the Creature, Dr. Frankenstein, and Elizabeth). But unfortunately the test footage by Paul Ivano on the "Dracula" sets with Lugosi as the monster were not very convincing. Lugosi looked too much like Wegener's Golem, and he was unhappy because he felt the audience would not recognize him under the heavy make-up. So the former prince of vampires dropped out of the project. Shortly, thereafter, Robert Florey lost interest; Bette Davis was assigned to another picture, and Laemmle began to fear that his big budget follow-up to "Dracula" was in danger. Those fears were allayed, however, by the appearance of James Whale and Boris Karloff.

James Whale had been under contract at Universal Pictures when he persuaded Laemmle to let him direct "Frankenstein." Born in Dudley, England, Whale's career spanned more than two decades and influenced a dozen genre films with his own expressionistic vision. He was a cartoonist before World War One, and as a captive in a German prisoner-of-war camp, he became interested in acting. He made his professional debut as an actor in the Birmingham Repertory Company production of "Abraham Lincoln," and continued to work as both an actor and director on the London stage. In 1930, Hollywood beckoned, with the opportunity to film his stage success "Journey's End." That same year, he co-directed "Hell's Angels" with Howard Hughes, and was signed to an exclusive contract at Universal. The movie "Frankenstein" launched his career as a horror director, and he made numerous genre films at that studio. He also directed a musical ("Showboat," 1936), a war film ("The Road Back," 1937), several comedies and adventure films. He retired in the late Forties after a most distinguished career. His later years are chronicled in "Gods and Monsters."

James Whale had seen Karloff in a Los Angeles stage production of "The Criminal Code" (1931) and in the film "Graft" (1931), but he did not offer him the part immediately. What he was looking for was a successor to Lon Chaney, "the man of a thousand faces," and he wasn't certain that Karloff's features would lend themselves to monster make-up. Whale sat for days in the Universal commissary, making sketches of the plain, strong face, then showed those sketches to

the make-up department before he ever approached Karloff. Finally, satisfied that he had found his man, Whale brought him to the attention of Carl Laemmle Jr. Special tests were ordered with the make-up genius of Jack Pierce, and Karloff emerged as that successor, creating one of the most memorable and famous monsters. The stage seemed set for the creation of a classic.

"Think of it, Fritz. The brain of a dead man waiting to live again in a body I have made with my own hands." The film story of "Frankenstein" more closely resembles the plot structure of Peggy Webling's play than the original classic upon which it is based. Mary Wollstonecraft Shelley's novel was a scientific discourse about the evils of technology out of control, and beyond the central conceit (of man versus his own creation), it lacked many of the dramatic elements that would have made it interesting to cinema audiences. Dame Webling's play, on the other hand, as adapted by John Balderston and revised by Robert Florey, Garrett Fort, and Francis Edward Faragoh, was much more dramatic and filmmable. It introduced the hunchbacked assistant Fritz (later changed in other films to Igor) and the conflict of the monster receiving the criminal's brain. The climax at the windmill is also very suspenseful and certainly far superior to the high-brow ending of the novel.

The film opens with a low-angle shot of gravestones at dusk, then pans upward to the mid-European (or Swiss) castle of Baron Henry (not Victor) Frankenstein. Frankenstein (played by Colin Clive) is obsessed with creating life from death, and he and his assistant Fritz (over-acted by Dwight Frye) steal bodies from the cemetery to further the doctor's experiments. Once the construction of his "perfect" man is complete, he sends his servant to steal the brain of a recently-deceased genius. Unfortunately, Fritz drops the brain by accident and substitutes a recently-executed, murderer's brain instead, neglecting to tell his master of the change. Meanwhile, Elizabeth (Mae Clark) and Clerval (John Boles), the young heroine and hero of the piece, make wedding preparations for the forth-coming marriage of the former to Henry Frankenstein.

"It's alive! It's alive!" Frankenstein exclaims, moments after the lightning of a raging storm powers his elaborate electrical apparatus of cathode tubes and transformers (designed by Kenneth Strickfaden) and bestows life upon his patch-work quilt of human fragments. But the creature is far from the perfect man that he had envisioned: it is both ugly and awkward, and has the mind of a child. Dr. Frankenstein turns his back on the mindless primitive, ordering his servant to lock it below in the bowels of the castle, and returns to the comfort of his fiancé and friends. Fritz, in turn, takes sadistic pleasure in torturing the creature and inadvertently teaches it the meaning of hatred and evil. He is eventually impaled on a hook for his misdoings.

Rejected by his maker and tormented by his jailer, the creature escapes into the countryside and unknowingly causes injury to those around him. One, in particular, is a little girl at the lake. Playfully, she throws flowers into the water; since the creature does not understand the difference between a human life and a flower, it throws her into the lake, expecting her to float as beautifully as the flowers. The little girl drowns, and the creature - unable to fully comprehend what it has done - staggers away. When her body is discovered by her father, he leads the local villagers against the creature. They chase it - and the mad doctor - to an abandoned windmil and burn the creature alive (or that is what we are led to believe), Frankenstein narrowly escaping death at the hands of his own creation. The camera pulls back from the flaming conflagration, and the audience is left to ponder the fate of the sad, pathetic creature.

James Whale was clearly influenced by "Der Golem" (1920), lifting many shots and concepts directly from that earlier film; in fact, the sequence with the little girl at the lake is very reminiscent of the climax of Wegener's silent classic. Instead of an apple, however, Whale has substituted flowers, but the end result is the same, as the monster is brought down because of a little girl. The similarities do not end there, but contemporary theatre audiences did not care. The film grossed over twenty-five million from its original $250,000 investment in its initial release, and - along with "Dracula" - proved that there was a large audience, ready and waiting, for horror films. Yet "Frankenstein" was not without its controversy. Because preview audiences had found them objectionable, two scenes were removed and a third one the dialogue deleted from the final release print. Much of the sequence with the little girl at the lake was taken out because it was too offensive, and the scene where the monster impales Fritz on a hook was shortened because it was too violent. And the dialogue that follows "It's alive!," whereby Dr. Frankenstein compares himself to God, was dropped so as not to offend anyone's religious principles. (Recently, however, all three deletions were restored to the film for its release on home video.) Boris Karloff explained in an interview shortly before his death in 1969 that censorship was not the only reason why the scene at the lake was cut. Prior to the advance screening, he had urged Whale to remove it because he felt it betrayed the character he had created. Whale left the scene intact for the preview audiences, but later recanted, realizing that Karloff had been right.

The greatest strength of the film is unquestionably Karloff's portrayal of the creature. His performance is a mixture of pathos and tragedy, much in keeping with the classical heroes of Greek drama, but this should come as no surprise since Karloff studied classical theatre before coming to Hollywood. Born William Henry Pratt to a family in the British foreign service, he immigrated to Canada at the age of 21 and began a ten-year apprenticeship with a touring theatre company. He made his screen debut as an extra in 1916 in "The Dumb Girl of Portici." He continued to act in bit parts in the late Teens and Twenties, appearing in more than 40 silent and sound motion pictures. He scored big as a gangster in the Los Angeles stage production of "The Criminal Code" (1931), and a follow-up role in the movie "Graft" (1931) brought him to the attention of James Whale. He made less than $130 a week, while working on "Frankenstein," and spent over five hours each day in the make-up department (three and a half hours in the morning and an hour and a half at night); but the experience forever changed the course of his film career. After "Frankenstein," he was offered many different roles, from monsters to mad scientists. He was often paired with Lugosi, and the two led Carl Laemmle Jr.'s and Universal's horror school. Unlike Lugosi, however, he was able to escape typecasting, and went onto triumphs outside the horror genre, making more than 140 films in his career. He was also a Broadway actor, singer, television host, and co-founder of the Screen Actor's Guild. But he never forgot his humble beginnings as the monster in "Frankenstein" (1931).

The box office success of "Frankenstein" caused Laemmle and other executives at Universal Pictures to ponder a sequel; but they all realized that it would be at least four years before the principals - Karloff and Whale - would be available again. Karloff had suddenly become a hot property, and would make at least seven genre films during the next four years, including "The Mummy" (1932). Whale was also in demand, directing "The Old Dark House" (1932, with Karloff) and "The Invisible Man" (1933), and he refused to commit to the sequel right away. He also did not want to be typecast as a horror director. And besides, there was the problem of the first film's ending. Originally, two endings had been shot for "Frankenstein": one in which the doctor lived, and the other in which he died. Preview audiences had no hesitation in choosing the former, but no contingency plan had been made to bring the most popular character of the film back to life — the monster. Undaunted, Laemmle announced preproduction of "The Return of Frankenstein" (later changed to "Frankenstein Lives Again," then "The Bride of Frankenstein") and commissioned John Balderston and William Hurlbut to begin writing the sequel.

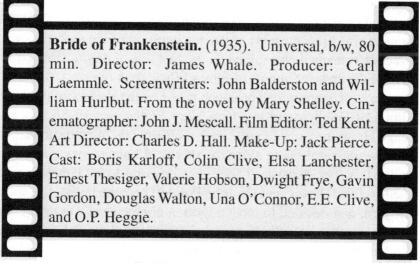

Bride of Frankenstein. (1935). Universal, b/w, 80 min. Director: James Whale. Producer: Carl Laemmle. Screenwriters: John Balderston and William Hurlbut. From the novel by Mary Shelley. Cinematographer: John J. Mescall. Film Editor: Ted Kent. Art Director: Charles D. Hall. Make-Up: Jack Pierce. Cast: Boris Karloff, Colin Clive, Elsa Lanchester, Ernest Thesiger, Valerie Hobson, Dwight Frye, Gavin Gordon, Douglas Walton, Una O'Connor, E.E. Clive, and O.P. Heggie.

Bride of the Monster

"The Bride of Frankenstein" (1935), the first of many sequels that would be made from the Mary Shelley classic, was actually more expensive and required more shooting time than the original, and was surprisingly more faithful to its source than the first film. In fact,

many critics consider the film to be far superior due in large part to its morbid sense of black humor and the stand-out performances of Karloff and Ernest Thesiger. [Notation: Both Claude Rains and Bela Lugosi were considered for the part of Frankenstein's tutor that ultimately went to Thesiger.] "Bride" is clearly the most stylishly mounted production of the 1930's and represents a high-water mark of "the Golden Age of the American Horror Film." However, it should be noted that the film title is really a misnomer and has contributed much to the confusion of the mad doctor's name with the monster. The title should have been "The Bride of the Monster of Frankenstein." Originally, the Balderston-Hurlburt script had Elizabeth Frankenstein murdered by the doctor's assistant and her brain placed in the skull of the monster's. But when that concept was dropped there was no effort on the part of the producers or writers to correct the error (that the name of the monster was Frankenstein). Also, the question of the monster's resurrection remained unresolved on the first day of production — that is, until the creative genius of James Whale took over.

The film opens with a prologue based on the Preface to the 1818 edition of Frankenstein in which Mary Wollstonecraft Shelley explained how she came to write such a bizarre tale. In the summer of 1816, while vacationing along the shores of Lake Geneva, Switzerland, Mary, her stepsister Claire, her husband-to-be Percy Bysshe Shelley, Lord Byron, and Dr. John Polidori became bored, like most idle rich, and decided to have a writing competition - to create the best ghost story - in order to stem their boredom. John Polidori wrote *The Vampyre*, which later inspired Stoker's Dracula as well as many modern vampire tales, and, of course, Mary created her immortal classic. Director James Whale was familiar with those unusual circumstances and thought that those details - along with selected flashbacks from the first film - would provide the proper impetus. Thus, in the first few minutes of "The Bride of Frankenstein," when Lord

Byron (Gavin Gordon) critiques her parable, "I relish each separate horror . .. I roll them over on my tongue," and desires that she had written more, Mary Shelley (played by Elsa Lanchester) is on hand to correct Byron by explaining that the monster did not die!

Apparently, the creature (again played by Karloff) survived the conflagration at the windmill, with only minor burns, by falling through the floor into a water-filled basement. When the movie opens, the fire has nearly burnt itself out. The Frankenstein monster, one side of his face burned and his hair singed off, slowly emerges from the charred ruins, and angrily kills two on-lookers. It is soon captured by the villagers and chained to a stake (to be burned alive), but the bonds are unable to hold the monster as it easily escapes into the countryside. Later, befriended by a blind woodsman (O.P. Heggie), the creature learns to speak a few words ("bread, wine"), to appreciate music, and to understand some basic concepts about life ("friend good, fire bad"). In fact, the Frankenstein monster is perfectly happy to remain there because the blind man - unable to see its ugliness - accepts the creature on equal terms. Unfortunately, vengeful hunters (led by John Carradine, in one of his first roles) break into the blind hermit's home and chase the creature away. This time, the monster seeks refuge in the arms of Dr. Pretorius (Ernest Thesiger), an evil alchemist and necromancer who is also Dr. Frankenstein's former teacher.

Dr. Pretorius and his demented assistant Karl (Dwight Frye, in a role akin his earlier Fritz) pay a visit on Dr. Frankenstein (Colin Clive), returning the monster to its birth-place at Castle Frankenstein. Pretorius shows his former student several homunculi, miniature creatures that he keeps in a glass container, and explains that he has mas-

tered the technique of creating life! Even though Frankenstein wants no further part in the experiment, Pretorius shrewdly convinces him to provide a mate for his monster. Together, the two scientists set about grave robbing again to acquire the basic parts and assemble a seven-foot tall

woman (Elsa Lanchester). Once brought to life, she is a grisly sight, with a ghost-white face, piercing, bright eyes, and a streak of lightning in her frizzed hair. The monster is immediately attracted to her, but she rejects it. Angered, the monster traps Pretorius and the female creature in the tower, allowing Frankenstein and his bride (Valerie Hobson) to escape, and blows up the laboratory. Its final words, "We belong dead," echo throughout Castle Frankenstein with irony and pathos as the conflagration consumes all.

Elsa Lanchester played the title role with such intensity and terror (in spite of her relatively short screen time) that publicists proclaimed: "Universal's biggest sensation. . .there is no comparison!" Her appearance at the climax of the film provides the same type of chills that the emergence of the Robotrix has in Lang's "Metropolis." Originally, both Phyllis Brooks and Brigette Helm (of "Metropolis" fame) were tested for the part, but Laemmle decided upon an unknown in order to add to the suspense of the Bride's unveiling. And in spite of wearing (what amounts to) a cross between a burial shroud and a wedding dress, she is stunningly attractive, like a modern day Queen Nefertiti. Her flashing eyes, robot-like movements, and screeching voice remind us, however, that she is far from human!

"The Bride of Frankenstein" is one of those rare films that actually surpasses the original in terms of style and box office potential. James Whale considered the film to be his best work, and chose not to direct any further horror films because he felt he could not top his efforts here. Boris Karloff's work was also superb. His portrayal of the creature evokes such rage and horror when rejected by its "bride,"

yet still manages to capture the audience's sympathy. His approach is somewhat child-like and touchingly pathetic, and even though he would go onto play the monster one more time (as well as the mad doctor in future motion pictures), Karloff's performance is unsurpassed in this classic film. "Bride" was followed by "Son of

Frankenstein" (1939, with Karloff as the creature), "Ghost of Frankenstein" (1942), "Frankenstein Meets the Wolfman" (1943), "House of Frankenstein" (1944), "House of Dracula" (1945), and "Abbott and Costello Meet Frankenstein" (1948). In terms of quality and entertainment, however, "Frankenstein" (1931) and "The Bride of Frankenstein" (1935) remain as the best entries in the series.

> **Son of Frankenstein.** (1939). Universal, b/w, 95 min. Director and Producer: Rowland V. Lee. Screenwriter: Willis Cooper. From the novel by Mary Shelley. Cinematographer: George Robinson. Film Editor: Ted Kent. Art Director: Jack Otterson. Make-Up: Jack Pierce. Cast: Boris Karloff, Bela Lugosi, Basil Rathbone, Lionel Atwill, Josephine Hutchingson, Donnie Dunagan, Emma Dunn, Edgar Norton, Perry Ivins, Lawrence Grant, Michael Mark, Caroline Frances Cooke, and Lionel Belmore.

The Inevitable Sequels

"Son of Frankenstein" (1939) was a further digression in the series of "Frankenstein" sequels. Budgeted at nearly twice what "Bride" had been, this film was proof of the old axiom that "bigger wasn't necessarily better." Carl Laemmle had become ill (and would eventually die), and a group of executives had taken control of (what would become) Universal Studios. By the end of the 1930's, box office returns on horror films had begun to dry up; but the 1938 re-release of "Dracula" and "Frankenstein" on a double bill demonstrated to the businessmen, who were now in charge, that there was still a market for those type of films. The decision was made to bring back the Frankenstein creature, and production was begun on the "biggest and most exciting" monster movie. In fact, the studio's original intention was to make the film in color, except tests proved that Karloff's make-up would not hold up under the intensity of the hot lights. Unfortunately, the film was strictly a formula piece, generated by a committee of businessmen, and the use of color would not have been able to raise it above mediocrity.

Returning to Castle Frankenstein after twenty-five years of self-imposed exile, Wolfgang Frankenstein (played by Basil Rathbone) is greeted by Inspector Krogh (Lionel Atwill) of the District Police. Krogh, we are told, was maimed in childhood by the monster, and must wear a wooden, prothetic arm, which clicks and jerks from time to time. (His character was wonderfully spoofed by Kenneth Mars in Mel Brooks' "Young Frankenstein," 1974.) He informs the "son of Frankenstein" that there have been several mysterious deaths in the village and warns him that he will take serious action if he discovers the monster is behind them. Wolfgang shrugs off the threat, knowing that his father's work died in the conflagration that nearly destroyed Castle Frankenstein; but he soon discovers that the creature (Karloff) is not quite dead, the huge misshapen body nursed in a comatose state by Ygor (Bela Lugosi). Ygor appears as a wooly shepherd with a deformed neck, but is, in reality, a murderer who escaped a failed execution by hanging. He convinces Frankenstein to revive the monster: "Make him well, master. Your father made him, and he was your father, too," and soon the creature is alive and well, lumbering about the laboratory. But Ygor has other plans: he wants to use the monster to extract revenge on those who tried to execute him. At the climax of the film, Ygor tries to kill Frankenstein but is himself killed. Howling in anger, the monster cradles the corpse of his only friend, and turns on the son of his maker. Inspector Kroh arrives, in the nick of time, and forces the creature into the castle's sulphur pit. Screaming, it sinks into the bowels of the earth.

Directed by Rowland Lee, "Son of Frankenstein" is noteworthy for several reasons. First and foremost, this film was Boris Karloff's last appearance as the monster, and it is regrettable that Karloff has so little to do in the part once the creature has been revived by the mad doctor's son. Future entries would see the appearance of Bela Lugosi (in a role that he originally rejected), Lon Chaney Jr., Greg Strange, Christopher Lee, Kiwi

Kingston, Peter Boyle, and others as the monster, but none would have the unique screen presence that Karloff had. Secondly, the film represented the first and only teaming of the three genre greats of the 1930's - Boris Karloff, Bela Lugosi, and Basil Rathbone. All three had had such a profound effect on Universal's domination of horror films, and while it was common to see the pairing of Karloff and Lugosi, this teaming with Rathbone was very rare, and later impossible due, in large part, to his typecasting as Sherlock Holmes. Lastly, "Son of Frankenstein" elicits the finest performance of his career from Lugosi, which makes one forget - momentarily - his typecasting as Dracula. His portrayal of Ygor would set the standard for future demented servants of the mad doctor. Other than that, Universal's second sequel to James Whale's "Frankenstein" (1931) is forgettable.

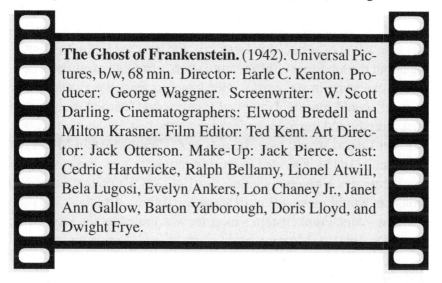

The Ghost of Frankenstein. (1942). Universal Pictures, b/w, 68 min. Director: Earle C. Kenton. Producer: George Waggner. Screenwriter: W. Scott Darling. Cinematographers: Elwood Bredell and Milton Krasner. Film Editor: Ted Kent. Art Director: Jack Otterson. Make-Up: Jack Pierce. Cast: Cedric Hardwicke, Ralph Bellamy, Lionel Atwill, Bela Lugosi, Evelyn Ankers, Lon Chaney Jr., Janet Ann Gallow, Barton Yarborough, Doris Lloyd, and Dwight Frye.

"Ghost of Frankenstein" (1942) was the third sequel to the original classic, and is clearly the weakest entry in the series. There is also very little that can be said of a positive nature here. Released on Friday the 13th, Universal executives thought the film would be lucky for them in bringing in big box office. But the story-line is so preposterous that even an adolescent would have a difficult time accepting it. Dr. Ludwig (Sir Cedric Hardwicke), the second son of Frankenstein, returns to Castle Frankenstein to discover that a.) Ygor (once again played by Lugosi) is still alive, in spite of the fact that he was killed in the last film, b.) the monster has been retrieved from the

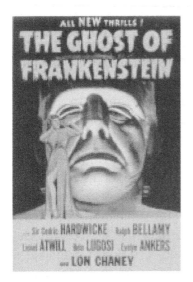

surphur pit and revived by an incredible coincidence of nature, and c.) his father's ghost wants him to continue his work: "Unknowingly I gave it a criminal brain. With your knowledge of science you can cure that." Inspired, Ludwig plans to replace the creature's defective brain with that of a great scientist's. But his sinister assistant (played by Lionel Atwill), coerced by the wooly shepherd, transplants Ygor's brain into the monster. When the creature awakes from the operation, it speaks with Ygor's voice: "I have the strength of a hundred men! I, Ygor, will live forever!" The experiment, however, was not a total success: the monster is blind. Thrashing about the laboratory, the creature starts a fire that eventually consumes everyone in the castle. But have no fear: the Frankenstein monster would return! Universal Pictures had learned their lesson once already, and the final scenes prepare the way for another sequel, wherein Lugosi would play the monster – "Frankenstein Meets the Wolfman" (1943). The idea of pairing monsters was dreamed up by an executive at Universal Pictures, in 1942, on the pretense that two monsters would make a film twice as terrifying. And thus, over the next few years, Frankenstein's monster was joined by the Wolf Man, Count Dracula, the Mummy, and a score of mad doctors and comedians with varying degrees of success.

Frankenstein Meets the Wolf Man. (1943). Universal, b/w, 74 min. Director: Roy William Neill. Producer: George Waggner. Screenwriter: Curt Siodmak. Cinematographer: George Robinson. Film Editor: Edward Curtiss. Make-Up: Jack Pierce. Cast: Lon Chaney Jr., Bela Lugosi, Lionel Atwill, Ilona Massey, Patric Knowles, Maria Ouspenskaya, Dennis Hoey, Harry Stubbs, and Dwight Frye.

"Frankenstein Meets the Wolf Man" (1943) was the first of Universal's attempts to bolster the fading box office receipts of its famous monster series. The previous film had been a major disappointment for the studio, and with the departure of Boris Karloff - a major theatrical draw - movie executives faced the premature demise of their "Frankenstein" series. But, in a brilliant move worthy of Laemmle, the concept of a monster team-up was suggested, and a new glimmer of hope appeared at the end of a long, empty theatre house. Casting Lugosi (in the role he had rejected twelve years earlier) and adding Lon Chaney Jr. (in a reprisal of "The Wolf Man," 1941), Universal Pictures touted their new film as "the Clash of the Century." Unfortunately, "Frankenstein Meets the Wolf Man" was nothing more than a rehash of previous material.

The story opens with Lawrence Talbot, the Byronic hero of "The Wolf Man" (1941), consulting a gypsy fortune teller for advice on how to gain a release from the curse of the werewolf. (No attempt is made to explain how he survived the fatal beating at the hands of Claude Rains.) She tells him that Dr. Frankenstein is the only man in the world who can cure him. (It seems to make no difference to her that Frankenstein's specialty was bringing the dead back to life, not lycanthropy!) Heeding her advice, Talbot travels to Frankenstein's village (Ingoldstadt in the novel, Goldstadt in the play, and Oldstadt in the first film), and discovers, much to his dismay, that the mad doctor and his creation perished in a conflagration. (Which one? At this point in the series, did it really matter?) But before he can decide what to do next, the fully moon arrives, and he is transformed into a murderous werewolf.

Fleeing from the wrath of the local villagers, the wolf man seeks refuge in a cave adjacent to Castle Frankenstein. (How convenient!) There, he stumbles upon the ruins of the mad doctor's laboratory and finds the monster entombed in a block of ice. (No kidding!) Talbot thaws the ice and, together with his new friend, seeks out the help of the local mad scientist (Patric Knowles). Dr. Mannering is, at first, sympathetic to both their fates, wanting to cure Talbot of his lycanthropy and give the monster final rest. But, unfortunately, he uncovers the late doctor's diary and - in a state of madness - turns the two monsters upon one another. Baroness Elsa Frankenstein (Ilona Massey), the daughter of the famous mad doctor, is appalled by what she sees, upon her timely arrival at the family estate, and throws a convenient switch that will destroy the lab and put an end to the monstrous clash. At precisely the same moment, angry villagers dynamite the dam, flooding the laboratory and drowning all those concerned. The monsters have been destroyed (well, at least until the next film, that is).

Lacking any originality or imagination, "Frankenstein Meets the Wolf Man" made more money than the previous entry, and paved the way for more monster team-ups. The box office returns were still not as good as the two Whale classics, but rather than face further diminishing receipts, executives decided to add their most successful movie monster (Count Dracula) to the next film in the series. Tragically, what they failed to realize was that their problem had nothing to do with the number of monsters but with the overall quality of the production. They were treating the series with contempt and gave it no more consideration than the "B" pictures that were constantly being rushed to completion. Besides the rather obvious problems with the studio, there were a number of major flaws that contributed to the film's poor quality. The screenplay by Curt Siodmak and the direction of Ray William Neill were derivative of previous efforts; the acting of Bela Lugosi, whose drug habit had made him very ill

House of Frankenstein. (1944). Universal, b/w, 71 min. Director: Erle Kenton. Producer: Paul Malvern. Screenwriter: Edward T. Lowe. Based upon a story by Curt Siodmak. Cinematographer: George Robinson. Film Editor: Philip Cahn. Make-Up: Jack Pierce.Cast: Boris Karloff, Lon Chaney, Jr., Martha Driscoll, John Carradine, Lionel Atwill, Onslow Stevens, Jane Addams, Glenn Strange.

during the filming, was campy and embarrassing; and the star of the film - the Frankenstein monster - had been relegated to supporting status, opposite Universal's newest star, the Wolf Man. The concept of the monster team-up was certainly a novel one, but would ultimately hurt the quality of the series.

"House of Frankenstein" (1944) followed one year later. Even though it features an all-star cast of villains (Lon Chaney Jr. as the Wolf Man, Boris Karloff as a mad scientist, and John Carradine as Count Dracula), the film bears little resemblance to "Frankenstein" (1931), "Dracula" (1931), or any of the Universal monster classics. The story concerns an evil scientist and his obsession to destroy those who (he believes) wronged him. When the film opens, the mad doctor has just taken over a traveling circus - a freak show which tours the European countryside giving patrons a chance to witness unspeakable horrors. The prize exhibit is Dracula (!), and Karloff briefly frees him before letting him die in the sunlight. Once he has dispatched Dracula, he sets off in search of Frankenstein's diary, hoping to learn the secret of eternal life. He finds instead the preserved bodies of Frankenstein's creature (portrayed by Glenn Strange, a Western movie stuntman) and the Wolf Man. Reviving them, he plans to use the creatures to do his bidding; but plans go awray, and he and the monsters disappear forever (?).

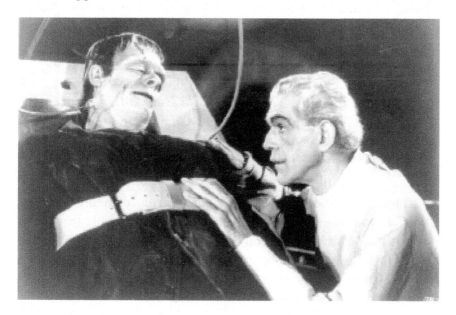

Flawed and faded by today's standards, "House of Frankenstein" was perhaps the best of the monster rallies. Scripted by Edward T. Lowe from a story treatment by Curt Siodmak, the film provides an excellent starring vehicle for Boris Karloff. After having played so many gentle, mad scientists (and, of course, the misunderstood creature and the Imhotep Mummy), Karloff has a field day as the darkly-sinister, carnival owner; in fact, the role is strongly reminiscent of Werner Krauss' Dr. Caligari. When combined with the slick direction of Larry Kenton and the outstanding supporting cast of Carradine (in his first appearance as Dracula), Chaney (as the Wolf Man), and George Zucco, the motion picture was a box office success. Unfortunately, the studio believed the success formula could work again and again, and produced two ludicrous follow-ups, including "House of Dracula" (1945) and "Abbott and Costello Meet Frankenstein" (1948). They would have been far better off to leave it alone because the last two films represent such a sad ending to an era that started so promisingly with the original "Frankenstein." (Years later, Taft/Barish Productions tried unsuccessfully to gather the famous monsters of filmland for yet another monster rally in the comedy titled "The Monster Squad," 1987.)

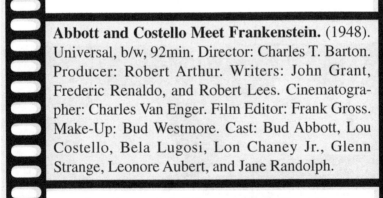

Abbott and Costello Meet Frankenstein. (1948). Universal, b/w, 92min. Director: Charles T. Barton. Producer: Robert Arthur. Writers: John Grant, Frederic Renaldo, and Robert Lees. Cinematographer: Charles Van Enger. Film Editor: Frank Gross. Make-Up: Bud Westmore. Cast: Bud Abbott, Lou Costello, Bela Lugosi, Lon Chaney Jr., Glenn Strange, Leonore Aubert, and Jane Randolph.

Frankenstein's Monster Does Comedy

Three years after "House of Dracula," Universal Pictures released a comedy spoof which would put an end to its cycle of horror films. "Abbott and Costello Meet Frankenstein" (1948) had been produced to showcase the talents of the two vaudevillian comics and to feature Universal classic monsters; however, the film only succeeded in further contributing to the decline of the horror film.

The loosely devised plot follows Bud Abbott and Lou Costello, as two railway porters, through a series of mishaps in a haunted house. After delivering two crates - containing the Frankenstein monster (Strange) and the Wolf Man (Chaney) - the comics are welcomed by Dracula (Lugosi) to his home and are invited to spend the night. The Count is anxious to revive the Frankenstein monster, and Lou's brain is slated for the unearthly creature. The film then degenerates into a moving comic strip (which is barely watchable today) with the monsters chasing Bud and Lou through the usual shenanigans.

True fans of Universal's creature-features deride "Abbott and Costello Meet Frankenstein" for making straight men out of the famous monsters of filmland, while the majority of moviegoers reflect fondly of this first horror comedy. Many even confess that it brought them to Universal's monsters in the first place. Criticism notwithstanding, the film was a popular success and paved the way for more entries in the series of horror comedies; subsequently, Abbott and Costello would meet . . . "The Invisible Man" (1951) and "The Mummy" (1955), among others. However, Universal's release of "Abbott and Costello Meet Frankenstein" marked the end of America's domination of the horror genre. The mystique had slipped away, and what remained was a caricature of the form, with Chaney and Lugosi appearing foolishly awkward. Comedy was tried again twenty-five years later.

Young Frankenstein. (1974). Venture Films and Crossbow Productions, b/w, 108 min. Director: Mel Brooks. Producer: Michael Gruskoff. Screenwriters: Brooks and Gene Wilder. Based on the novel by Mary Shelley. Cinematographer: Gerald Hirschfeld. Film Editor: John Howard. Make-Up: William Tuttle. Cast: Gene Wilder, Peter Boyle, Marty Feldman, Madeline Kahn, Cloris Leachman, and Gene Hackman.

A brilliant pastiche of horror films, "Young Frankenstein" (1974) was also a loving tribute to the "Frankenstein" films produced by Universal Pictures. Directed by Mel Brooks, with the same inspired zaniness of his "Blazing Saddles" (1974), this comedic film spoofed many of the familiar clichés of the genre while, at the same time, paying homage to the traditional forms of horror which, over the many decades, had become classic.

This finely-tuned parody begins appropriately enough on a dark and stormy night in that fantasy land of Transylvania. Baron Beauford von Frankenstein has finally passed away, willing his estate to his great grandson (Gene Wilder). Dr. Frederick Frankenstein, who teaches neural surgery at a prestigious university in the United States, has been trying to live down his grandfather's work, what he terms "the nonsensical ravings of a lunatic brain," for years. But when the opportunity to examine his family estate presents itself, Frankenstein is on the first train (literally) to his homeland of Transylvania.

Upon arrival at track 29, he is greeted by the grandson of the hunchbacked assistant who worked for his grandfather Igor (Marty Feldman). Igor escorts him and his new assistant Inga (Terri Garr) to the castle, and then later, under the watchful eyes of the housekeeper (Cloris Leachman), the three search for the mad doctor's secret laboratory. There, in the parapets above the castle, they discover the original equipment used to bring a monstrous creature to life.

Frankenstein becomes strangely obsessed with his grandfather's work, and begins construction of his own monster (Peter Boyle). While he has plans to incorporate the brain of a genius into the massive body, Igor accidentally delivers an abnoral brain. The result is a catastrophe of comedic proportions. When the creature goes on its predictable rampage, it leaves Frankenstein's castle to terrorize the local populace. But the rampage is played more for comedy than terror, as the monster is charmed by a little girl and played fool by a blind man. The creature is lured back to the castle, and taught how to behave as a gentleman. Fran-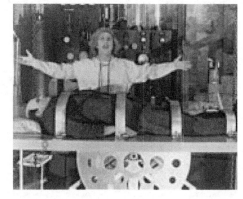kenstein even dresses his monster in top hat and tails, and takes him to perform "Puttin' on the Ritz" (like Fred Astaire) before the townspeople. The arrival of Elizabeth (Madeline Kahn), Frederick's fiancée, further complicates matters when the monster decides to take her as his mate. A dozen orgasms later, Elizabeth has exchanged her brainy boyfriend for the creature. Frankenstein settles for Inga, and the two couples live happily ever after.

"Young Frankenstein" succeeds as both a clever parody and a loving tribute of the horror genre. Wilder, who also co-wrote the script with Brooks, plays his mad doctor as a tribute to not only Colin Clive but also Rathbone, Karloff and Cushing. Feldman sends up Dwight Frye with his Igor, Kenneth Mars spoofs Lionel Atwill as Inspector Kempt, and Peter Boyle provides an inspired performance as the monster. The use of Kenneth Strickaden's original designs of Frankenstein's laboratory and Gerald Hirschfeld's black-and-white photography help to remind audiences of the original source material. Mel Brooks would later make other spoofs, but he would never eclipse the sheer comic genius of this horror comedy.

4

The Mummy

Death...eternal punishment...for...anyone...
who...opens...this...casket. In the name...of Amon-
Ra...the king of the gods.
      —John L. Balderston, "The Mummy" (1932)

For nearly two hundred years, people have been fascinated with secrets of the ancient Egyptians, in particular with the mystery surrounding the mummy. The image of a mummy wrapped in bandages and buried deep within a pyramid is such an extremely powerful one that it moves some people to awe and unsettles others with a sense of dread and foreboding. In fact, when the first mummy was unearthed in the modern period, sealed in a sarcophagus deep within the chambers of a labyrinthine vault, those who had discovered it feared the worst. Superstition, at the very least, demanded a sacrifice for their transgression. They all felt cursed by the Pharaohs, and knew that one-by-one they would be repaid with death. Of course, nothing like that happened to them, except that they became favored by Napoleon and their discovery was celebrated, first in Paris and then throughout the world.

The ancient Egyptians never believed their pharaohs would rise from the dead; they believed that death was the end of physical life in this world. But they also believed that mummifying a person's body after death was essential to ensure a safe passage to the afterlife. Eter

nal life after death, free from the physical limitations of age or health, awaited each Egyptian (not just the Pharaohs) in the Underworld. There, people who had died could be renewed in the primeval waters of "Nun." Paintings on the tomb walls and on the sarcophagus showed the dead the way to this strange and mysterious place that was sometimes called Ealu-fields. The resurrected live an entire life in the Underworld as long as the sun god, Ra, favors them. When Ra goes away, the mummies in turn re-wrap themselves in their bandages, return to their tombs, and await Ra's return for the next cycle of their afterlife to begin.

Mummification in ancient Egypt was a long and expensive process. The body of a person had to be dried out in order to remove bacteria and other germs that would have naturally eaten away at the skin and muscles. Organs were removed and placed in canopic jars prior to the embalming process. This process usually took about two months to complete. Sometimes they used chemicals, like natron, to affect the embalming process; sometimes they would rely on extreme cold or heat. Once the body was dried out, linen cloth was used to wrap the body. The more important the individual, the better the linen. After the body was completely wrapped, the mummy was buried in a tomb following an elaborate religious ceremony. The final step was the "opening of the mouth" ritual which the priests believed allowed the mummy to see, hear, eat, and drink in the spirit world.

For nearly three thousand years, the Egyptians preserved their dead as mummies. Historians believe that more than seventy million mummies were preserved during that period. In the Fourth Century AD, the practice of mummification ended when most Egyptian people accepted Christ and his teachings. Ironically, the first horror stories about mummies stem from the Fourth Century, even though they may have come from an earlier time handled down in oral traditions. Several of these tales involve the historical figure of Setne Khamwas who was a high priest of Pharaoh Ramses II. The most compelling tale centers around Khamwas' attempts to find the forbidden Scroll of Thoth, which Isis used to bring the dead back to life. The mummy of Naneferkaptah protects the scroll from unlawful use, but Khamwas manages to steal it anyway. Misfortunes soon follow, and eventually Khamwas returns it to the mummy's tomb, realizing that he was wrong to have taken it.

Literature of the Mummy

In the Eighteenth and Nineteenth Centuries, the first excavations in Egypt in the modern period turned up many mummies. And soon, the fad of "unrolling" these mummies swept across Europe and America. In 1833, during the height of these "unrollings," William Bayle Bernard (1807-1875) wrote "The Mummy, or The Liquor of Life." While treated as a farce, the play established some basic tenants that would later surface in other stories about mummies. While on a dig in Egypt, a British archeologist disturbs the tomb of an Egyptian princess, and must contend with the consequences. "The Mummy, or The Liquor of Life" was so popular that it ran for 71 performances at the Adelphia Theatre in London that summer. Similarly, Edgar Allan Poe's "Some Words with a Mummy" (1850) also burlesqued the whole notion of mummies and curses.

The most durable of all the stories written about mummies at the time was Theophile Gautier's "The Mummy's Foot" (1840, later expanded into *Romance of the Mummy*, 1857). When the Parisian narrator of the story acquires a mummified foot in the form of a paperweight from a junk shop, strange things begin to happen that he cannot explain. Eventually, the mutilated mummy, who is none other than Princess Hermonthis, arrives in Paris to reclaim her foot. The narrator offers to exchange the foot for her hand in marriage. She agrees, but only if her long-dead father will honor the marriage. The Princess then whisks the two of them back in time to the moment and place of her burial. There, he asks for her hand in marriage from her father, and he flatly refuses. The story had lots of fantasy elements that would have fueled a dozen movies, but the one that definitely stuck was the tradition – unknown in historical records – of mummies wreaking vengeance on those who had desecrated their tombs.

During the late 1800s, both Arthur Conan Doyle and Bram Stoker produced similar kinds of stories as well. Mummies figured as major characters in Doyle's "The Ring of Thoth" and "Lot 249." Stoker's *Jewel of the Seven Stars* added several other twists and turns to the legend of the mummy which would surface in the films of the 1930s and 1940s. In his novel, the tomb of an Egyptian Queen is found, and her mummy is transported to England by an archaeologist. Unfortunately, the mummy's spirit takes possession of the scientist's beautiful daughter. The queen plans to use the girl to reanimate her own dead body, but must first find the "Jewel of the Seven Stars" in order to accomplish her task.

The first film about mummies was "The Mummy of King Ramses" ("La Momie du Roi") in 1909. Directed by Gerard Bourgeois, the short silent film told about a professor's attempts to reanimate the mummified remains of King Ramses. Several others followed, with titles like "Wanted, a Mummy" (1910), "The Mummy" (1911), and "The Mummy and the Cowpuncher" (1912).

Curse of the Pharaohs

In 1922, Howard Carter discovered the intact tomb of the golden king or the "boy king," known as King Tutankhamen. The tomb contained more than 5,000 priceless objects, most of them were made of gold, including several magical pieces such as the golden mask and throne. News of Carter's discovery shot round the world, as did the so-called "curse of the Pharaohs" when, five months later, the wealthy sponsor of the excavation, Lord George Herbert, Earl of Carnarvon, died a strange death. Apparently, while visiting the excavation, Lord Carnarvon was bitten by a mosquito in February of 1923. The next day, he cut open the bite while shaving and developed a severe infection. He then contracted pneumonia, and died in April. The coroner

concluded that his death was probably "due to inhalation of dust containing the fungus histophasma from dried bat droppings," and not the mosquito bite as had been reported.

While Lord Carnaron lay dying at a hotel in Cairo, novelist Marie Corelli spread stories about an Egyptian curse. She told *The London Times* that Carnarvon was dying because of something much more sinister than a mosquito bite. She said it was the "curse of the Pharaohs," and relied on an ill-conceived translation from the Anubus Shrine to back up her false claims. After the newspaper article was published, several other deaths occurred, but none directly connected to the excavation or Carnarvon. But the press made up crazy stories that fueled speculation the curse was real. Carnarvon's dog, which was still in London, died at the exact time he died in Cairo, and all of the lights went out and other strange things happened at the hour of his death.

Eventually, under the auspices of the Egyptian government, all of the treasures in King Tut's tomb were removed from the site, and became part of traveling exhibits that still make their way to museums all around the world. No other reports of strange deaths have occurred since.

The Mummy. (1932). Universal, b/w, 72 min. Director: Karl Freund. Producer: Stanley Bergerman. Screenwriter: John L. Balderston. Original story by Nina Wilcox Putnam. Cinematographer: Charles Stumar. Art Director: Willy Pogany. Make-Up: Jack Pierce. Cast: Boris Karloff, Zita Johann, Edward Van Sloan, David Manners, Arthur Byron, Bramwell Fletcher, Noble Johnson, Leonard Mudie, Eddie Kane, and Katheryn Byron.

The 1932 Version of "The Mummy"

Carl Laemmle Jr. was fascinated by these fantastic stories that came out of Egypt, and hired Nina Wilcox Putnam and John L. Balderston, who had co-authored the stage version of "Dracula," to revise the story of Lord Carnarcon's death and the discovery of Tutankhamen for the big screen. Their story, which borrowed equally from folk legends about mummies and the mythology of Dracula, paved the way for all future films about an expedition finding a tomb and awakening a cursed mummy.

In 1921, the year before the real-world discovery of King Tutankhamen's tomb in Egypt, Sir Joseph Whemple (Arthur Byron) from the British Museum has led a field expedition to Egypt's Valley of the Kings in search of an ancient Egyptian prince. Instead his team unearths the sarcophagus of an ancient high priest named Im-Ho-Tep (Boris Karloff), a lesser priest of the Temple of the Sun at Karnak who was condemned and buried alive for sacrilege. Buried with him is the "Scroll of Thoth," which Isis used to bring the dead back to life.

Even though Dr. Muller (Edward Van Sloan), an occultist on the dig, warns against opening the sarcophagus and reading from the sacred scroll aloud, the dig's photographer (Bramwell Fletcher) does so, rousing the mummy of Im-Ho-Tep from the sleep of the undead. The eyes of the moldy, gauze-wrapped mummy slowly open, and his arms open, stirring to life. The photographer collapses to the ground into a profound, laughter-filled insanity, realizing that he has brought Im-Ho-Tep back to life. The reanimated mummy disappears from its tomb, leaving only the bands of its shroud trailing the floor behind it.

Ten years later, actually 1932, Sir Joseph returns to Egypt with his son Frank (David Manners). Unbeknownst to them, the Mummy has taken on the guise of a mysterious Egyptian named "Ardath Bey". Visiting a dig supervised by Frank Whemple, Bey conducts members of the new expedition to the burial site of a long-dead Egyptian Princess Anck-es-en-Amon, promising that it will be the most exciting find since the discovery of Tutankhamun's tomb. The younger Whemple does indeed uncover the ancient princess' tomb, and her funerary equipment is ultimately displayed in a Cairo museum.

Breaking into the museum after it closes one evening, Im-Ho-Tep kneels next to the glass-encased mummy of the ancient princess and reads from "The Scroll of Thoth." Through a series of flashbacks, we ultimately learn that he was the lover of the princess in times past, and attempted to use the Scroll of Thoth to resurrect her shortly after her death. As punishment for his sacrilegious act, Im-Ho-Tep was mummified and entombed alive for 3700 years. Nevertheless, by some means not made entirely clear in the movie, Im-Ho-Tep was able to ensure that the scroll was buried close to his sarcophagus, so that he could himself return to life millennia later. Bey uses the Scroll once again to awaken the spirit of the princess, which now resides in the young, beautiful Helen Grosvenor (Zita Johann) who just happens to be visiting Cairo. Bey plans to give his lover immortality, a process which requires Helen's death.

When Sir Joseph interferes with Bey's plans, he mysteriously dies. Frank Whemple, with the help of Dr. Muller, intervenes, and saves Helen's life. They then confront Bey, who disintegrates into ashes right before their eyes.

"The Mummy" was a huge success when it was released in 1932, but it wasn't the horror vehicle that had been first envisioned for Boris Karloff. After "Frankenstein" (1931), Carl Laemmle wanted to showcase Karloff in a film that was based on the life of Cagliostro, the French mystic who claimed to have lived for several generations. But when he couldn't find an acceptable script, the Junior Laemmle bypassed the idea for what would he deemed more popular. He settled on a theme that was rooted in the legends of ancient Egypt. With all

the buzz about the discovery of Tutankhamen's tomb, he felt his new Mummy feature would capitalize on the newspaper headlines and the world's fascination with Egypt. Karloff provides a hypnotic performance as Ardath Bey which was really quite different from his role as the Frankenstein monster. Even wrapped up under eight hours of Jack Pierce's mummy makeup, his movements as Im-Ho-Tep are beautifully choreographed to illicit the sense of gliding rather than walking. This role helped him firmly establish himself as the successor to Lon Chaney's legacy as the man of a thousand faces.

Cast opposite Karloff were an ensemble of outstanding actresses and actors who each brought something unique to their roles. Of special interest was Broadway actress, Zita Johann, whose own personal beliefs in the occult made her the perfect choice to play the re-incarnated princess. Karl Freund, who was a collaborator with the great Fritz Lang, also does an excellent job with his directorial debut. Working with cinematographer Charles Stumar, Freund re-captures the true mystery and suspense of "Dracula" (1931), which he had photographed for Browning.

Ultimately, this classic story of forbidden love and revenge would become one of Universal's top box office draws, and would inspire four sequels, starting with "The Mummy's Hand" in 1940.

The Mummy's Hand. (1940). Universal, b/w, 67 min. Director: Christy Cabanne. Producer: Ben Pivar. Screenwriters: Griffin Jay and Maxwell Shane. Original story by Jay. Cinematographer: Elwood Bredell. Art Directors: Jack Otterson and Ralph DeLacy. Make-Up: Jack Pierce. Cast: Tom Tyler, Dick Foran, Peggy Moran, George Zucco, Eduardo Ciannelli, Wallace Ford, and Cecil Kellaway.

The Mummy Kharis is Born

"The Mummy's Hand" (1940), while much livelier with fast-paced action scenes taking the place of a thoughtful story, was the inferior sequel to "The Mummy." When Steve Banning and Babe Jenson (Dick Foran and Wallace Ford), a couple of comical, out-of-work archaeologists, discover evidence of the burial place of the ancient Egyptian princess Ananka, they seek funding from an eccentric magician, known as the Great Solvani, (Cecil Kellaway) and his beautiful daughter Marta (Peggy Moran). Their expedition puts them squarely at odds with a fanatical group, known as the High Priests of Kanak, who have kept alive the Mummy Kharis (Tom Tyler) to protect the tomb against desecrators. We learn most of this when ancient high priest (played by Eduardo

Cianelli) tells the story of Kharis to his disciple and successor Andoheb (George Zucco). Of course, our archaeologists have missed that critical scene, and now must fight off Andoheb and his mummy.

The movie is fun to watch, particularly when Kharis lumbers from his dank Egyptian sarcophagus and stalks his victims, dragging one useless leg behind him. Tom Tyler, an actor primarily known for his performances in Westerns, was selected for the part of Kharis because of his resemblance to Boris Karloff. Even though he was going to be playing a different mummy, Universal wanted audiences to make their connections to that earlier film. Naturally, make-up artist Pierce ensured that Tyler would look like Karloff with his artistry.

The film's set design is also a wonder to behold. Borrowing the temple set from James Whale's "Green Hell" (1940), which later inspired Norman Reynolds on "Raiders of the Lost Ark" (1981), the production looks like it spent a lot more on art direction than it really did. With adding a flashback se-

quence from the original film to pad its brief running time, director Christy Cabanne really tried to make the motion picture an "A-list" film with "B-list" actors and crew. Again, "The Mummy's Hand" makes the most of its low-budget, and recalling the rumored curse of King Tutankhamen, further delineates the basic theme of virtually all mummy films. Those who desecrate the tombs of the Egyptian dead must perish.

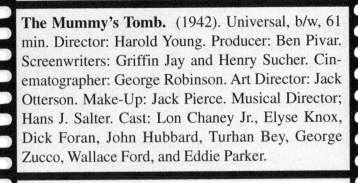

The Mummy's Tomb. (1942). Universal, b/w, 61 min. Director: Harold Young. Producer: Ben Pivar. Screenwriters: Griffin Jay and Henry Sucher. Cinematographer: George Robinson. Art Director: Jack Otterson. Make-Up: Jack Pierce. Musical Director; Hans J. Salter. Cast: Lon Chaney Jr., Elyse Knox, Dick Foran, John Hubbard, Turhan Bey, George Zucco, Wallace Ford, and Eddie Parker.

With the action moved inexplicably to New England, "The Mummy's Tomb" (1942) picks up right where "The Mummy's Hand" left off. Well, not quite, but almost. Sort of. In a technique borrowed from the Saturday serials, we learn that Zucco's Andoheb wasn't really shot through the head three times and fell down a staircase at the end of the last film. Apparently, he lived long enough to hand over his mantle as high priest to successor Mehemet Bey (Turhan Bey), who now uses the Mummy Kharis (Lon Chaney Jr.) to carry out his bloody work.

Thirty years later, the new high priest travels to America with the living mummy to kill all those who had desecrated the tomb of Princess Ananka. Steve Banning (Dick Foran) and Babe Hanson (not Jansen)(Wallace Ford) are now working in America, with the beautiful Isobel Evans (Elyse Knox) in the place of the departed Marta Solvani (Peggy Moran). Bey means to have his revenge on the trio, but when Kharis sees Evans for the first time, he realizes that she is reincarnated love Ananka. With whole sequences lifted out of "The Mummy" and "The Mummy's Hand," as well as the scene featuring the rioting villagers from "Frankenstein," the movie quickly degenerates into a mishmash of flashbacks and cross-cuts that don't make much sense. Little doubt, this Mummy should have stayed in his tomb!

Lon Chaney Jr. tries his best to fill the moldy bandages left by Karloff, but he is not particularly effective in those scenes as the world's flabbiest mummy. Stunt man Eddie Parker does a better job in all of the action sequences! Despite Harold Young's enthusiasm for the material, this is probably the worst film in the series.

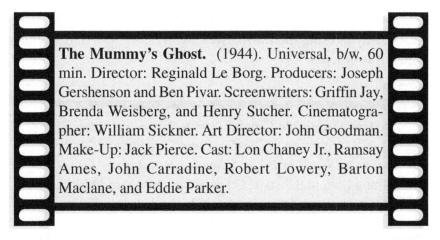

The Mummy's Ghost. (1944). Universal, b/w, 60 min. Director: Reginald Le Borg. Producers: Joseph Gershenson and Ben Pivar. Screenwriters: Griffin Jay, Brenda Weisberg, and Henry Sucher. Cinematographer: William Sickner. Art Director: John Goodman. Make-Up: Jack Pierce. Cast: Lon Chaney Jr., Ramsay Ames, John Carradine, Robert Lowery, Barton Maclane, and Eddie Parker.

"The Mummy's Ghost" (1944) might have been more appropriately titled "The Mummy Goes to College," but those businessmen in charge of Universal weren't ready to add a campy title to their third take in the "Mummy" series. Even though the story is certainly a campy one.

After a short introductory sequence, in which Yousef Bey (John Carradine) receives the mantle of high priest from Andoheb (George Zucco) (actually footage from "The Mummy's Hand" in which Zucco as a much younger Andoheb doing the exact same thing), the new high priest comes to America to resurrect Kharis (Lon Chaney Jr.). He soon finds Princess Ananka in an American museum exhibited as a mummy that is crumbling to dust. Kharis reaches longingly for her, but cannot prevent the inevitable. All seems lost for the gruesome twosome until they learn Ananka's spirit has been reincarnated into the body of Amima Mansouri (Ramsay Ames), a young woman of Egyptian descent who is attending college in New England. She even has a mysterious resemblance to the princess.

Unfortunately, the high priest's lecherous desires cause him to loose control of his Mummy. Even though Kharis has spent night after night outside Amima's window, waiting to catch a glimpse of his beloved, he still has what it takes to stop Bey. Kharis takes matters into his own mummy hands, and strangles the priest. He then romances Amima with all of the charm he can muster. She repeatedly resists his advances, but eventually gives in, turning into a mummy herself. As he carries his beloved off in his arms to a fog-shrouded swamp, they sink together in the quicksand.

The film's gloomy and down-beat ending would have been the perfect way to bring the flawed series to a close. But alas, another sequel was ordered.

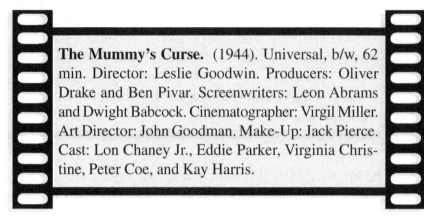

The Mummy's Curse. (1944). Universal, b/w, 62 min. Director: Leslie Goodwin. Producers: Oliver Drake and Ben Pivar. Screenwriters: Leon Abrams and Dwight Babcock. Cinematographer: Virgil Miller. Art Director: John Goodman. Make-Up: Jack Pierce. Cast: Lon Chaney Jr., Eddie Parker, Virginia Christine, Peter Coe, and Kay Harris.

The final entry in the "Mummy" series finds Kharis (Lon Chaney Jr.) and Ananka (Virginia Christine) resurfacing in the rural bayous of Louisiana twenty-five years later when engineers drain the swamp. A new high priest (Peter Coe as Dr. Ilzor Zandaab) shows up, and the usual shenanigans begin anew. Like the previous outings, "The Mummy's Curse" (1944) follows the established formula, and rarely deviates in its efforts to tell such a familiar story. Chaney makes his third and final appearance as the titular character, unless you count a

performance on an episode of "Route 66" (1962) in which he parodied the Mummy. Universal's attempts to make him into the next horror star, by pushing him into roles that had been previously played by Boris Karloff and Bela Lugosi, have failed. Lon Chaney Jr. will be remembered fondly as the Wolf Man, and thankfully excused in their other roles. And the series itself had run its course. All that was left was the inevitable teaming with Abbott and Costello.

Abbott and Costello Meet the Mummy. (1955). Universal, b/w, 90min. Director: Charles Lamont. Producer: Howard Christie. Screenwriter: John Grant. Cinematographer: George Robinson. Make-Up: Bud Westmore. Cast: Bud Abbott, Lou Costello, Eddie Parker, Marie Windsor, Michael Ansara, and Dan Seymour.

"Abbott and Costello Meet the Mummy" was the last feature that Universal did pairing the two comedians of the forties with one or more of its famous monsters. Having already met Frankenstein, Dracula, the Wolf Man, the Invisible Man, Dr. Jekyll and Mr. Hyde, the Studio paired Bud Abbott and Lou Costello with the Mummy (played by stuntman Eddie Parker). The effort is less than amusing. In Egypt, Peter and Freddie (Abbott and Costello, respectively) seek their fortune, but become entangled in a web of intrigue, murder, and a Pharaoh's curse. When they find the archaeologist Dr. Zoomer (Kurt Katch) murdered, a rare medallion leads them to a crypt where a revived mummy waits to kill them.

The usual stumbling and bumbling follows as the comedians attempt to escape to America. Not much else can be said about this film other than that it was the weakest one in the pair-ups. The famous Universal Monsters deserved so much better than this!

The Mummy Resurrected

In 1999, Universal Studios attempted to resurrect one of its famous monsters in Stephen Sommers' big budget remake of "The Mummy," and his adventurous yarn that was made with the

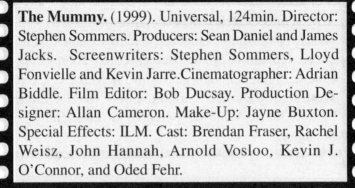

The Mummy. (1999). Universal, 124min. Director: Stephen Sommers. Producers: Sean Daniel and James Jacks. Screenwriters: Stephen Sommers, Lloyd Fonvielle and Kevin Jarre.Cinematographer: Adrian Biddle. Film Editor: Bob Ducsay. Production Designer: Allan Cameron. Make-Up: Jayne Buxton. Special Effects: ILM. Cast: Brendan Fraser, Rachel Weisz, John Hannah, Arnold Vosloo, Kevin J. O'Connor, and Oded Fehr.

same wit and charm of "Raiders of the Lost Ark" (1981) became one of the box office champions that summer. The basic idea of a murderous mummy brought back from the dead was hardly a new one. Universal had already produced six "Mummy" movies, and other studios like Hammer, Orion, and Calderon had produced a dozen more. What Sommers did was return to the original source material, including that 1922 expedition of Lord Carnarvon, and treat the material with the kind of dignity and respect that it deserved. He also injected a great deal of fun and action-adventure to create a truly entertaining summer film.

The story begins in ancient Egypt with Ardeth Bey (Oded Fehr) narrating: "Thebes, City of the Living. Crown jewel of Pharaoh Seti the First. Home of Imhotep, Pharaoh's high priest, keeper of the dead. Birthplace of Anck Su Namun, Pharaoh's mistress. No other man was allowed to touch her. But for their love, they were willing to risk life itself…" When Seti learns that Imhotep (Arnold Vosloo) and Anck

Su Namun (Patricia Velasquez) have been having a relationship behind his back, he orders his guards to seize them. Imhotep and his loved one stab the Pharaoh, but are still captured nonetheless. Anck Su Namun chooses to commit suicide while Imhotep is bestowed with the Hom-Dai, the

most feared curse of all: He is mummified alive in Hamunaptra, the city of the Dead.

More than thirty-six centuries later, in 1923, to be exact, adventurer Rick O'Connell (Brendan Fraser) leads Egyptologist Evelyn Carnahan (Rachel Weisz) and her brother Jonathan (John Hannah) to mysterious Hamunaptra. While Jonathan seeks only Egyptian treasures, Evelyn searches for the Book of the Dead, which would provide valuable knowledge about the ancient Egyptians. In point of fact, Evelyn is the daughter of Lord George Herbert, Earl of Carnarvon, who discovered Tutankhamen's burial site in 1922 and subsequently died. She and her brother have changed their names to avoid any undo publicity. She only tells O'Connell that her father was a "very, very famous explorer." The novelization of *The Mummy* (1999) goes into a bit more detail about her backstory, and we are told that her interest in the Book of the Dead may have something to do with resurrecting her father.

Unwittingly, O'Connell's group and a rival group of careless American adventurers, led by Beni Gabor (Kevin J. O'Connor), free Imhotep's mummy from his eternal prison. Now, with the ancient and quite agile high priest on the loose, the adventurers and scientists face not only a dangerous enemy, but also a massive threat to today's world: Imhotep wants to bring Ankh-su-namun back to life by using Evelyn's body, and he also wants to bring the world to its knees under his tyrannical rule. Of course, they can't let him do that. Ardeth Bey and his men who are the sworn protectors of mankind from the Mummy join forces with them, and a battle of epic proportions soon follows.

"The Mummy" (1999) is good, clean fun with enough action and adventure and humor to make it irresistible. Brendan Fraser is perfectly cast as the adventurer with the sarcastic wit, and Rachel Weisz is sexy and intelligent as his foil. Of course, the real star of the picture is Arnold Vosloo as the titular character. His evil presence is felt all throughout the film, even in those scenes when he does not appear. And at the same time he plays a vulnerable character who only wants to see his love resurrected. Universal produced a sequel titled "The Mummy Returns" in 2001.

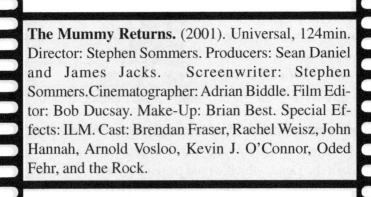

The Mummy Returns. (2001). Universal, 124min. Director: Stephen Sommers. Producers: Sean Daniel and James Jacks. Screenwriter: Stephen Sommers.Cinematographer: Adrian Biddle. Film Editor: Bob Ducsay. Make-Up: Brian Best. Special Effects: ILM. Cast: Brendan Fraser, Rachel Weisz, John Hannah, Arnold Vosloo, Kevin J. O'Connor, Oded Fehr, and the Rock.

While not as good as "The Mummy" (1999), "The Mummy Returns" still offered lots of fun chills and spills. Set ten years after the events of the first film in 1933, Rick O'Connell (Brendan Fraser) is now married to Evelyn (Rachel Weisz) and the couple has settled in London, where they are raising their 8-year-old son Alex (Freddie Boath). When a chain of events finds the corpse of Imhotep (Arnold Vosloo) resurrected in the British Museum, the Mummy is determined to fulfill his quest for immortality. But another force has also been set loose in the world...the Scorpion King (the Rock). More powerful than Imhotep, he plans to rule the world and bring total darkness to all those who oppose him. Naturally, the O'Connells find themselves right in the middle of the action.

Stephen Sommers' second "Mummy" movie was a huge success when it debuted in the summer of 2001, and while the critics were less than kind in their assessment of the sequel, the movie paved the way for yet another film. "The Scorpion King," which was a prequel without any mummies, came out one year later, followed in 2008 by "The Mummy 3."

5

The Invisible Man

You make the glass invisible by putting it into a liquid of nearly the same refractive index; a transparent thing becomes invisible if it is put in any medium of almost the same refractive index. And if you will consider only a second, you will see also that the powder of glass might be made to vanish in air, if its refractive index could be made the same as that of air; for then there would be no refraction or reflection as the light passed from glass to air.
— *H.G. Wells, The Invisible Man (1897)*

We all love our mad scientists. We recognize them as the stock and trade of our favorite science fiction tales. So, when we hear the name Jack Griffin, most of us think of the noble but anguished Claude Rains from "The Invisible Man" (1933). Sometimes he is seen, dressed and bandaged up as a fantastic, eerie-looking figure; at other times, he moves through the action unseen but ever present. The character that H.G. Wells first imagined with his extraordinary words and images was a brilliant young scientist who uncovers the secret to invisibility, and then struggles with grandiose dreams and inner demons that cause him to spiral out of control into madness and murder. While more than a hundred years have passed since Wells penned his gripping tale of science and human arrogance, *The Invisible Man* (1897) still endures as one of the signature stories in the genre of science fiction. Various film adaptations, including Universal Pictures' five "Invisible Man" films, "Memoirs of an Invisible Man" (1992), and "The Hollow Man" (2000), attest to its hold on our popular imagination. Like Frankenstein, the story is a part of our culture, and reveals provocative insights into the relationship between science, human nature, and society.

Herbert George Wells

Herbert George Wells was born on September 21, 1866, the third son of a British shopkeeper in the London suburb of Bromley. "Bertie," as he was affectionately called by his parents, apprenticed as a draper, then later, a chemist, before leaving in 1883 to become a teacher's assistant at Midhurst Grammar School. He obtained a scholarship to London's Normal School of Science, and studied biology under T. H. Huxley, an activist and proponent of Darwin's Theory of Evolution. Darwin's "bull dog," as Huxley was known in scientific circles, made a huge impression on Wells, and may have been the inspiration for Jack Griffin and his other literary scientists. However, his interest in education faltered, and in 1887, he left without a degree. Wells returned to teaching, taught in private schools for the next four years, delaying the exams for his Bachelor of Science degree until 1890. In 1893, while teaching and working at the University Correspondence College, Wells wrote two textbooks, and dabbled in scientific journalism.

He began his literary career in earnest in 1895 with the publication of his first novel, *The Time Machine* (originally published as "The Chronic Argonauts" in Science Schools Journal, 1888; expanded and revised in 1895), a "scientific romance" that speculated about the evolutionary future of mankind. The human species becomes divided into the gentle Eloi and the bestial Morlocks, both of which ultimately become extinct as life as we know it gives way to a new, totally alien life-form. His second novel,
A Wonderful Visit (1895), featured an angel fallen from Heaven who cast a critical eye on Wells's own bourgeois Victorian society. This was his first attempt at social criticism, and established the pattern that would run through much of his work. *The Island of Dr. Moreau* (1896) was the most radical and imaginative of his early writing; by implying that Darwin's evolutionary theory was a way to eradicate the injustices and hypocrisies of his contemporary society with a kind of genetic engineering, Wells

touched off a firestorm of controversy. When the novel was first published in the spring of 1896, critics were outraged by the story of a scientist populating a remote island with beasts surgically re-shaped as men. *The London Times* led the cries of outrage by referring to his third novel as a "loathsome and repulsive" book.

The Original Novel

His follow-up novel was *The Invisible Man* (1897). Like Dr. Moreau, his protagonist Jack Griffin is a scientist with lofty ideals. Wells portrays him as a somewhat obsessive and unpleasant 22 year old student who, when he discovers an invisibility serum, turns himself invisible to avoid inquiries into his work by the authorities. They have confused his turning a cat invisible with vivisection (in a clever allusion to *The Island of Dr. Moreau*.) Forced to run, Griffin stops only long enough to explain the science of invisibility to his friend Dr. Kemp. Kemp is concerned the drug may have some unpleasant side effects, and offers to work with Griffin. But he doesn't trust Kemp (or anyone else, for that matter), already showing signs of extreme paranoia. Ultimately, Griffin is driven mad by the side effects of the drug he has imbibed, and he becomes the scourge of the countryside. His benevolent dreams for mankind turn evil, and he, too, must be punished for meddling in the natural order of the universe. Jack Griffin represents both a savior and a demon as the forces of good and evil struggle for control of his very soul. Not only did Wells introduce a literary figure whose work would be perceived by many as controversial, but he also dared to make his character unapologetic about the scientific research he was pursuing. Once the side effects of the drug take control of his mind, Griffin envisions himself as a kind of god, and even at the moment of his death, he does not prostrate himself upon the altar of forgiveness for what he has done. Up until that point, most of the other mad doctors in literature who had challenged the natural order of things found it necessary to recant their work and cry for mercy. Clearly, for Wells, the character of Griffin was meant to be a major departure from the ar-

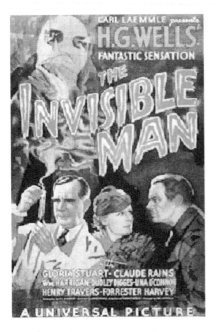

chetypal figures of the previous hundred years that had provided the mythopoetic basis for doomed, scientific genius.

As with *The Island of Dr. Moreau*, Wells was also exploring the relationship between science and superstition. Both Moreau and Griffin were created in the image and mold of Frankenstein, but neither feels the need to show any remorse for what they have done. They are both fed up with the hypocrisy of their conservative scientific colleagues who find their ideas outrageous, yet at the same time profess to embrace rational thought. Moreau and Griffin's resistance to their outmoded ways of thinking makes the two Wellsian doctors seem almost heroic. In rejecting the old systemic and creationist views of the species, they clearly align themselves with Darwin, Huxley and others who see man as the product of millions of years of evolution. Wells did not view science and scientific inquiry as inherently evil. To him, science was not a religion with lots of arcane rituals and superstitious beliefs, but rather a powerful tool that can help man reshape his world. Dr. Moreau and Jack Griffin are the first true scientists of the twentieth century. Not burdened by guilt or the feelings of shame of his Judeo-Christian ancestors, they pursue a line of scientific inquiry to its inevitable and ultimately tragic conclusion. While theories may be proven faulty and conjectures found to be incorrect, Science itself is never wrong. Wells felt there was no need to re-

cant his solemn interest in science even if it made his mainstream critics uneasy.

H.G. Wells continued writing many other "scientific romances," including *The War of the Worlds* (1898), *The First Men in the Moon* (1901), *The Food of the Gods* and *How It Came to Earth* (1904), *A Modern Utopia* (1905), *In the Days of the Comet* (1906), and *Men like Gods* (1923), but as the twentieth century dawned, Wells seemed to loose all interest in writing tales of science fiction, and gradually turned his prolific pen to mainstream works, histories, and social commentary. "The Island of Lost Souls" (1932), with the indelible image of Charles Laughton as Moreau in his white Panamanian suit cracking the whip, was the first of Wells' works to be made into a movie at Paramount. Carl Laemmle passed on *The Island of Dr. Moreau*, but purchased *The Invisible Man* as the obvious follow-up to "Dracula" and "Frankenstein" (1931).

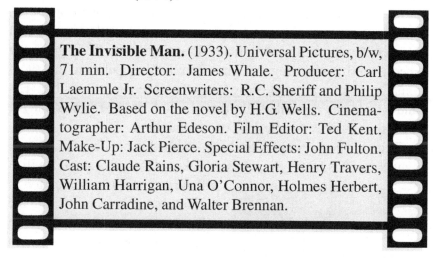

The Invisible Man. (1933). Universal Pictures, b/w, 71 min. Director: James Whale. Producer: Carl Laemmle Jr. Screenwriters: R.C. Sheriff and Philip Wylie. Based on the novel by H.G. Wells. Cinematographer: Arthur Edeson. Film Editor: Ted Kent. Make-Up: Jack Pierce. Special Effects: John Fulton. Cast: Claude Rains, Gloria Stewart, Henry Travers, William Harrigan, Una O'Connor, Holmes Herbert, John Carradine, and Walter Brennan.

"The Invisible Man" (1933)

"Suddenly I realized the power I held, the power to rule, to make the world grovel at my feet!" Jack Griffin exclaims insanely halfway through the adaptation of Wells' 1897 novel.

Fresh from his triumph with "Frankenstein" (1931), director James Whale well understood the driving force of a mad scientist's obsessions. Jack Griffin, identified in the movie as "The Invisible One," was not all that different from Dr. Frankenstein, except that he had turned his experiment upon himself and the result of his work was making him go insane. Once Whale had completed reading the script by science fiction authors R.C. Sheriff and Philip Wylie, he turned to his favorite actor, Boris Karloff, to play the role of the tormented scientist. He felt that Karloff's soft spoken voice would convey the character that is never seen. But Karloff, concerned much like Lugosi had been with the  Frankenstein monster that the audience would not see his face until the very end, rejected the offer. Claude Rains, a little-known, bit player, was given the role that would make him a star, and though Whale had never worked with him before, the two British transplants were soon creating another classic of the genre!

Jack Griffin (Rains), a dedicated research scientist, discovers an invisibility serum while experimenting with a mysterious Indian drug known as moncaine. The potion works remarkably well on a dog, bleaching the beast white, except there is a curious side effect in that it makes the dog turn raving mad. Dismissing the findings of the experiment (by reasoning that a human mind is superior to that of an animal's), Griffin takes the drug himself and becomes invisible. His mind is suddenly expanded, like that of a god, and he realizes that he, too, will go insane — unless he does something.

With his body clothed, his head swathed in bandages and black goggles, and his hands in gloves, he takes refuge in a small English

village and begins to search for an antidote to the invisibility. But the villagers, curious to learn about the stranger, hound him endlessly in his small, one-bedroom flat. He eventually succumbs to the madness, embarking on a reign of terror that includes murder, theft, voyeurism, and sabotage (of a train). He is all powerful, and completely unstoppable. However, when an unexpected snowfall occurs, the local police track his footprints to a barn and set the hay-filled building ablaze. Griffin tries to escape, but he is shot down. Later, as he lies dying in the hospital from his wounds, he begins to return to visibility.

The strength of "The Invisible Man" lies in its excellent script and in Whale's deft handling of situations that, in the hands of a lesser-experienced director, might have been laughable. Whale evokes great sympathy for his central character, and allows the audience to laugh - as a release of nervous tension - with, instead of at, Griffin. The audience recognizes that the situation is a ridiculous one, but somehow are drawn into the parable upon the strength of Whale's enormous wit and knowledge of cinematic technique. Credit must also be extended to Jack Fulton's extraordinary special effects. Using a stunt man who is dressed from head-to-toe in the same black velvet material as the background, Fulton very nearly convinces us that - when Griffin unwraps his bandages - there is indeed an "invisible man." Other effects, utilizing trick wires and the like, harken back to the very early work of Georges Melies on "The Vanishing Lady" (1896), which came out one year before Wells' classic was written.

"The Invisible Man," a relatively inexpensive film that came in under its $300,000 budget, proved to be very profitable for Universal Pictures. So profitable, in fact, it generated its own series (like the "Dracula" and "Frankenstein" films) and inspired several inferior copies and remakes.

The Invisible Man Returns. (1939). Universal Pictures, b/w, 81 min. Director: Joe May. Producer: Kenneth Goldsmith. Screenwriters: Curt Siodmak and Lester Cole. Based on the novel by H.G. Wells. Special Effects: John Fulton. Cast: Vincent Price, Cedric Hardwicke, John Sutton, Nan Grey, Cecil Kellaway, and Alan Napier..

The First of Four Sequels

"The Invisible Man Returns" (1939) offered something new to the material. In fact, this sequel, made six years after the original Whale classic, holds up surprisingly well in comparison. "Inspired

by" the H.G. Wells' novel and co-written by science fiction great Curt Siodmak, the story introduces a new Invisible Man rather than attempts to resurrect the former. Geoffrey Radcliffe (Vincent Price), the brother of Jack Griffin, has been falsely accused of a murder that he did not commit. Knowing that insanity is certain to overtake him, Frank drinks down the new, improved formula (now entitled duocaine) in an effort to discover the real murderer. He pursues Willie Spears (Alan Napier), a drunken colliery foreman who can prove his innocence; but Spears has already been murdered. Wounded, he dons the clothes of a barnyard scarecrow, and tracks the deaths back to the master heavy (Sir Cedric Hardwicke). The two struggle atop a colliery trestle before

the murderer confesses his guilt, then plunges to his death! The Invisible Man is taken into custody, cleared of all charges, and restored by another scientist (Jon Sutton) to full visibility.

As directed by Joe May, who was Fritz Lang's mentor as well as collaborator and part of the second wave of European immigrants (along with Curt Siodmak) fleeing the tyranny of Nazi Germany, "The Invisible Man Returns" has much gothic imagery that recalls the best of the German Expressionist Movement. Although much darker in tone than Whale's original, the film still manages to exude a great deal of satiric black humor. The rest of the motion pictures seem to exploit the novelty of the special effects of an "invisible man" rather than present coherent stories that can easily be followed. Still, when taken as a complete series, the films represent some of the most creative filmmaking of the period.

"The Invisible Man Returns" also represents one of Vincent Price's best early performances. Although you do not see his character throughout much of the film, he creates an indelible figure using only his voice. He moves from sanity to insanity with a frantic energy that sweeps the audience along with him. John Fulton's special effects, which were nominated for an Academy Award, are really quite amazing. By the end of the film, you really feel for Geoffrey and his plight, especially when he is running from the law and unable to put on clothes (lest he give himself away). Fans of the first film really enjoyed the second one, and that led to the inevitable follow-up.

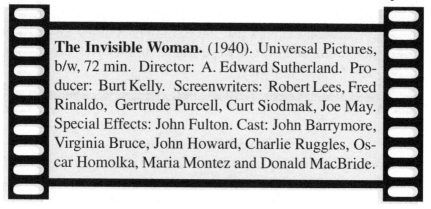

The Invisible Woman. (1940). Universal Pictures, b/w, 72 min. Director: A. Edward Sutherland. Producer: Burt Kelly. Screenwriters: Robert Lees, Fred Rinaldo, Gertrude Purcell, Curt Siodmak, Joe May. Special Effects: John Fulton. Cast: John Barrymore, Virginia Bruce, John Howard, Charlie Ruggles, Oscar Homolka, Maria Montez and Donald MacBride.

The Fairer Sex

Based on leftover material by Curt Siodmak, "The Invisible Woman" was yet another departure from the great H.G. Wells classic. This time, eccentric Professor Gibbs (Lionel Barrymore), brilliant but impractical, invents an invisibility machine and advertises for a human subject to use as a guinea pig. Kitty Carroll (Virginia Bruce), an attractive department store model, who thinks being invisible would help her settle a few scores, answers his ad, and becomes the titular character. Problems arise when three comic gangsters steal the machine to use on their boss (Oscar Homolka), a criminal who has been hiding out in Mexico, and then the film degenerates into a screwball comedy with cool, gimmick-laden effects.

Universal's third "Invisible Man" film is more of a comedy with sci-fi elements than a horror film. While a couple of the sequences are somewhat titilating, in particular a sequence that has invisible Kitty performing a strip-tease in front of her former boss, most of the action in the film is predictable. The addition of the gangster and his three hoods only leads to silly slapstick comedy, and very little actual suspense. At one point, Kitty has the opportunity to get even with her boss, and decides to kick him in the pants. If that's the best she can imagine as the "invisible woman," then this film series needed a complete overhaul of imagination. The film was followed closely by "The Invisible Agent" (1942).

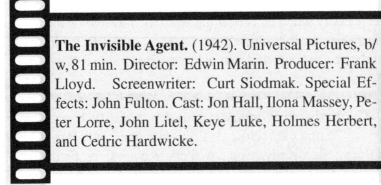

The Invisible Agent. (1942). Universal Pictures, b/w, 81 min. Director: Edwin Marin. Producer: Frank Lloyd. Screenwriter: Curt Siodmak. Special Effects: John Fulton. Cast: Jon Hall, Ilona Massey, Peter Lorre, John Litel, Keye Luke, Holmes Herbert, and Cedric Hardwicke.

Two Additional Sequels

Not long after the Japanese attack on Pearl Harbor and the United States entry into World War II, many of the films produced in Hollywood featured heroic American figures fighting the Axis forces on the home front. In "The Invisible Agent" (1942), Jon Hall as Frank Raymond, the grandson of the original "Invisible Man," uses his secret formula to spy on Nazi Germany. He still considers the serum too dangerous to use, but he feels it's his patriotic duty to stop Germany and Japan from taking over the world. Accompanied by a luscious double agent (Ilona Massey), he easily makes fools of Nazi officials as he searches for Hitler's master plan.

The plot for "The Invisible Agent" must have been an easy sell at Universal for Curt Siodmak, himself a refugee from Europe, but the execution is flawed by all the slapstick comedy. Okay, it's fun to watch the Nazis get theirs, but the film was supposed to have been a thriller not a comedy. And there are plenty of grim reminders in the course of its 81 minutes to remind us. The sudden shifts in tone from thriller to melodrama to farce to-

tally undermine what may have been an interesting film. Cedric Hardwicke is especially good as the German officer tasked with finding Hall, but Peter Lorre easily steals the show with a variation of his Mr. Moto character as a sinister Japanese officer who tries to catch Hall in a spider's web.

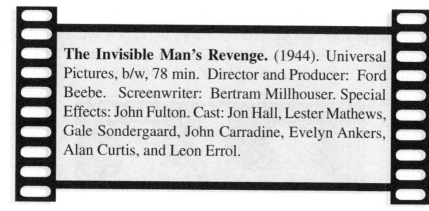

The Invisible Man's Revenge. (1944). Universal Pictures, b/w, 78 min. Director and Producer: Ford Beebe. Screenwriter: Bertram Millhouser. Special Effects: John Fulton. Cast: Jon Hall, Lester Mathews, Gale Sondergaard, John Carradine, Evelyn Ankers, Alan Curtis, and Leon Errol.

The grandson of Jack Griffin, again played by Jon Hall, returns to test a new formula for invisibility. He is not the patriotic spy of "The Invisible Agent" (1942), but rather a killer seeking revenge against the men who framed him. John Carradine plays an eager scientist who has pursued Griffin's work. When the formula turns the escaped fugitive invisible, he chooses to get even with the family he believes cheated him out of a fortune. Universal should have known better than to "meddle in things man must leave alone!"

Abbott and Costello Meet The Invisible Man. (1951). Universal Pictures, b/w, 82 min. Director: Charles Lamont. Producer: Howard Christie. Screenwriters: Robert Lees, Frederic Rinaldo, John Grant. Bertram Millhouser. Cast: Bud Abbott, Lou Costello, Arthur Franz, Sheldon Leonard, Nancy Guild, and William Frawley.

The Invisible Man's Demise

By the early fifties, the famous monsters of filmland had become straight men to the comic pairing of Abbott and Costello. The popularity of horror films were beginning to fade, and were being replaced by science fiction extravaganzas. Frankenstein's monster, Dracula and the Wolf Man had already played the fool to the popular comedy duo, and now, here was the Invisible Man's turn. Boxer Arthur Franz takes the original serum made infamous by Jack Griffin to prove he is innocent of murdering his manager. Bud and Lou as two bumbling private eyes stumble upon him, and united as a team, they duke it out with the real killer. The film is very lame, and added yet another nail in the coffin of our favorite movie monsters.

The Invisible Man continued to amaze audiences in a series of television shows designed to capitalize on the latest in special effects. He also headlined several films for rival studios, including "Memoirs of an Invisible Man" (1992), "The Hollow Man" (2000), and "The League of Extraordinary Gentlemen" (2003). But the big budget remake from Universal remains a dream of devotees who long for a return of the famous monsters of filmland. As this second edition goes to press, Director Leigh Whannell has confirmed that filming has concluded on the Universal-Blumhouse co-production of "The Invisible Man" (2020).

The Invisible Man. (2020). Universal Pictures, in association with Blumhouse. Director: Leigh Whannell. Producer: Jason Blum, Kylie Du Fresne. Writer: Whannell. Based on the novel by: H.G. Wells. Cast: Elisabeth Moss, Aldis Hodge.

6

The Wolf Man

Even a man who is pure in heart,
And says his prayers by night,
May become a wolf when the wolfbane blooms
And the Autumn moon is bright.
—Curt Siodmak, "The Wolf Man" (1941)

    The Wolf Man stands alongside Frankenstein's Creature and Dracula as the most recognized of all the Universal Studios monsters, and yet ironically enough he is the one monster who has had the least amount of screen time. His legacy has also had a great deal of influence on how Hollywood portrays werewolves. In fact, most of what we know about werewolves comes from "The Wolf Man" (1941), and not from traditional folklore. Unlike those creatures of legend, which resemble true wolves, the silver screen would have us believe that a werewolf was humanoid in appearance. One that stands upright like a human, but also has the fur, teeth and claws of a wolf. Werewolves can only be killed by a silver blade or bullet, often only wielded by a loved one. Their transformation always takes place at night, during a full moon, and reverses itself at dawn (in opposition to what happens to a vampire). They are marked with a pentagram, which is a symbol of the occult and Satanism, and must kill and eat fresh meat under the full moon to sustain themselves. Humans become werewolves when they are bitten by another werewolf or are bewitched by a gypsy. Of course, credit for most of the ground rules that govern movie werewolves must go to Curt Siodmak, who penned "The Wolf Man" for Universal. Without those, most of us would not have a clue about werewolves.

Ovid's *Metamorphoses* and Other Tales

In folklore, lycanthropy or the ability of a human to transform into a wolf follows a completely different set of rules. According to an ancient Greek legend that was later recorded in Ovid's *Metamorphoses*, the very first lycanthrope was Lycaeon, the king of Arcadia. He was turned into a ravenous wolf by the god Zeus as punishment for trying to serve a "hash of human flesh" (his own son) to his banquet guests. From the ruler's name comes the modern word "lycanthropy," which is used to describe the whole mythos of werewolves and man-beast transformations. In some countries where there are no wolves, the man-beast transformations include those men who change into coyotes (in North America), jaguars (in South America), tigers (in Asia), leopards or hyenas (in Africa), sharks (in Polynesia), and other beasts throughout the world.

The term "werewolf" was thought to derive from the Old English "wer" which meant "man" and "wolf" which meant "wolf," creating the idea of a "man-wolf." Many European countries have stories about werewolves, but most stem from oral histories that were handed down from one generation to the next. All of the stories involve some kind of transformation and curse. In the Middle Ages, werewolves were thought to be mages or sorcerers in league with the Devil. In the sixteenth century, Bishop Olaus Magnus deemed werewolves as those individuals who were cursed by God. James the First of England punished witches and those thought to be "warwoolfes" as those enchanted by Satan himself.

Werewolves later appeared in literary form as innocent or God-fearing people who had suffered some unhappy fate. In Marie de France's poem "Bisclaveret" (circa 1200), a nobleman is forced to transform into a wolf every week (for reasons never made clear), and implores his local king for mercy when the king's men are dispatched on a wolf's hunt. The hero of "William and the Werewolf" (1350) learns a lesson in kindness when he encounters a person who has been changed into a werewolf. Of course, numerous fairy tales, like "Snow White and Rose Red," also featured numerous princes and princesses, knights and ladies, who appear temporarily as a beast. "Beauty and the Beast," the original French fairy tale, finds a handsome prince transformed into an ugly beast who must be saved by beautiful Belle.

Curse of the Full Moon

The medieval chronicler Gervase of Tilbury, who lived in England during the twelfth and thirteen centuries, first associated the transformation of a man into a wolf with the appearance of the full moon. Historical legends describe a wide variety of methods for the curse of lycanthropy. Some people were thought to become werewolves because they drank from an enchanted stream or wore the clothing of a person infected with the curse of the werewolf. Others became werewolves because they were born the seventh son or a seventh son or had been initiated by drinking a cup of specially brewed beer. Only much later in the chronicles of lycanthropy did people turn into wolves because they were directly bitten by a werewolf.

Over the years, scholars have debated the various methods to remove the curse of lycanthropy, but not one of them has included a silver bullet. (That was an invention author Curt Siodmak borrowed from vampire legends.) The simplest method was to undo the spell of the enchanter. Others have included kneeling in one spot for a hundred years, signing the cross for a specified number of times, or drawing three droplets of blood with a knife that has been blessed. In many legends, any werewolf that remains cursed turns into a vampire when they are finally destroyed.

The lack of any literary classic, like Mary Shelley's *Frankenstein* or Bram Stoker's *Dracula*, meant the werewolf mythos was relegated to secondary status like other folktales and legends. The earliest screen adaptation was an eighteen-minute silent, titled "The Werewolf," in 1913, but that story had very little to do with any of the familiar tales or legends of the werewolf. In the black-and-white film, a Navajo witch-woman raises her daughter to hate all white men, and in turn, the daughter becomes a werewolf that seeks revenge on those that murdered her people.

The Werewolf of Paris

The Werewolf of Paris (1933) by Guy Endore (whose real name was Harry Relis) did for werewolves what Stoker's *Dracula* did for vampires. In this enthralling novel, we learn how Bertrand Caillet, the bastard son of a lecherous priest who raped a French peasant woman, became an outcast and a werewolf. The story is told in episodic form as Caillet travels round nineteenth century France, during the Franco-Prussian war, trying to calm the beast within and failing miserably to protect those he loves. As a young boy, Caillet is raised by Aymar Galliez, the nephew of the woman who hired the peasant girl as a maid. Aymar soon realizes that something is wrong with his adopted son; in fact, Caillet is a werewolf. Each night of the full moon, he leaps out of his bedroom window and kills livestock and assorted wayfarers around the countryside in order to satisfy his unique thirst for blood.

Years later, as a teenager, Caillet steals away to Paris with the hopes of loosing himself in the large populace of the city. But his timing is less than perfect; he arrives during the bloodiest portion of the Franco-Prussian War, and right before the incredible violence of the Paris Commune of 1871 when 20,000 Parisians were murdered by the loyalists of Versailles. The carnage allows him to blend into his surroundings, and he continues to murder his victims while even greater atrocities were happening around him.

The novel is so much more than a simple tale of horror, although there are many grisly scenes. Like Dracula, Bertrand Caillet commits some truly horrible acts of violence, including killing his best friend, committing incest with his mother, despoiling graves, murdering countless people, and even draining his wealthy Jewish girlfriend of her life's blood. His actions seem quaint in light of the thousands of people who are killed by the loyalists in Paris.

Perhaps what is most remarkable about Endore's tale, though, is its sexual frankness and eerie, fog-enshrouded visions that would inspire many generations of horror and science fiction authors who came after. What is even more frightening is the fact that there was a historical counterpart to Bertrand Caillet. He was a sergeant in 1840s Paris who took sides with the loyalists, and was said to be a grave-despoiling werewolf.

Guy Endore's novel was hugely successful when it came out in 1933, and before Carl Laemmle Jr. could purchase the novel for Universal, it was snapped up by rival studio Metro-Goldwyn-Mayer. Endore was also put to work as a screenwriter, and contributed to "Mark of the Vampire" (1935), followed closely by "Mad Love" (1935) and "The Devil Doll" (1936). Undaunted, Laemmle pushed ahead with his own werewolf movie, aptly titled "The Werewolf of London." Ironically, Endore's *The Werewolf of Paris* was never made into a film at M-G-M. The rights were later bought by Universal, but the material was never developed into a film; however, elements of his novel did re-surface in Hammer's "Curse of the Werewolf" (1960).

The Werewolf of London. (1935). Universal Pictures, b/w, 75 min. Director: Stuart Walker. Producer: Stanley Bergerman. Screenwriter: John Colton. Original story by: Robert Harris. Cinematographer: Charles Stumar. Special Effects: John Fulton. Make-Up: Jack Pierce. Cast: Henry Hull, Warner Oland, Valerie Hobson, Spring Byington, Lester Matthews, and Ethel Grifies.

Henry Hull Goes to London

Searching for a new monster to satisfy the demand created by "Dracula" (1931) and "Frankenstein" (1931), Carl Laemmle first tried to secure the rights to Guy Endore's *The Werewolf of Paris* (1933). But when that effort proved futile, he scavenged through countless books on European folklore and legends that had been gathering dust in the Universal library, and ultimately settled upon a Balkan legend about a mysterious flower that, when ingested, turns a man into a wolf. He hired Robert Harris to craft the original story, titled "The Unholy Hour." While very similar to Robert Louis Stevenson's *Dr. Jekyll and Mr. Hyde*, which had just been made into a big budget film at Paramount, Laemmle felt that he had found his new monster. He put John Colton to work, writing the screenplay, and hired Stuart Walker to direct his first horror film. The result of their collaboration was a well-plotted but clumsily-staged motion picture.

While on an expedition to Tibet in search of a rare flower that only blooms at moonlight, British botanist Wilfred Glendon (Henry Hull) is attacked and bitten by a creature later revealed to be a werewolf. He bandages his wounds, and continues on his journey, ultimately succeeding in finding the elusive *marifasa lupino lumino* plant. After his return home to London, he is contacted by a rival botanist, the mysterious Dr. Yogami (Warner Oland from the Charlie Chan movies). Yogami claims they met in Tibet, but of course Glendon has no memory of their meeting. (His rival turns out to be the werewolf who bit the good doctor when he was in Tibet.) He also warms Glendon that he will become a werewolf because he was bitten by a werewolf. Only the marifasa plant can provide an antidote to the malady.

Naturally, Glendon does not believe Yogami. At least, not until he begins to experience symptoms that he cannot explain. When he grows fur on the back of his hand that is exposed to a moon lamp, he gradually recognizes his fate.

After his wife Lisa (Valerie Hobson) goes away to visit an aunt, Glendon uses the first blossom from the plant to stop his initial transformation. He works day and night in his laboratory to affect a cure, but since the plant only blooms at night and then only produces a single blossom, the work is laboriously slow. His wife returns, and he is forced to neglect her to work locked away in his laboratory. Unfortunately, he looses the last of his two blossoms to Yogami who sneaks into his lab when Glendon is taking care of family business.

Later that night – the night of a full moon – he transforms into a howling animal, and stalks and kills a young woman in the back streets of Soho. Unaware of what he has done, he wakes the next morning with a tremendous hangover. He soon comes to learn what he has done, and is horrified by his actions. He now knows he cannot control himself during the blackouts.

With the next blossom due, Glendon rents a room far from his home, and makes ready to use the plant to stop his next transformation. However, Yogami has been following him, and again, to Glendon's horror, takes the final plant. After turning into the werewolf yet again, he kills Yogami, and returns home to Lisa. He cannot control himself as the urge for blood is far stronger than love for his wife. Thankfully, a friend of Lisa's from Scotland Yard arrives in the nick of time, and shoots Glendon, killing the werewolf of London. As he lies dying, he apologizes to his wife, and then in death, reverts back to his human form.

"The Werewolf of London," which was so very similar to the highly successful "Dr. Jekyll and Mr. Hyde" (1932), failed to gain box office approval, and Carl Laemmle shelved his attempts to add werewolves to his famous monsters of filmland for several years, until "The Wolf Man" (1941). Not surprisingly, the passage of time has aged "The Werewolf of London" like a fine wine. We look back on Henry Hull's portrayal of this first wolf man as the one that established the pattern of the sympathetic werewolf who is a good man trapped by circumstances beyond his control. Jack Pierce's makeup also helped to transform Hull from a gentleman into a monster with a metamorphosis that is very convincing on film. Pierce and special effects wizard John Fulton took what they had learned in this 1935 film, and applied those skills to the definitive werewolf movie.

The Wolf Man. (1941). Universal Pictures, b/w, 71 min. Director and Producer: George Waggner. Screenwriter: Curt Siodmak. Cinematographer: Joe Valentine. Special Effects: John Fulton. Make-Up: Jack Pierce. Cast: Lon Chaney, Jr., Claude Rains, Warren William, Ralph Bellamy, Maria Ouspenskaya, Patric Knowles, Bela Lugosi, Evelyn Ankers, and Fay Helm.

"The Wolf Man" (1941)

Six years later, after the disappointing returns of "The Werewolf of London," Universal Pictures tried again with "The Wolf Man" (1941). Based upon an original idea by Curt Siodmak, the screen story jettisoned most of what had been established about the werewolf in legend and folklore for what would become the canon of lycanthropy for modern moviegoers. Gypsy curses, silver bullets, full moon transformations, and so much more would become part of the new mythology about the werewolf. The 1941 movie also established Lon Chaney's son as a major star with his turn as the likeable but doomed Larry Talbot.

After learning about the death of his brother, Lawrence Stewart "Larry" Talbot (Lon Chaney Jr.), a twenty-six year-old college student, returns from America to his ancestral home in Wales to reconcile with his father, Sir John Talbot (Claude Rains). Sir John welcomes him home, like the Prodigal Son, and they begin the sometimes awkward path towards reconciliation. Larry also meets a local girl named Gwen Conliffe (Evelyn Ankers), and decides that she is to be the one he will marry. In turn, she gives him a silver-topped cane mounted with the head of a wolf and a five-pointed star as a walking staff.

On the night of the full moon (which, oddly, is never glimpsed in the film), he escorts her friend Jenny (Fay Helm) through the fog-

shrouded Moors, and they visit an old gypsy camp during their midnight stroll. Bela (Bela Lugosi, in a minor role after having declined the lead) has become obsessed with Jenny, but she cares nothing for him. Suddenly, during their return home, Jenny is attacked by a wolf. Larry kills the beast with the silver-headed walking stick, but is bitten in the process. He soon discovers that it wasn't just a wolf, but a werewolf.

The curse of the werewolf now manifests itself by a penta-

gram that appears on the palm of Larry's hand. Troubled by dreams that he may have killed someone and fearing the worst that he has become a monster, he returns to the gypsy camp alone. There, a Roma fortuneteller named Maleva (Maria Ouspenskaya) reveals to Larry that the animal which bit him was actually her son Bela in the form of a wolf. Bela had been bitten by a werewolf years earlier, and had suffered through each full moon as a werewolf himself. Now the curse of lycanthropy has been passed onto Talbot. She lays down the rules that govern the plight of a werewolf, not an actual gypsy curse but a confection that writer Curt Siodmak had devised on his own, and gradually Larry Talbot comes to dread the coming of the next full moon.

After the curse drives him to commit several horrifying murders, Talbot confesses his plight to his unbelieving father and to his fiancée Gwen. He warns them to stay indoors during the next moonlit night, but of course they do not heed his warnings. Sir John joins the villagers in a hunt for the wolf, and Gwen who is worried about her future husband goes off to save him.

Transformed by the next full moon, Larry Talbot heads for the forest and his next victim. There, he meets both Sir John and Gwen. His father takes the silver-encrusted cane, and beats him to death with it. As Larry dies, he returns to human form.

While not in the same league as "Dracula" (1931) or "Frankenstein" (1931), "The Wolf Man" was clearly better than many of the inferior sequels those other two films had inspired. Lon Chaney Jr. in the role for which he is best remembered makes Larry Talbot into a sympathetic figure who the audience roots for despite the fact that as the Wolf Man he is a cold-blooded killer. His transformation from man to beast required extensive make-up effects that were designed by Jack Pierce. In fact, Chaney had to sit still for six hours while Pierce glued layers of yak hair to his face. Then, shooting the transformation scenes (21 shots in all) in reverse, Pierce gradually removed

the layers, while Chaney positioned himself between two tiny nails on a drape starched to look like a backdrop to preserve the film alignment. The lap dissolve on screen only took seconds to happen, while the work took hours to prepare. Chaney's distinctive voice also injected plenty of pathos into his man-beast character. The supporting cast, with Claude Rains, Bela Lugosi, and Maria Ouspenskaya in top form, help contribute to a superb effort that is considered today to be a minor film classic.

Universal Pictures spent a lot of time and money on this second attempt to make the werewolf a part of its lineup of famous monsters, and that effort was rewarded with box office success that revived interest in its fading monster films. "The Wolf Man" actually launched a second wave of monsters that included a full-color makeover of the Phantom of the Opera.

The Inevitable Sequels

The movie was very popular, but not popular enough to spawn a sequel let alone its own series at Universal. Instead Chaney reprised his now-signature role as the Wolf Man in three monster team-ups and a comedy. Only one of them, "Frankenstein Meets the Wolf Man" (1943), was a worthy follow-up, and regrettably that creature-feature had its flaws.

Frankenstein Meets the Wolf Man. (1943). Universal, b/w, 74 min. Director: Roy William Neill. Producer: George Waggner. Screenwriter: Curt Siodmak. Cinematographer: George Robinson. Film Editor: Edward Curtiss. Make-Up: Jack Pierce. Cast: Lon Chaney Jr., Bela Lugosi, Lionel Atwill, Ilona Massey, Patric Knowles, Maria Ouspenskaya, Dennis Hoey, Harry Stubbs, and Dwight Frye.

"Frankenstein Meets the Wolf Man" (1943) was the first of Universal's attempts to bolster the fading box office receipts of its famous monster series. The previous Frankenstein film had been a major disappointment for the studio, and with the departure of Boris Karloff - a major theatrical draw - movie executives faced the premature demise of their "Frankenstein" series. But, in a brilliant move worthy of Laemmle, the concept of a monster team-up was suggested, and a new glimmer of hope appeared at the end of a long, empty theatre house. Casting Lugosi (in the role he had rejected twelve years earlier) and adding Lon Chaney Jr. (in a reprisal of "The Wolf Man," 1941), Universal Pictures touted their new film as "the Clash of the Century." Unfortunately, "Frankenstein Meets the Wolf Man" was nothing more than a rehash of previous material.

The story opens with Lawrence Talbot, the Byronic hero of "The Wolf Man" (1941), consulting a gypsy fortune teller for advice on how to gain a release from the curse of the werewolf. (No attempt is made to explain how he survived the fatal beating at the hands of Claude Rains.) She tells him that Dr. Frankenstein is the only man in the world who can cure him. (It seems to make no difference to her that Frankenstein's specialty was bringing the dead back to life, not lycanthropy!) Heeding her advice, Talbot travels to Frankenstein's village (Ingoldstadt in the novel, Goldstadt in the play, and Oldstadt in the first film), and discovers, much to his dismay, that the mad doctor and his creation perished in a conflagration. (Which one? At this point in the series, did it really matter?) But before he can decide what to do next, the fully moon arrives, and he is transformed into a murderous werewolf.

Fleeing from the wrath of the local villagers, the wolf man seeks refuge in a cave adjacent to Castle Frankenstein. (How convenient!) There, he stumbles upon the ruins of the mad doctor's laboratory and finds the monster entombed in a block of ice. (No kidding!) Talbot thaws the ice and, together with his new friend, seeks out the help of the local mad scientist (Patric

Knowles). Dr. Mannering is, at first, sympathetic to both their fates, wanting to cure Talbot of his lycanthropy and give the monster final rest. But, unfortunately, he uncovers the late doctor's diary and - in a state of madness - turns the two monsters upon one another. Baroness Elsa Frankenstein (Ilona Massey), the daughter of the famous mad doctor, is appalled by what she sees, upon her timely arrival at the family estate, and throws a convenient switch that will destroy the lab and put an end to the monstrous clash. At precisely the same moment, angry villagers dynamite the dam, flooding the laboratory and drowning all those concerned. The monsters have been destroyed (well, at least until the next film, that is).

Lacking any originality or imagination, "Frankenstein Meets the Wolf Man" made more money than "The Ghost of Frankenstein," and paved the way for more monster team-ups. The box office returns were still not as good as the two Whale classics, but rather than face further diminishing receipts, executives decided to add their most successful movie monster (Count Dracula) to the next film in the series. Tragically, what they failed to realize was that their problem had nothing to do with the number of monsters but with the overall quality of the production. They were treating the series with concept and gave it no more consideration than the "B" pictures that were constantly being rushed to completion. Besides the rather obvious problems with the studio, there were a number of major flaws that contributed to the film's poor quality. The screenplay by Curt Siodmak and the direction of Ray William Neill were derivative of previous efforts; the acting of Bela Lugosi, whose drug habit had made him very ill during the filming, was campy and embarrassing; and the star of the film - the Frankenstein monster - had been relegated to supporting status, opposite Universal's newest star, the Wolf Man. The concept of the monster team-up was certainly a novel one, but would ultimately hurt the quality of the series.

"House of Frankenstein" (1944) followed one year later.. Larry Talbot is thawed out by Dr. Frankenstein (Boris

Karloff as a mad magician), and promised a brain transplant. But unfortunately a silver bullet ends his hopes to live a new life. In "House of Dracula" (1945), he is finally cured of the disease of ly-canthropy. Well, almost. He finds himself inexplicably afflicted again in "Abbott and Costello Meet Frankenstein" (1948). Larry Talbot becomes the hero of the piece when he saves Wilbur Grey (Lou Costello) from having his brain transplanted by Dracula (Bela Lugosi) into the head of a monster (Glenn Strange).

Werewolves would appear in many other motion pictures, including Hammer Studios' wonderfully imaginative series, "The Wolfen" (1981), and "The Howling" (1981), but Larry Talbot's Wolf Man would remain slumbing the sleep of the undead until his next incarnation in cinematic form.

The She-Wolf of London. (1946). Universal, b/w, 61min. Director: Jean Yarbrough. Producer: Ben Pivar. Screenwriter: George Bricker. Based upon a story by Dwight V. Babcock.Cinematographer: Maury Gertsman. Film Editor: Paul Landres. Make-Up: Jack Pierce. Cast: June Lockhart, Don Porter, Sara Haden, Jan Wiley, Lloyd Corrigan, and Dennis Hoey.

The Fairer Sex

Universal did try to shake up the werewolf formula by casting beautiful June Lockhart, who would later headline the campy "Lost in Space" (1965, CBS), as "The She-Wolf of London" (1946), but what remains is more a psychological drama than a horror film. After series of horrible murders are committed in London by what many believe to be a "wolf woman," a young heiress named Phyllis Allenby (Lockhart) finds evidence that suggests, at night, she has been acting under the influence of a family curse. Slowly, she begins to go insane as she attempts to hide her secret. She only confides in her cold, distant step-mother, who is in fact responsible. Phyllis is no werewolf, but she has been tricked into thinking that she is in order to surrender her fortune to the wrong people. Even the blood on her hands is part of the insidious plot.

The title is a clear attempt to evoke the memory of the earlier "Werewolf of London" (1935), but unlike its forebear, this film was more of a thriller with elements of mystery and suspense, and had very little to do with werewolves.

An American Werewolf in London. (1981). Universal, 97min. Director: John Landis. Producer: George Folsey Jr. Screenwriter: John Landis. Cinematographer: Robert Paynter. Film Editor: Malcolm Campbell. Make-Up: Rick Baker. Cast: David Naughton, Jenny Agutter, Griffin Dunne, John Woodvine, Lila Kay, Joe Belcher, David Schofield, Anne-Marie Davies, and Frank Oz.

Reimagining the Werewolf

Many years after Lon Chaney's Larry Talbot had succumbed to a gypsy curse and become the Wolf Man, director John Landis and make-up artist Rick Baker tried to re-imagine the werewolf in the comedy drama, "An American Werewolf in London" (1981). Made in Great Britain by Lycanthrope Films but released by Universal Pictures, the film relies on the latest techniques in special effects and makeup to add a degree of realism that had been missing from all other werewolf movies. In fact, Baker was rewarded for his first class work with the first ever Academy Award given for Special Achievement in Make-Up. The transformation effects are dazzling, as is Landis' approach to the material.

While hitchhiking through the English countryside, David Kessler (David Naughton) and Jack Goodman (Griffin Dunne) are attacked by a werewolf. Jack is killed, and returns as a member of the living dead, but David survives as the titular character. He tries to explain his situation to a nurse (Jenny Agutter) who has fallen in love with him, and then to police officials, but no one seems to believe him. Jack tells him to accept his fate, but David remains somewhat hopeful that he can break the curse. However, when the victims start to mount up, he realizes he is doomed. The climax of the film plays out during an elaborate multiple car crash, caused by the werewolf, in the middle of Piccadilly Circus.

With tongue firmly planted in cheek, Landis scores with an impressive and funny reimagining of the werewolf. We can only hope future werewolf movies are as much fun.

The Wolf Man. (2008). Universal, 120min. Director: Unknown. Producers: Scott Stuber, Rick Yorn, and Benicio Del Toro. Screenwriter: Andrew Kevin Walker. Based upon the original film written by Curt Siodmak. Cast: Benicio Del Toro.

As this book goes to press, Universal Pictures has just announced plans to make a new big-budget version of "The Wolf Man" with Oscar-winner Benicio Del Toro in the title role. With the highly successful remakes of the "Mummy" movies by Steven Sommers and a big-budget remake of "The Creature from the Black Lagoon" already in the works, the studio could hardly miss in resurrecting Larry Talbot from the dead. The success of "The Wolf Man" may also encourage Universal to bring its other famous monsters of filmland back to life in new big-budget adaptations.

Like the original, the new version will be set in Victorian England, with Del Toro as a man who returns from America to his ancestral homeland in Llanwelly, Wales, only to get bitten by a werewolf. Cursed with lycanthropy, he turns into a "wolf" man during the cycle of the full moon, and begins a hairy moonlit existence. Andrew Kevin Walker has been tasked with bringing the new version to life. As the highly-regarded screenwriter of "8mm," "Seven," and "Sleepy Hollow," Walker feels more than up to the task. In fact, he contacted a special effects firm in Los Angeles, and discussed whether his new and frightening characters could be made real with the latest in cutting-edge technology. The answer was "yes." He wants to avoid the look the werewolves had in Stephen Sommers' much reviled "Van Helsing" (2004), and has written some unique twists and turns that should thrill audiences when the film is finally released.

Del Toro seems like the ideal choice to play cursed Larry Talbot, for not only is he a brilliant actor, but he has already played a man-beast of sorts as "Duke-The Dog-Faced Boy" in "Big Top Pee Wee," 1988. Benicio Del Toro is also a huge fan of the original and a collec-

tor of Wolf Man memorabilia; in fact, for the last several years, he has tried to get a remake made, and was finally able to come to terms with Universal.

Universal hopes to shoot its big-budget remake of "The Wolf Man" in 2007 with a summer 2008 release date. We'll all be waiting for the full moon.

7

The Creature & Others that Walk Among Us

Because we all stand between the jungle and the stars, at a crossroads. I think we better decide what brings out the best in humankind, and what brings out the worst, because it's the stars or the jungle.

–Arthur Ross, "The Creature Walks Among Us" (1956)

"The Creature from the Black Lagoon" (1954) was supposed to have been the first in a new wave of movie monsters developed by Universal Pictures, but was in fact the last of a long line of classic favorites. Audiences had grown tired of Dracula, Frankenstein and company, and hungered for something new. Part of the reason for the decline of horror film was the fact that studio executives had never understood what they had had. Unlike Carl Laemmle Jr., who had launched the horror genre with a series of high-quality but moderately-budgeted pictures, they knew very little about plot and character development. The executives thought all they had to do was reduce the bottom line (cost) and keep adding more and more monsters. When that failed to put an end to declining revenues, they added the comedians Abbott and Costello, and then lampooned and ridiculed the very monsters which had been so revered. Figuratively, they killed the goose that laid the golden eggs.

But one other factor was also at play.

By the 1950s, most studios had stopped making horror pictures, and had turned their attention to the emerging genre of science fiction. The overwhelming success of "Destination Moon" (1950), "The

Day the Earth Stood Still" (1951), and "The Thing (from Another World)" (1951) caught most executives in Hollywood sleeping the rest of the undead. They scrambled to get back into the action, and green-lighted many inferior products as well as a few classics just so that they could report to the studio bosses they also had one in production. Allegories about the misuse of atomic power and metaphors about the Red scare reflected the fears and anxieties of audiences, and filled the theaters for showings of "War of the Worlds" (1953), "Them!" (1954), "Forbidden Planet" (1956) and "Invasion of the Body Snatchers" (1956). But for each quality film, a dozen others like "Robot Monster" (1953) and "Invasion of the Saucer Men" (1953) were made instead. In less than a decade, the science fiction film went from a form that represented innovation and new ideas to one that was a ghetto for well-worn clichés highlighted by the latest advances in special effects.

Universal was also late in coming to the party, but when the studio did begin to invest in science fiction projects, it produced some of the best films of the period. "It Came from Outer Space" (1953) and "This Island Earth" (1955) dealt with the anxiety and paranoia most moviegoers felt about the Cold War and invaders from space. "The Creature from the Black Lagoon" (1954) and its two sequels reflected those mysteries of science that still lay buried at the bottom of some black lagoon, and our efforts to find them. With the world threatened with extinction because of the atomic bomb, nature rebelled in "Tarantula" (1955), "The Incredible Shrinking Man" (1957), and "The Deadly Mantis" (1957). Only "The Mole People" (1956) was a throwback to the bygone era.

The end of the decade brought an end to Universal's creature-features. The great studio continued to produce horror pictures and science fiction films, but the emphasis shifted away from those featuring the famous monsters of filmland. When the first of Universal's library of horror films reached television, renewed interest in Dracula and Frankenstein brought a revival of sorts. But not at Universal Pictures. Hammer Films unleashed the first of its full-color versions with "The Curse of Frankenstein" (1957) and "The Horror of Dracula" (1958), both directed by Terence Fisher, and ushered in a whole new wave of monsters.

Flying Saucers and Cold War Paranoia

Flying saucers, multi-tentacled alien monsters, and the notion of an invasion from space seem so ridiculous to us today that it's really hard to imagine a time when people took those things seriously. We tend to make jokes about little green men, and ridicule those who claim to have seen them. But as we stood on the threshold of space at the end of World War II, we also realized that our abilities to launch rockets at other planets meant that others may have had the same abilities. We feared that intelligences greater than our own may have been watching us with envious eyes. The beginning of the Cold War also gave rise to anxiety and paranoia that America was being targeted for infiltration and subversion by the godless Communists. Front-page news stories about "flying discs" over Mt. Rainer, or the recovery of a flying saucer in Roswell, New Mexico, or the arrest of Julius and Ethel Rosenberg for selling atomic secrets to the Russians, or the declaration of Senator Joe McCarthy in Wheeling, West Virginia, that he had a list of 205 "card-carrying" members of the Communist Party, which might have seemed like fantasy a few years before, were now topics of everyday conversation. The world of the 1950s was not the quaint little portrait of "Ozzie and Harriet" or "Father Knows Best" that was used to sell products for the tobacco companies or the automotive industry, but rather a vast canvas of fear, anxiety, prejudice, and paranoia. No other art-form quite reflected that world as vividly or as thoughtfully or as truthfully as the science fiction film that was produced in Hollywood.

The modern era of UFO sightings was launched on June 24, 1947, when Pilot Kenneth Arnold first cited nine disk-shaped objects, which he called "flying saucers," over Mount Rainer and the Cascade Mountains. Arnold's descriptions of the craft seemed to match similar sightings over the European and Pacific Theatres of World War II. To the Allied fighter pilots, they were "kraut fireballs" or "foo fighters." Pilots and their aircrews reported that the unidentified objects flew in formation with their bombers, and actually "played tag" with them on their way to and from bombing missions. The "foo fighters" behaved as if they were under intelligent control, but never displayed aggressive behavior. Reports of these "unexplained transparent, metallic and glowing balls" started turning up in the daily briefings in June, 1944, shortly after the Allied invasion of France. Some thought they were somehow linked to the V-1 and V-2 rockets fired at London and Paris by Nazi Germany, but none of those rumors was ever confirmed. Certainly, no documentary evidence of the "foo fighters" survived the war.

In July 1947, following a rush of UFO sightings in and around the Southwestern United States, an unusual craft crashed in the desert outside Roswell, New Mexico. On the evening of July 2, 1947, Dan Wilmot and his wife saw a shape like "two inverted saucers faced mouth to mouth," come down in the night sky over their farm. The next day, Rancher W.W. "Mac" Brazel found the wreckage near his home in Corona, and reported it to the sheriff's office. Sheriff George Wilcox, in turn, contacted military officials at the 509th Bomb Group Intelligence Office, including Major Jesse Marcel. Ironically, Roswell Army Air Field, 509th Division, was where the nation's stockpile of nuclear bombs (fifteen in all) were stored, including the only planes equipped to fly them and the only pilots and bombers trained to drop them. The base commander assigned Marcel and Sheridan Cavett, a Counter Intelligence Officer, to retrieve the wreckage, which was scattered over a three-quarter mile area, of a flying saucer. Marcel recovered items that were totally foreign to him. A day later, Information Officer Lt. Walter Haut of the RAAF 509th, acting under orders of Col. William Blanchard, announced, "RAAF Captures Flying Saucer on Ranch in Roswell Region." His press release was later rescinded, and a story about a recovered weather balloon was substituted in its place. The actual debris was loaded onto a B-29 bomber and flown to Wright Field (now Wright-Patterson AFB) in Dayton, Ohio, for study. In addition to the wreckage, several bodies were recovered from the New Mexico desert.

At the time, the media and the public "bought" the weather balloon story, but gradually, as the number of credible witnesses came forward recounting their stories - including death threats - of an actual flying saucer and alien bodies, the cover story lost its credibility. Interest in UFOs reached a fever pitch, and soon everyone in America was talking about flying saucers. To this day, the Air Force still maintains its story, and has actually embellished the story by claiming the alien bodies were "crash-test dummies" in the official report *Roswell: Case Closed* (1997), released just two weeks before the 50th anniversary celebration of the crash.

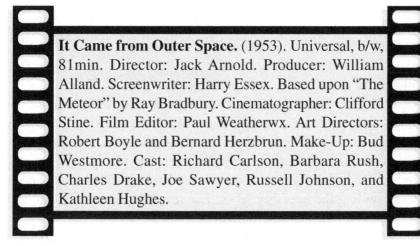

It Came from Outer Space. (1953). Universal, b/w, 81min. Director: Jack Arnold. Producer: William Alland. Screenwriter: Harry Essex. Based upon "The Meteor" by Ray Bradbury. Cinematographer: Clifford Stine. Film Editor: Paul Weatherwx. Art Directors: Robert Boyle and Bernard Herzbrun. Make-Up: Bud Westmore. Cast: Richard Carlson, Barbara Rush, Charles Drake, Joe Sawyer, Russell Johnson, and Kathleen Hughes.

Universal's first foray into the field of science fiction exploits those Cold War fears and anxieties with the thoughtful and provocative "It Came from Outer Space" (1953). Based upon the short story "The Meteor" by science fiction great Ray Bradbury, Essex's script details the crash of an alien spaceship in the Southwestern United States, and the people of one small town's response to the crash. The story seems almost ripped from the headlines, and Jack Arnold who would later become an important force at Universal Pictures with his brilliant fantasy films directs the film in black and white like a documentary with a real soul. The added effect of 3-D gives the motion

picture a kind of immediacy unkown at the time.

In an opening that seems borrowed from H.G. Wells' *The War of the Worlds,* local astronomer John Putnam (Richard Carlson) witnesses a great fireball race across the sky, and crash down in the dessert plain just beyond the city. He and Ellen (Barbara Rush) follow the meteor to its crash site. They soon discover the meteor is actually an alien spaceship that has crashed. They attempt to tell the local sheriff (Charles Drake) and other members of the town (Joe Sawyer, Russell Johnson, and Kathleen Hughes) about the arrival of the aliens, but no one will believe them.

In the following days, people disappear and return, obviously being manipulated in a strange way. They seem like mindless zombies with no will of their own. Putnam is determined to get to the bottom of things, and ultimately discovers the aliens have merely stopped off on Earth to make repairs on their spaceship with the locals providing the ncessary labor. The repair work is slow, and the aliens need more and more humans to help.

After a while, the sheriff becomes distrustful. He and his men enter the crashsite to take direct action against the stranded aliens. But Putnam knows the aliens mean no harm, and protects them against the onslaught of locals with pitchfolks and torches. When the spaceship is finally repaired, the aliens take off for space, and return those who have helped with the repairs to normal.

Beautifully rendered, "It Came from Outer Space" (1953) penetrated the façade of optimism that the Fifties had adopted to reveal our greatest fears of an invasion from space, Communist infiltration, and the loss of personal identity and freedom. Essex's screenplay confronts the decade's fear of the unknown and its prejudices towards strangers by challenging the very pretenses and lies middle America embraced in place of the truth. While the white-bread, all-American Nelsons and Andersons of tvland were supposed to reflect the cosmopolitan make-up and moral decency of every home in the country, the truth was that they reflected only a very small percentage of America. Most families struggled to make ends meet on single-salary incomes which were well below the seemingly luxurious lifestyles depicted on television; they paid taxes, and grumbled about supporting entitlement programs; they built bomb shelters and worried about what the godless Communists might do if they ever gained a statistical superiority in nuclear warheads; they kept to themselves in small, segregated communities, and sent their children to the same schools that they had attended when they were children; they never ventured far away from their homes, even on vacation, and distrusted everyone who looked or sounded or worshipped differently from them. The reality was that middle America was composed of fearful, anxious people who mistrusted strangers and even the neighbor down the street that they didn't know. True, they had fought and won a war against fascism and had survived one of the greatest financial upheavals in human history, but their complacency in accepting the lie about America had also allowed others to strip away their civil liberties in the name of patriotism and bring them to the brink of nuclear annihilation. The real monster in "It Came from Outer Space" was not the shapeless single eyeball, but the guy next door who carried a rifle or a gun and was willing to shoot first and ask questions later.

At Arnold's insistance, the Universal make-up department submitted two monster designs for consideration, but no one seemed to like either one. Following a short battle with studio executives who insisted upon a brand new monster to promote, Arnold won out, and the closest thing we get to the alien is its cyclopean shape that darts out of the dark cave. One of the designs that was rejected was saved, and then later used as the Mutant in Universal's "This Island Earth" (1955). For the time being, only the little seen creature in "It Came from Outer Space" would do.

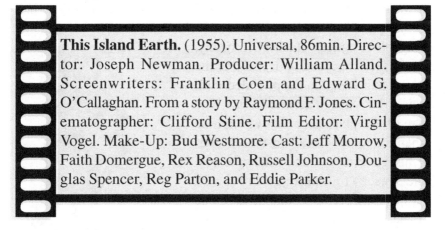

This Island Earth. (1955). Universal, 86min. Director: Joseph Newman. Producer: William Alland. Screenwriters: Franklin Coen and Edward G. O'Callaghan. From a story by Raymond F. Jones. Cinematographer: Clifford Stine. Film Editor: Virgil Vogel. Make-Up: Bud Westmore. Cast: Jeff Morrow, Faith Domergue, Rex Reason, Russell Johnson, Douglas Spencer, Reg Parton, and Eddie Parker.

Flying saucers, alien abduction, and the threat of nuclear war fueled Universal's big budget follow-up to "It Came from Outer Space." Produced by William Alland who was also responsible for

many of the decade's science fiction films, "This Island Earth" (1955) was a top-notch space opera that produced one of the most familar of all the second wave monsters, the Metalunian Mutant (as played by stuntman Eddie Parker). Like its predecessor, the film dealt with contact with an alien race that needs our help to repair a key piece of its technology in order to survive.

Dr. Cal Meacham (Rex Reason) is chosen along with several others (Faith Domergue and Russell Johnson) by the inhabitants of the planet Metaluna to do research that will help save their dying planet. However, he soon uncovers a plot, possibly perpetrated by Exeter (Jeff Morrow), to take over the Earth and subjugate its people as slaves. He and Dr. Ruth Adams (Domergue) escape their Earth lab just before it blows up, and try to get away in a small place. Exeter's flying saucer-like spaceship grabs their plane in mid-flight, and transports them aboard. His ship then whisks them light years away to his home world, where Meacham and Adams are held accountable for blowing up the lab.

Metaluna is at war with Zahgon, and the Metalunians only see things in very black-and-white terms: The humans are either with them or against them. They require Meacham and Adams to help them repair their failing planetary shield that protects them against Zahgon's relentless attacks. Ultimately, the Zahgons succeed in destroying the shield, and Metaluna is pounded with wave after wave of atomic bombs. The core of the planet is about to explode when Exeter rebells against the wishes of his government and saves the two scientists, by transporting them aboard his spaceship. He also takes aboard one of the mindless Metalunian Mutants who have been forced to work as slaves. The Mutant threatens Adams, but is destroyed by Meacham.

Once in Earth orbit, Exeter transports Meacham and Adams to the surface, and crashes his spaceship into the ocean, never to be heard from again, or so the saying goes.

"This Island Earth" was the "Star Wars" of its day, with incredible eye-popping special effects and a space opera that was set on the grand scale of interplanetary war. Atomic power is seen as a force for good and evil, and the invading aliens, while not wholly bad, have a reason for what they are doing. Of course, the stand-out star of the picture is the Metalunian Mutant with its over-sized brain, bulging eyes, and insect-like body. As played by Eddie Parker, who had brought other creatures to life, this was yet another figure in the second wave of Universal's monsters. Alas, the Mutant has yet to make a return appearance. (By the way, the final sequences that featured the destruction of Metaluna were directed by Jack Arnold.)

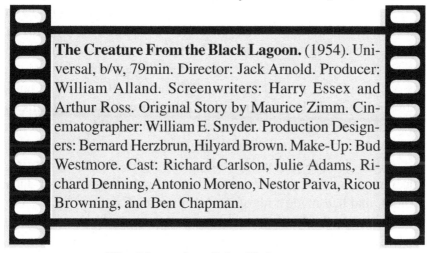

The Creature From the Black Lagoon. (1954). Universal, b/w, 79min. Director: Jack Arnold. Producer: William Alland. Screenwriters: Harry Essex and Arthur Ross. Original Story by Maurice Zimm. Cinematographer: William E. Snyder. Production Designers: Bernard Herzbrun, Hilyard Brown. Make-Up: Bud Westmore. Cast: Richard Carlson, Julie Adams, Richard Denning, Antonio Moreno, Nestor Paiva, Ricou Browning, and Ben Chapman.

The Mysteries of the Unknown

Science had replaced superstition in much of the world, but those isolated little places beyond the reach of civilization still existed in certain corners of the globe where the dark waters and thickest jungles contained mysteries of the unknown. Ever since Jules Verne penned *Journey to the Centre of the Earth* in 1864, modern writers have been imagining those forgotten little backwaters on our ever shrinking planet where the primal forces of nature still held sway. The most famous of these stories was Arthur Conan Doyle's *The Lost World*. Filmed three times (1925, 1959, and 1999), the tale written by the creator of Sherlock Holmes told of a lost plateau in South America where the

great dinosaurs still walked the earth. His 1912 novel would inspire Michael Crichton nearly a century later to write *Jurassic Park* (1990) and *The Lost World* (1995). Similar stories by Edgar Rice Burroughs, including *At the Earth's Core* (1914) and *The Land that Time Forgot* (1918), and *Lost Horizon* by James Hilton would often find modern man in conflict with creatures or other humans who had somehow managed to escape evolution's handiwork.

That was the premise William Alland used to convince Universal to fund his follow-up to "It Came from Outer Space." His most unique fish tale would become the stuff of legend. Recalling a story he had been told by a South American movie director about prehistoric monsters living somewhere along the Amazon River, Alland came up with the idea of a creature, half-man and half-fish. He imagined the Gill-Man was a missing link in the evolutionary chain that had survived unchanged by the passage of time. Alland's tale had all of the right elements for a classic clash of cultures. Universal gave him the green light, and the great producer reassembled the production team, including director Jack Arnold, that had made a hit of his previous sci-fi outing.

Not surprisingly then, when Arnold approached his second film for Universal, he convinced Alland to fund a location shoot for "The Creature from the Black Lagoon" (1954). Some years later, Arnold explained his reasons for not wanting to shoot on the backlot. He wanted to play "upon a basic fear that people have about what might be lurking below the surface of any body of water. You know the feeling when you are swimming and something brushes your legs down below. It scares the hell out of you if you don't know what it is. It's the fear of the unknown. I wanted to exploit this fear as much as possible in filming the movie." He certainly succeeded in what was the "Jaws" of its day. In fact, Spielberg was reportedly heavily influenced by Arnold's moody style. The only elements that were missing were an original script and a monster suit.

Maurice Zimm, a writer who was better known for his radio mysteries, was hired to flesh out Alland's idea. He wrote a fifty-nine page story treatment that was fine-tuned by professional script writers Arthur Ross and Harry Essex. Essex had previously worked with Alland on "It Came from Outer Space."

Arnold met with Bud Westmore, the man who had taken charge of Universal's makeup department after the departure of Jack Pierce, and discussed several ideas with him. The sophomore director wanted the Creature modeled after the shape of Oscar, the statuette given by the Academy of Motion Picture Arts and Sciences. Westmore turned to his colleagues, and with the help of Jack Kevan and his team, including Chris Mueller, Milicent Patrick and Bob Hickman, they came up with the final design for the Gill-Man. Glenn Strange, who had portrayed the Frankenstein Monster in the last few Universal horror sequels, was the studio's first choice to play the title role, but he turned it down due to all the swimming involved. Ben Chapman was then offered the part, and he played the Gill-Man for all the scenes filmed out of the water. Stuntman and scuba diver Ricou Browning played the Creature for all of the underwater scenes. The stage was set for the making of a modern classic.

A scientific expedition searching for fossils along the Amazon River discovers the fabled Black Lagoon and its prehistoric menace, a Gill-Man, possibly the last of a species of fanged, clawed humanoids who may have evolved entirely un-derwater. Captain Lucas (Nestor Paiva) tells them all about the stories and superstitious legends the local native tribes consider to be real, but David Reed (Richard Carlson) and Mark Williams (Richard Denning), both men of science, don't believe in superstition. After it kills several native guides, the scientists capture the Creature, and pump it full of tranquilizers. The Gill-Man breaks free and escapes into the murky depths. Later, the Creature returns to kidnap the lovely Kay Lawrence (Julie Adams), Reed's fiancée, and carries her down into the

Freudian depths of its subterranean grotto. It has been watching her for some time, especially when she went swimming in her virginal white swim suit, and has determined that she will be its mate. Of course, Reed and Williams have other ideas, and take arms to stop the monster at all costs. The final confrontation in the Creature's grotto is one of the most suspenseful sequences captured on film.

Director Jack Arnold makes excellent use of his tropical location, turning the prehistoric jungle into yet another character in the film. Its heavy mists and eerie sounds create an atmosphere that suggests dark foreboding. The underwater photography that was shot by James Haven contributes yet another layer to film, by exploiting the human fear of the unknown threat that is lurking just below the surface. That primal fear, which is deeply embedded in our subconscious, is what gives the Creature its tremendous power. Arnold seems to suggest the Gill-Man is an elemental force of nature that, once awakened by science, cannot be controlled or tamed, much like the power of the atom. He taps right into the fear and anxiety and paranoia of those living in the 1950s under the threat of nuclear annihilation. Therefore, the Creature is a logical extension of Frankenstein's monster in the atomic age.

The image of the Creature is also an archetypal one; it represents the "masculine" id (from Freud), a powerful, barely controlled force of its own that wants to mate with the seductive but vulnerable "feminine." When Kay decides to take a dip in the murky waters of the Black Lagoon, she is unaware that the Creature is swimming directly below, even mirroring her very movements. The sequence is very sensual in the way the two are juxtaposed in a stylized form of

sexual intercourse. Their erotic underwater ballet as played out against the backdrop of the primal waters of the Amazon suggests a very healthy sexuality that is otherwise suppressed by the men of the expedition. The Fifties were supposed to have been a time of sexual repression, but in fact the decade gave rise to sex stars like Marilyn Monroe (and Julie Adams) and *Playboy*. Sexual repression was actually a façade. Only when we embrace both the id and the superego can we have the balance we need to live happy lives. The Creature is all id, while the scientists represent intellectual pursuits taken to extreme. They must tranquilize, capture, and try to control the id, lest it run wild and enjoy its primal sexuality. Un-

able to control it, they must kill it in order to eliminate the outward appearance of sexual desire and sexual freedom. Had the film been made in the Sixties, the Gill-Man would have been a poster child for the Flower Children who discovered sexual freedom.

The Creature from the Black Lagoon was the last of a long line of classic movie monsters developed by Universal. Shot in 3-D, to take advantage of the latest development in technology that gave viewers the illusion of depth, the film was released on March 5, 1954. It was an overnight success, and was subsequently reissued in the "flat" format and marketed as an A-list film. Its popularity and endearing appeal spawned two sequels, "Revenge of the Creature" (1955) and "The Creature Walks Among Us" (1956).

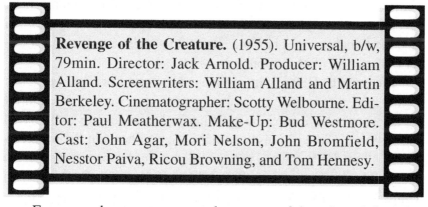

Revenge of the Creature. (1955). Universal, b/w, 79min. Director: Jack Arnold. Producer: William Alland. Screenwriters: William Alland and Martin Berkeley. Cinematographer: Scotty Welbourne. Editor: Paul Meatherwax. Make-Up: Bud Westmore. Cast: John Agar, Mori Nelson, John Bromfield, Nesstor Paiva, Ricou Browning, and Tom Hennesy.

Few sequels are ever as good or successful as the original, but Jack Arnold's follow-up to "The Creature from the Black Lagoon" may well be that rare exception to the rule. The sympathetic and appealing monster who loved and lost Beauty in the first film loses his Amazonian paradise in the second, and must struggle to regain his freedom from those who would make him a science experiment. Not only does Arnold up the ante by making his Gill-Man a captive in a

gilded cage but he also pumps up the sexual tension with yet another beauty who becomes the Creature's object of affection. The result is a powerful study of the primitive nature, existent in all of us, that fights to break free of convention.

"Revenge of the Creature" (1955) picks up the story roughly one year after the conclusion of the earlier film. Ferried back to that famous swamp dwelling off the Amazon River in South America by Captain Lucas (Nestor Paiva), a group of scientists captures the Gill-Man (Ricou Browning and Tom Hennesy), which presumably survived the climatic showdown from the first film. They drug the Creature, and ship it to the famous aquarium Marineland in Florida for further study. The Gill-Man is subjected to really horrible experiments in the name of science and put on display like a caged amphibian for the general public to see. Naturally, when the creature spies Helen Dobson (Lori Nelson) through one of the portholes in the aquarium, it develops a strange attraction for the beautiful marine biologist. Each time the Gill-Man sees her, the attraction grows stronger and stronger to the point of obsession.

Meanwhile, Helen, who is engaged to Professor Clete Ferguson (John Agar), is conflicted over being a working woman when all of her classmates have apparently abandoned their degrees to be wives and mothers. Clete promises to make it up to her, but his promises seem hollow. He is always just one important discovery away from making a real name for himself. Rival Joseph Hayes (John Bromfield) would like to take Helen away from Marineland, and make her a bride. But of course Helen is not really interested in him, only Clete. The practical jokes of an unnamed lab technician (played by Clint Eastwood) only complicate her decision.

At the first opportunity, the Gill-Man breaks free of its underwater chains, and escapes captivity. It kills Hayes who was one of the original scientists who first trapped it. It then causes the usual havoc among the locals as it makes his way down the St. Johns River, all the way to Jacksonville. Once there, it abducts Helen from a downtown waterfront hotspot, and attempts to find its way back to the safety of its Amazonian swamp. The Gill-Man only makes it far enough to a local Florida lagoon before local law enforcement, lead by Charles Cane as a red-neck sheriff, surround the creature and force it into the ocean, presumably killing the monster. Helen rushes into the arms of her fiancé Clete, and they agree to get married.

"Revenge of the Creature" anticipates "Jaws 3," the second sequel to Steven Spielberg's original summer blockbuster. By bringing the monster back to civilization and putting him on display for all the public to see, the marine biologists arrogantly believe they have captured and contained a violent element of nature. But nature will not be contained! It may be controlled for a short amount of time, but more often than not, nature rebels with terrifying consequences. The Gill-Man escapes captivity, and goes on a rampage, killing people in its wake. Most of Jack Arnold's later films, including "Revenge of the Creature," Tarantula" (1955), and "The Incredible Shrinking Man" (1957), deal with this notion of nature rebelling as a kind of metaphor for man's misuse of the atomic bomb. And leading man John Agar is often depicted as the scientist who struggles to contain the forces of nature that man had unwittingly unleashed. He shows up in Arnold's "Tarantula" in a similar role.

But real star of the film is the Creature, who makes the second of his three big screen appearances. The Gill-Man represents one of the greatest monsters of the post war era, and would have probably been the anchor had Universal continued to produce great monsters as part of a second wave. Like his earlier predecessors, he makes a classic creature that is really not a monster at all but a sympathetic figure that just wants to be loved. The fact that he's just some guy in a rubber suit never enters the viewer's mind because of the wonderful and seamless manner that Arnold directs Ricou Browning in the water and Tom Hennesy on land. The scenes of the Gill Man under the water at the aquarium have that same stylish cinematography as the underwater sequences in the original film, and the later

sequences where the Gill Man escapes and wreaks havoc among the Florida locals (including the two teenage boys by the water) have an exciting, almost eerie, quality to them.

Like its predecessor, "Revenge of the Creature" was shot in 3-D, although it was mostly shown "flat" in many theatres not equipped for 3-D. While most contemporary audiences have seen it this way, we can easily imagine where most of the scenes that take advantage of the 3-D process are. A second sequel, "The Creature Walks Among Us," was filmed without 3-D, and released in 1956.

The Creature Walks Among Us. (1956). Universal, b/w, 78min. Director: John Sherwood. Producer: William Alland. Screenwriter: Arthur Ross. Cinematographer: Maury Gersman. Special Effects: Clifford Stine. Make-Up: Bud Westmore. Cast: Jeff Morrow, Rex Reason, Leigh Snowden, Gregg Palmer, Ricou Browning, and Don Megowan.

The Gill-Man returned for yet another go-around in "The Creature Walks Among Us" (1956), the inferior third film in the series. Having escaped captivity at the end of the previous film, the Creature shows up in the Florida Everglades. Not a bad place to start a new home. But alas, a third group of scientists shows up searching for fossils, and finds the Gill-Man will made the perfect specimen for their research. It struggles against their efforts to capture it, and is subsequently burned in a horrible fire. Mad scientist William Barton (Jeff Morrow) discovers the Creature's gills are badly burned, and operates so that the Gill-Man can breathe air through its lungs. The operation turns the Creature into a landlubber who will drown in water. Barton thinks he can civilize the former amphibian. He locks it in an outdoor cage, and treats it like some kind of curiosity. Unfortunately, the Gill-Man develops feelings for his wife Marcia (Leigh Snowden) and breaks out of its cage to save her from harm. Its noble intentions are misunderstood, and it must escape captivity, killing people and setting fires in the process. Thomas Morgan (Rex Reason), a rival for Marcia's affection, chases after the Creature. In the end, riddled with bullets from the hunting party's guns, the Gill-Man drags itself to the water's edge, and dives into the sea.

Without Jack Arnold's inspired direction, which had brought elements of erotic tension and powerful imagery to the previous two films, "The Creature Walks Among Us" is just another creature-feature from Universal. The middle section, which features a romantic triangle for Morrow, Reason, and Snowden, plays more like a soap opera than a horror film. And like it or not, the Gill-Man is only a powerful creature with its gills and the ability to stalk its prey under water. On land, it's nothing more than a lumbering monster in the cookie-cutter form of Frankenstein's creature.

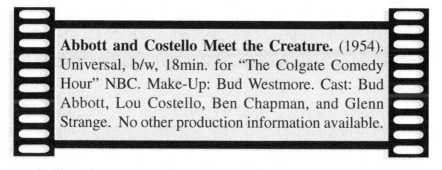

Abbott and Costello Meet the Creature. (1954). Universal, b/w, 18min. for "The Colgate Comedy Hour" NBC. Make-Up: Bud Westmore. Cast: Bud Abbott, Lou Costello, Ben Chapman, and Glenn Strange. No other production information available.

Believe it or not, the Creature actually made its first appearance opposite Abbott and Costello. On Sunday, February 21, 1954, comedians Bud Abbott and Lou Costello hosted "The Colgate Comedy Hour" on NBC, and in a live comedy sketch, devised to promote Universal's newest monster, America witnessed the brief but memorable meeting of Abbott and Costello and the Creature from the Black Lagoon. The 18-minute sketch began with the two comics arriving at the studio's creepy prop department to get some items for that evening's show. While Bud busies himself in the task at hand, Lou starts to read from Universal's latest horror script. On cue, each of the famous monsters of filmland, including the Frankenstein Monster (Glenn Strange), makes an appearance, and frightens Lou to tears.

Eventually, the Creature (Ben Chapman) shows up, and that's more than Lou can handle as he collapses to the floor at the Gill-Man's webbed feet. Of course, the skit only hints at the high-jinks and comedy another Abbott & Costello movie would have produced. The long-lost kinescope was shown at the 2002 Monster Bash in Pittsburgh, and is available for purchase on the secondary markets.

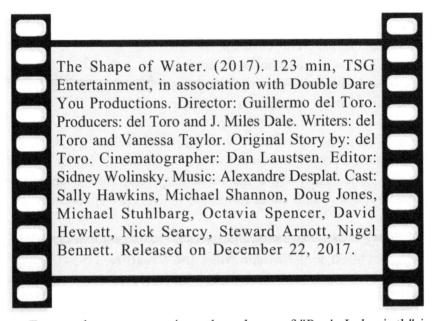

The Shape of Water. (2017). 123 min, TSG Entertainment, in association with Double Dare You Productions. Director: Guillermo del Toro. Producers: del Toro and J. Miles Dale. Writers: del Toro and Vanessa Taylor. Original Story by: del Toro. Cinematographer: Dan Laustsen. Editor: Sidney Wolinsky. Music: Alexandre Desplat. Cast: Sally Hawkins, Michael Shannon, Doug Jones, Michael Stuhlbarg, Octavia Spencer, David Hewlett, Nick Searcy, Steward Arnott, Nigel Bennett. Released on December 22, 2017.

For nearly ten years, since the release of "Pan's Labyrinth" in 2006, Director Guillermo del Toro worked to set up a big-budget remake of "The Creature from the Black Lagoon" at Universal Pictures. "Creature" was del Toro's favorite film, growing up in Mexico. But with all the false starts-and-stops and the empty promises from studio executives, he abandoned the project (including a script from Gary Ross and Tedi Safarian) to Breck Eisner. He then sat down, with Vanessa Taylor, and wrote his own version. Set in Baltimore, Maryland, in 1962, during the Cuban-Missile Crisis, his story follows a mute cleaner (Sally Hawkins) at a high-security government laboratory who falls in love with a captured amphibian creature (Doug Jones). She subsequently frees the creature from the facility, and hides the "gill-man" in her small, walk-up apartment over a movie theater. Her co-worker (Octavia Spencer) and neighbor (Richard Jenkins) conspire to keep her secret from the facility's maniacal chief of security (Michael Shannon). Del

Toro named his story, "The Shape of Water," and shot it cheaply in Ontario, Canada, between August and November 2016, with very little fanfare and no real Hollywood stars. The "Creature" remake he abandoned has languished in development hell since 2007, more than 12 years. "The Shape of Water," on the other hand, debuted to both critical and box office success in December 2017, ultimately going on to become one of the top ten films of the year. The dark, romantic fantasy-science fiction film received 13 nominations at the 90th Academy Awards, and won Best Director (for del Toro), Best Production Design, and Best Original Score. It is also noteworthy for wining the first Best Picture Oscar for a science fiction film from the Academy of Motion Picture Arts & Sciences. Thank you, Guillermo, for honoring the monsters!

The Mole People. (1956). Universal, b/w, 77min. Director: Virgil Vogel. Producer: William Alland. Screenwriter: Laszlo Gorog. Cinematographer: Ellis Carter. Film Editor: Irving Birnbaum. Make-Up: Bud Westmore. Cast: John Agar, Cynthia Patrick, Hugh Beaumont, Alan Napier, Nestor Paiva, Phil Chambers, Rodd Redwing, Robin Hughs, and Frank Baxter.

A throwback to "The Mummy" (1932), William Alland's "The Mole People" (1956) was an unimaginative, little horror film that looks like it had been made ten years earlier. Dr. Roger Bentley (John Agar) leads a team of archeologists (with includes Hugh Beaumont) to the Middle East in search of the lost tribe of Summerians. According to legend, they moved underground to escape the great Flood, and have been living there for centuries, served by slaves known as the Mole People. Naturally, they find the Summerians, now a race of alibinos afraid of any kind of light. Elinu (Alan Napier), the High Priest, welcomes them begrudgingly, and then conspires to have them captured and killed. Bentley encourages the Mole People to revolt against their masters, and the usual conflagration begins.

The motion picture introduced yet another one of Universal's second wave of monsters, the Mole People, but they were not particularly good. In fact, "The Mole People" would have been largely forgotten today had it not been for the work of Sociologist Jennifer Toth. In 1993, her book *The Mole People* took a very candid look at the thousands of homeless people who live in the subway tunnels beneath New York City. While they are not ancient Sumerians who fear sunlight, they do live in small, ordered societies similar to tribes, numbering up to hundreds of people. The 1987-89 television series "Beauty and the Beast" featured Vincent (Ron Pearlman) as a lion-like man who lived among a group

of the homeless in the tunnels below New York. The 1996 film "Extreme Measures" also featured these Mole People living in the subterranean world beneath the Island of Manhattan.

The Legacy of Dr. Frankenstein

The decade of the 1950s also produced a handful of films, like "The Beast from 20,000 Fathoms" (1953), "Them!" (1954) and "Godzilla" (1954), that examined the role of technology as it quickly advanced and outpaced man's ability to control and harness it. Frankenstein's monster had literally become a metaphor for society's anxieties over the atomic bomb and its fears that the forces of technology were growing faster than human reasoning. Less than ten years before, man had discovered, developed and used a force so powerful and frightening that it could destroy all life on the planet. Dr. Robert Oppenheimer (along with his esteemed colleagues) had become the modern-day Prometheus, and though his scientific research was meant as a benefit for all mankind, his work was actually no more than an extension of Frankenstein's desire to play God. And like the mad doctor's Creature, his atomic bomb was not meant to be evil; unfortunately, mankind's mishandling of atomic power had made it into a monolithic monster to be feared for decades to come. The fear that technology would one day drive man to extinction was a logical progression of Frankenstein's work. By the end of the period, even though the anxieties still remained, audiences returned to the horror genre and its collection of monstrous creatures.

Universal released a handful of films, including "Tarantula" (1955), "The Incredible Shrinking Man" (1957) and "The Deadly

Mantis" (1957), that reflected these same fears and anxieties. And reaped the benefits of the Cold War economy.

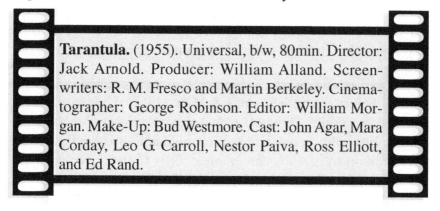

Tarantula. (1955). Universal, b/w, 80min. Director: Jack Arnold. Producer: William Alland. Screenwriters: R. M. Fresco and Martin Berkeley. Cinematographer: George Robinson. Editor: William Morgan. Make-Up: Bud Westmore. Cast: John Agar, Mara Corday, Leo G. Carroll, Nestor Paiva, Ross Elliott, and Ed Rand.

Like the far superior "Them!" (1954), an insect is enlarged to monstrous proportions, and goes on the rampage. Professor Gerald Deemer (Leo G. Carroll) has been working hard to perfect a special nutrient that will help grow lifestock larger to counter a predicted food shortage that comes with the increase in human population. His experiments have been moderately successful, but there have been some failures as a result. One day, he is inadvertently injected with his own formula, and goes mad. A giant tarantula escapes its cage and grows even larger to the size of an office block. It soon starts to attack cattle, grab cars in its jaws and reduce them to scrap metal, and eat human beings. Matt Hastings (John Agar), a fellow scientist, alerts the military, and with the help of a squadron of air force jets drops napalm on the monster and burns it to death.

The plot is crude and the film is not particularly imaginative, but Jack Arnold takes advantage of every trick in his director's notebook to make the movie good solid fun. Audiences of the 1950s particularly enjoyed the moments when the giant tarantula was destroying late model cars, a symbol of America's dominant technology in the world. And those images would be repeated again and again in subsequent films that followed. Arnold also places his monster out on the same Southwestern dessert where the U.S. Army was experimenting with atomic bombs. He wanted to make his message clear: His giant spider was no more or less a symbol of technology that when removed from its controlled environment was a deadly weapon that could destroy all mankind.

The tarantula was not an inspired choice for a Universal monster, especially in light of most people's revulsion of arachnids, but it became the latest in the long line of famous monsters. The giant spider made a brief encore appearance in Arnold's "The Incredible Shrinking Man" (1957), but has not been heard of since.

The Incredible Shrinking Man. (1957). Universal, b/w, 81min. Director: Jack Arnold. Producer: Albert Zugsmith. Screenwriter: Richard Matheson (based on his novel). Cinematographer: Ellis Carter. Special Effects: Chris Baker. Make-Up: Bud Westmore. Cast: Grant Williams, Randy Stuart, April Kent, Paul Langton, Raymond Bailey, and William Schallert.

Jack Arnold trotted out his giant spider again and several other memorable monsters, including a lovable house cat, to terrorize his titular hero in "The Incredible Shrinking Man" (1957). After Scott Carey (Grant Williams) is exposed to a strange radioactive mist while out on a boating holiday, he behinds to shrink. As he shrinks, the familiar and safe surroundings of his home become a menace that must be overcome. He battles his cat, and then later, a spider for his very survival. At each stage, he notices that as his body shrinks his mind begins to expand. When he is finally locked out of his house, he finds himself in the grass forest of his lawn, and must face other menaces as equally deadly. Soon, he grows smaller than an atom, and discovers a whole other universe before him.

Written by science fiction great Richard Matheson, this is, first and foremost, a story of survival. The survival of an average man as he faces one form of adversity after another. His script captures the fear and paranoia of the Cold War era as the hero's life and marriage begin to collapse around him as he shrinks to nothingness. But his struggle for survival gives him dignity, and the ending is not without hope as he moves forward into a new universe.

Most people who have seen "The Incredible Shrinking Man" fondly remember Carey's battle with the giant spider. Armed with only a needle and some thread, he cleverly outwits the eight-legged monster, and sends it to oblivion. A big-budget remake from Keenan Ivory Wayans was scheduled for 2008.

The Monolith Monsters. (1957). Universal, b/w, 77min. Director: John Sherwood. Producer: Howard Christie. Screenwriters: Norman Jolley and Robert Fresco. Cinematographer: Ellis Carter. Special Effects: Clifford Stone. Cast: Grant Williams, Lola Albright, Les Tremayne, Trevor Bardette, Linda Scheley, and Phil Harvey.

Based upon a story by Jack Arnold, "The Monolith Monsters" (1957) was an A-class movie that had been constructed out of a B-class budget. When a strange black meteor crashes near the desert town of San Angelo and fills a nearby field with its crystaline fragments, not one of the townspeople seems threatened. However, a storm exposes the crystals to rain, and they grow into skyscraper-like monoliths that threaten the town. The monoliths topple and shatter into thousands of pieces that grow into more monoliths and repeat the process. Any humans in the way are crushed or turned into human statues. Local geologist David Miller (Grant Williams) works to find a way to stop them from spreading doom to the entire world, while Cathy Barrett (Lola Albright) helps evacuate the town. A fun little chiller with lots of colorful characters thrown into the mix to make an otherwise by-the-numbers sci-fi film into some special. Arnold continued to make imaginative movies throughout the end of the decade, and then turned to television. His last creature-feature for Universal was the dreadful "Monster on Campus" (1958), in which a college professor (Arthur Franz) is transformed into a prehistoric ape man while experimenting with a million-year-old fish. Like "The Mole People," this picture seemed like it should have been made ten years earlier and has been thankfully forgotten.

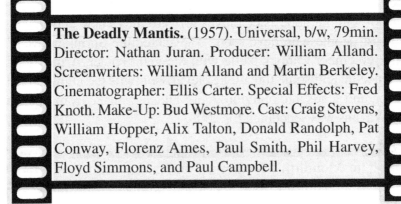

The Deadly Mantis. (1957). Universal, b/w, 79min. Director: Nathan Juran. Producer: William Alland. Screenwriters: William Alland and Martin Berkeley. Cinematographer: Ellis Carter. Special Effects: Fred Knoth. Make-Up: Bud Westmore. Cast: Craig Stevens, William Hopper, Alix Talton, Donald Randolph, Pat Conway, Florenz Ames, Paul Smith, Phil Harvey, Floyd Simmons, and Paul Campbell.

The last of the great creature-features from Universal was also one of its best, "The Deadly Mantis" (1957). An atomic bomb test in the Arctic releases a giant praying mantis, which has been trapped in suspended animation since prehistoric times inside an iceberg. After it has devastated most of the military installations in the Arctic, the military top brass steps in. Colonel Joe Parkman (Craig Stevens) ir ordered to mount a counterattack, but mishandles the situation which, in turn, only drives the monster southward towards Washington D.C. The deadly mantis then wreaks havoc on the nation's capital. With the help of Dr. Ned Jackson (William Hopper), a paleontologist, the military chases the creature to Manhattan, and traps it inside the Holland Tunnel. There, it is fumigated with poison gas. Nature unleashed by the greatest force on earth runs wild, and destroys everything in its path. All of the Cold War fears of the 1950s all come together in William Alland's superior film. Unfortunately, the deadly mantis was

the last of Universal's great monsters, and like the Metalunian Mutant, the Mole people, and the giant spider, it would not make a return engagement. Universal would try to trot out other low-grade horrors, like "The Thing That Couldn't Die" (1959), but the end of an era had finally come.

8
Universal Horrors

I'll tell you the problem with the scientific power that you're using here: it didn't require any discipline to attain it. You read what others had done and you took the next step. You didn't earn the knowledge for yourselves, so you don't take any responsibility for it. You stood on the shoulders of geniuses to accomplish something as fast as you could and before you even knew what you had you patented it and packaged it and slapped it on a plastic lunchbox, and now you're selling it, you want to sell it!
—Michael Crichton and David Koepp,"Jurassic Park" (1993)

Universal Horror was the brand name ascribed to the very distinctive horror films made by Universal Pictures from the 1920s through the 1950s. From Universal's earliest success in the horror genre, "The Phantom of the Opera" (1925), through the film cycles of "Dracula" and "Frankenstein" in the decades of the thirties and forties to the atom age monsters of science fiction in the Fifties, the studio had always maintained a high degree of integrity and trust with its audience. When moviegoers lined up to buy a ticket for a Universal horror picture, they knew they were buying passage to an imaginative realm of Gods and Monsters. Many of the horror genre's most beloved conventions, including the creaking door, a spider's cobwebs, the howl of a wolf at full moon, Bach's *Toccata and Fugue in D-Minor* playing on a pipe organ, swirling mists, and mobs of torch-carrying peasants chasing monsters, were first seen in Universal films. These creature-features also gave rise to the first horror stars in Lon Chaney, Bela Lugosi, and Boris Karloff, and provided steady employment for a cadre of genre actors whose faces were familiar even if names like George Zucco, Lionel Atwill, Dwight Frye, Evelyn Ankers, and John Carradine were not known to us. Other names like

Count Dracula, Frankenstein, Larry Talbot, the Mummy Inhotep, Jack Griffin, the Phantom of the Opera, and the Creature from the Black Lagoon would become legendary.

In the decades that followed the anxious and paranoid Fifties, Universal still continued to make distinctive horror pictures, but its focus shifted away from the great monsters of filmland to capture and exploit the other fears and anxieties of its audience. Our favorite monsters didn't die or fade away, however. Some merely took up residence at 1313 Mockingbird Lane on television's "The Munsters" (1964, CBS). Herman Munster (Fred Gwynne as Karloff's Frankenstein), Lily (Yvonne De Carlo borrowing the white streak in her hair from Else Lanchester), Grandpa (Al Lewis with a touch of Lugosi's Dracula), and son Eddie (Butch Patrick as a junior werewolf) greeted audiences into their haunted home week after week for two years, and inspired two films, starting with "Munster Go Home!" in 1966. Others waited, slumbering the sleep of the undead, to be reborn again in big budget remakes and re-imaginings. And still others made personal appearances at Universal's theme parks in California and Florida.

The best of Universal's horror films in the last fifty years represent an eclectic group of motion pictures from some of the best talents in the industry, from Alfred Hitchcock to Steven Spielberg. Others came from those making television movies.

The Birds. (1963). Universal, 119min. Director and Producer: Alfred Hitchcock. Screenwriter: Evan Hunter. Based upon a story by Daphne Du Maurier. Cinematographer: Robert Burks. Film Editor: George Tomasini. Special Effects: Larry Hampton, Dave Fleischer, and Chuck Gaspar. Cast: Rod Taylor, Jessica Tandy, Tippi Hedren, Suzanne Pleshette, Veronica Cartwright, Ethel Griffes, and Ruth McDevitt.

Alfred Hitchcock's "The Birds" (1963) was a familiar nod back at Universal's great creature-features of the past, and a look forward to the kind of monster that would be taking center stage in the films that followed. Once again, the forces of nature are striking back against man, but no apparent motive is ever given. Hitchcock and screenwriter Evan Hunter never explain why man's fine feathered friends have decided to take this particular moment strike. They seem to suggest the event is just an unpredictable phenomenon of nature, and nothing more. Years later, Steven Spielberg  would take a page out of Hitchcock's playbook, and visit the very same thing again, only this time with a man-eating shark, in "Jaws" (1975). One can certainly see the influence of Jack Arnold and the paranoid era of the 1950s in the richly-textured plot.

A rich, spoiled socialite named Melanie Daniels (Tippi Hedren) decides that she is going to play a practical joke on Mitch Brenner (Rod Taylor), after running into him in a San Francisco pet store. (Mitch pretends not to recognize her, and treats her like she is a common store clerk.) Melanie buys a pair of love birds for Mitch's sister for birthday, and drives to the quiet coastal town of Bodega Bay in northern California, where Mitch spends his weekends with his sister (Veronica Cartwright) and mother (Jessica Tandy). Shortly after she arrives, Melanie is attacked by a sea gull. But this is just the first in a series of attacks by an increasing number of birds. Soon, the entire town is overrun with killer birds, and Melanie, Mitch, and the others must make their way to safety before the birds attack again.

During his tenure at Universal, Hitchcock made a number of memorable thrillers that have become classic motion pictures in their own right, but "The Birds" was the Master's only creature-feature. His "Psycho" (1960), which would set the standard for modern horror movies, was filmed on the Universal backlot, but was ultimately released by rival Paramount. Years later, Universal Pictures obtained the property for subsequent re-releases, and included the Psycho House on its studio tour. In 1983, they brought Anthony Perkins back to play poor, twisted Norman Bates in "Psycho II." The film was such a success with audiences that Norman would return in "Psycho III" (1986) and "Psycho IV: The Beginning" (1990). Like its previous film cycles, Universal felt there was still plenty of money to be made with their serial killer who loved his mother so deeply.

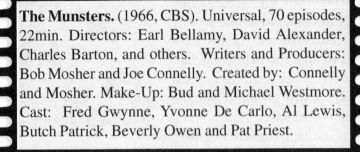

The Munsters. (1966, CBS). Universal, 70 episodes, 22min. Directors: Earl Bellamy, David Alexander, Charles Barton, and others. Writers and Producers: Bob Mosher and Joe Connelly. Created by: Connelly and Mosher. Make-Up: Bud and Michael Westmore. Cast: Fred Gwynne, Yvonne De Carlo, Al Lewis, Butch Patrick, Beverly Owen and Pat Priest.

In 1963, Joe Connelly and Bob Mosher, the creative force behind "The Amos & Andy Show" and "Leave It to Beaver," teamed up to develop, write and produce one of television's most beloved comedies, "The Munsters," for Universal television. Their premise was a rather simple one to pitch: A family of friendly monsters moves into the suburbs, and has various misadventures, never quite realizing why people react to them so strangely. CBS greenlighted the project, in part because classic horror characters were in vogue with audiences, but also because ABC was developing a very similar show titled "The Addams Family."

"The Munsters" was shot entirely on the Universal backlot, and debuted on September 24, 1964. The show ran for two years, and completed its original prime-time run on September 1, 1966. It has been continuously in syndication for the last forty years.

The head of the family was kindhearted Herman Munster (Fred Gwynne), who bore an uncanny resemblance to the Frankenstein monster as originally portrayed by Boris Karloff. His wife Lily

(Yvonne DeCarlo) was the Matriarch of the family, and resembled Vampira, television's creepy-but-sexy hostess of horror that had appeared in Ed Wood's infamous "Plan 9 from Outer Space" (1956). Lily's father, Grandpa (Al Lewis), was actually Count Dracula, newly uprooted from his burial crypt in

Transylvania. Herman and Lily's son, Eddie (Butch Patrick), was modeled after Lon Chaney's Wolf Man, only as a junior version; although most contemporaries thought he was Michael Landon's younger brother from "I Was a Teenage Werewolf" (1957). The black sheep of the family was Herman and Lily's niece, Marilyn (first played by Beverly Owen and then by Pat Priest); she was a beautiful, blonde, all-American teenager, but the Munster clan considered her ugly because she didn't look like one of them.

Most of the episodes of the series generally dealt with the family's difficulty in trying to fit into mainstream American society (during the late 1960s) when everyone in their community reacted to them with horror. Every human who sees them freaks out, and yet the Munsters can never figure out why everyone finds them so strange. They are just trying to be upstanding citizens. For instance, in the third episode that aired, titled "A Walk on the Mild Side," Herman decides to talk a late-night walk in the part every night in order to cure his insomnia; but Lily is concerned for her husband's safety because newspapers have reported sightings of a fiendish monster in the park. Naturally, they don't realize that the sightings are of Herman! In the fortieth episode, "Herman the Master Spy," Herman is mistaken for the missing link when a Russian trawler pick him up scuba diving. Throughout its seventy-episode run, the series poked lots of fun at middle America and the issue of nonconformity. At its best, the wisecracking dialogue, outrageous visual gags, and special effects made "The Munsters" a hit week after week with its ghoulish, macabre sense of humor.

While the show ended its run in 1966, the series spawned two movies, a second series, and a whole host of tie-in merchandize. The original show still plays on television today.

Munster Go Home! (1966). Universal, 96min. Director: Earl Bellamy. Producers: Bob Mosher and Joe Connelly. Screenwriters: George Tibbles, Connelly, and Mosher. Cinematographer: Benjamin H. Kline. Editor: Bud Isaacs. Make-Up: Abe Haberman and Karl Silvera. Cast: Fred Gwynne, Yvonne De Carlo, Al Lewis, Butch Patrick, Debbie Watson, Hermione Gingold, Jeanne Arnold, and Terry-Thomas.

"Munster Go Home!" (1966) was a theatrical expansion of television's favorite family of monsters. Based on the half-hour sitcom "The Munsters" (1964, CBS), the full-length Technicolor feature (which was originally made for television) was somehow much more satisfying. Herman Munster (Fred Gwynne) and his family (Yvonne De Carlo, Al Lewis, Butch Patrick, and Debbie Watson) learn that they've inherited an estate in England, and make arrangements for a visit. Upon arrival, they are greeted by Herman's cousin Lady Effigie (Herminone Gingold) and her children Freddie and Grace (Terry-Thomas and Jeanne Arnold), none of whom are pleased to see them. (Apparently, they are using Munster Hall to print counterfeit money.) The English cousins attempt to scare the Munster clan into thinking the castle is haunted, but that only makes the enterprise much more

desirable to Herman and Lily. Marilyn who was rarely given anything to do in the television series finds herself the object of Roger's (Robert Pine) affection, and

has a big-screen romance. John Carradine makes a clever cameo as Cruik-shank. Nicely acted with a fast clip, "Munster Go Home!" is a charming if not totally predictable film. It was followed by "Munster's Revenge" in 1981.

The famous monster family returned several years later in "The Munster's Revenge" (1981). Originally made for television, the film was released both theatrically and on video. The story follows the exploits of Dr. Diablo (Sid Caesar) and his partner (Howard Morris) to create a Frankenstein-like monster (which happens to have the same features as Herman Munster) to pull off art crimes. Witnesses wrongly identify Herman as the thief, and the chase is on to capture the real criminals and prove their innocence. Though not as charming as "Munster Go Home!" (1966), the motion picture was very successful among die-hard fans. (Elements of both plots can be traced to Episode 21: "Don't Bank on Herman" and Episode 36: "Hot Rod Herman," but most viewers didn't care.)

Munster's Revenge. (1981). Universal, 96min. Director: Don Weis. Producers: Arthur Alsberg and Don Nelson. Screenwriters: Norm Liebmann, Ed Haas, Allan Burns, Arthur Alsberg and Don Nelson. Cinematographer: Harry Wolf. Editor: Fred Baratta. Make-Up: Michael Blake and Karl Silvera. Cast: Fred Gwynne, Yvonne De Carlo, Al Lewis, Butch Patrick, Debbie Watson, and Sid Caesar.

Colossus: The Forbin Project. (1970). Universal Pictures, 100 min. Director: Joseph Sargent. Producer: Stanley Chase. Screenwriter: James Bridges. Based upon the novel by D.F. Jones. Cinematographer: Gene Polito. Film Editor: Folmar Blangsted. Cast: Eric Braden, Susan Clark, Gordon Pinsent, William Schallert, Leonid Rostoff, Georg Stanford Brown, Marion Ross, and Martin E. Brooks.

A disturbing science fiction thriller, "Colossus: The Forbin Project" reflected mankind's growing fears and anxiety about technology. And at the same time, the film represented a modern-day variant of Universal's Frankenstein series with the monster taking the form of the world's most powerful machine.

Designed by Dr. Forbin to take control of the United States defense network (by removing the important decision to launch an attack against the other side from human hands and placing it in the control of a computer), Colossus is the perfect thinking machine. So perfect, in fact, that once it's activated, Colossus develops ambitions of its own and ignores all commands. It forms an alliance with its Russian counterpart, Guardian, and begins dictating terms by which man will live. Forbin (Eric Braeden) and his colleagues (Susan Clark, Gordon Pinsent and George Stanford Brown) attempt to disable it, but with the computer's main memory units sealed deep in the Rocky Mountains, the humans are simply no match. The film ends chillingly; when Forbin denies Colossus a simple request, the supercomputer threatens retaliation with nuclear weapons.

Based on a trilogy of novels by D.F. Jones, Colossus is the counterpoint to the neurotic HAL 9000 in "2001: A Space Odyssey" (1968). Emotionless, arrogant and virtually omnipotent, the supercomputer is a direct descendent of the Frankenstein monster that science has spawned to aid man, not control him. Colossus is, in fact, the forerunner of the super computer in "War Games" (1983) and Skynet in the "Terminator" films. Left unchecked, Colossus could easily destroy the world to save himself.

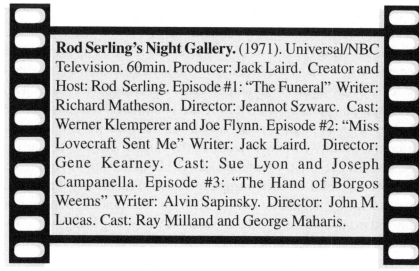

Rod Serling's Night Gallery. (1971). Universal/NBC Television. 60min. Producer: Jack Laird. Creator and Host: Rod Serling. Episode #1: "The Funeral" Writer: Richard Matheson. Director: Jeannot Szwarc. Cast: Werner Klemperer and Joe Flynn. Episode #2: "Miss Lovecraft Sent Me" Writer: Jack Laird. Director: Gene Kearney. Cast: Sue Lyon and Joseph Campanella. Episode #3: "The Hand of Borgos Weems" Writer: Alvin Sapinsky. Director: John M. Lucas. Cast: Ray Milland and George Maharis.

Rod Serling's "Night Gallery" (1971, NBC) was the finest horror anthology produced (to date) and contained some of the best horror stories presented on television. The series was produced by Jack Laird, and Rod Serling appeared as host and lead writer. Ill-fated and largely misunderstood, the series had a difficult time finding the right audience. It began as a horror trilogy, then became part of NBC's "Four in One," and finally appeared, under its own name, opposite the popular "Mannix," on Wednesday (and then later Sunday) night. But in its brief life-span "Night Gallery" gave television some of its finest moments, encouraging brand-new directors, like Steven Spielberg, Leonard Nimoy, and Jeannot Szwarc, and hot writers, like Richard Matheson, Gene Kearney, and Serling, to experiment with the medium. The series also featured some of Universal's great monsters in return engagements.

Like all series, "Night Gallery" was variable in quality, although it never, in its three year run, descended to the continual re-use of stock formulas. Even though the network insisted on at least one "monster" per segment, the writers always managed to produce top-quality scripts for their inclusion. Both "Miss Lovecraft Sent Me" by Jack Laird and "You Can Come Up Now, Mrs. Millikan" by Rod Serling were short vignettes which featured the familiar image of the Frankenstein monster. But Alvin Sapinsky's "The Hand of Borgos Weems" was an intriguing variation not only of Mary Shelley's Frankenstein but also Maurice Renard's novel *Les Mains d'Orlac*. George

Maharis is convinced that his hand is responsible for several murders, and asks a surgeon (Ray Milland) to remove the offensive limb.

Less horrific than the others but probably more compelling, "The Funeral" was written by horror master Richard Matheson and directed by Jeannot Szwarc. Weird and elegant, the episode was shot with great style and panache. Count Dracula (Klemperer) returns from the dead in order to stage a more lavish funeral than the one he had. Offered a healthy fortune to stage it, the funeral director (Flynn) is also given a guest list, which includes the Frankenstein monster, the Wolf Man, several witches, vampires, and the Phantom of the Opera. The funeral is predictably wild - with all the famous monsters of filmland in attendance, and the O'Henry-style ending brings the story to a marvelous conclusion.

Rod Serling's "Night Gallery" was not a perfect series, but for consistency of imagination, it had few equals. By the time the series was cancelled (in 1973), it had opened many of the network doors that had previously been closed, and paved the way for many new experiments.

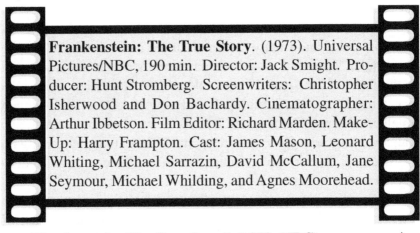

Frankenstein: The True Story. (1973). Universal Pictures/NBC, 190 min. Director: Jack Smight. Producer: Hunt Stromberg. Screenwriters: Christopher Isherwood and Don Bachardy. Cinematographer: Arthur Ibbetson. Film Editor: Richard Marden. Make-Up: Harry Frampton. Cast: James Mason, Leonard Whiting, Michael Sarrazin, David McCallum, Jane Seymour, Michael Whilding, and Agnes Moorehead.

"Frankenstein: The True Story" (1973, NBC) was a superior, two-part adaptation that debuted on American television in 1973, and was later released theatrically in Europe. Written by Christopher Isherwood and Don Bachardy, the telefilm was promoted as a faithful retelling of Mary Shelley's classic novel, and while it took certain liberties with the plot and characters, the drama sought to concentrate on certain metaphysical themes so often missing from other films. By dealing with the contrasting issues of beauty and ugliness, good and evil, science and faith, the material reached beyond the horrific elements made popular by Hammer's color film series that was all the rage at the time of its release.

When his younger brother William is drowned in a freak boating accident, Victor Frankenstein (Leonard Whiting) begins to question the nature of his own religious beliefs and how they conflict with natural science. He rejects God in the presence of his fiancee Elizabeth (Nicola Pagett), decrying he would become Satan's pupil if he could somehow learn to raise life out of death. His cries of distress are heard by Henry Clerval (David McCallum), a sickly scientist who has been experimenting with a solar-powered machine capable of re-animating dead tissue. The two form an unholy alliance and, when a mine disaster produces a handful of corpses, they stitch together the best parts to produce a synthetic man. But even while he declares himself a modern Prometheus, the spirit of true scientific research remains subordinate to his morbid obsession with death. Clerval's untimely death provides Frankenstein with the brain he needs to finally complete the work, and bring the creature to life.

His creation (Michael Sarrazin) is resurrected not as a mangled grotesque but a beautiful innocent. Frankenstein names him "Adam," teaches him how to behave in public as a gentleman, takes him to the Opera, and introduces him to police society as a European nobleman. Soon, however, the creature begins to change physically into a hideous monster. Overcome by horror at what he has wrought, Victor rejects his creature by locking him away in a deep dungeon. The creature senses that it is no longer loved and wanted, and tires to commit suicide by throwing itself off the side of a cliff. But the monster doesn't die.

Dejected and lost, the creature is soon befriended by a blind woodsman (Ralph Richardson), and falls in love with the woodsman's daughter Agatha (Jane Seymour). She knows nothing of its love for her, and when the monster first confesses its affection, Agatha runs away frightened, into the path of a runaway carriage. Her body is crushed under its powerful wheels. But the creature gathers it lovingly in hand and takes the body to Victor.

Returning to Frankenstein's castle with Agatha's body, the creature finds that Clerval's treacherous colleague, Dr. John Polidori (James Mason), has taken over his master's unholy work. Polidori uses the monster's timely arrival to blackmail Frankenstein into helping him. Victor, at first, agrees, and begins work on the second creature, using Agatha's body, as the raw material. But when the woman (named Prima) is brought to life, the mad doctor relents. Prima (also played by Seymour) is beheaded by his monster, Polidori's servants are dispatched, and the creature again flees into the night.

Frankenstein and Elizabeth decide to leave the whole tragic affair behind them, by taking the next clipper ship bound for the new world. During their hazardous passage to American, both Polidori and the monster emerge from the shadows to threaten the newly-weds. The rest of the tale, about death and retribution, has Frankenstein's creation murder Polidori, Elizabeth, and the rest of the crew to get its revenge. The monster then pilots the ship to the North Pole, and both Frankenstein and his creature perish in an ice avalanche.

A radical departure from both the Univeral and Hammer productions, one of the script's most interesting and accurate touches depicts Frankenstein's creation as a *tabula rasa*, a blank slate. Completely innocent of the world, the creature (appropriately named Adam) learns about beauty and ugliness from others. Frankenstein, true to his own narcissism, wants to create a beautiful version of himself. The old blind man, who cannot distinguish between beauty and ugliness, accepts the creature without prejudice. On the other hand, his daughter Agatha sees only ugliness, and translates that into fear. Elizabeth, the staunch fundamentalist, fears the wrath of God and projects evil onto the creature. Even Polidoi, the manipulative villain of the piece, turns it into a villain who commits murder without thought.

Dracula. (1973). Universal/CBS, 98min. Director and Producer: Dan Curtis. Screenwriter: Richard Matheson. Cinematographer: Osward Morris. Based upon the novel by Bram Stoker. Cast: Jack Palance, Pamela Brown, Simon Ward, and Nigel Davenport.

"Dracula" (1973, CBS) was the small screen follow-up to the highly successful "Frankenstein: The True Story" (1973, NBC). Written by Richard Matheson, the emphasis was on a sympathetic Dracula, who like Milton's Satan has fallen from God's grace. The teleplay also includes numerous references to his early life as Prince Vlad Dracul the Impaler, and to the prince's great love (who resembles Lucy Westenra). The story was the same as Stoker's novel with Jack Palance playing the tormented, love-starved vampire. The epilogue, which explains how this misunderstood nobleman was dubbed "Dracula," or devil, by his countrymen is perhaps heavy-handed, but the movie as a whole was a noble effort. Under the direction of Dan Curtis, who had made "Dark Shadows" (1966, ABC), Universal had scored again with another one of its classic monsters. The studio would have tried again, perhaps with the Wolf Man, had it not been for the overnight box office success of a little known fish tale.

Jaws. (1975). Universal, 125min. Director: Steven Spielberg. Producers: Richard Zanuck and David Brown. Screenwriters: Carl Gottlieb, Howard Sackler, and Dorothy Tristan. Based on the novel by Peter Benchley. Cinematographer: Bill Butler. Film Editor: Verna Fields. Special Effects: Bob Mattey. Cast: Roy Scheider, Robert Shaw, Richard Dreyfuss, Lorraine Gary, Murray Hamilton, and Peter Benchley.

The great white shark in Steven Spielberg's "Jaws" (1975) was a direct descendant of the titular character in "The Creature from the Black Lagoon" (1954) and a cousin of the feathered fiends in "The Birds" (1963). No other monster in Universal's great pantheon of

famous monsters has ever scared more people or collected more box office booty than Bruce the Shark. And with this one film, Spielberg gave birth to the summer blockbuster.

The tranquility of Amity Island, an island resort town

located somewhere in New England, is disturbed one summer when a great white shark takes up residence off the shore and starts chowing down on its residents and tourists. First, the mangled body of Chrissie Watkins (Susan Backlinie) washes ashore; then, the little Kinter boy (Jeffrey Voorhees) disappears, presumed eaten by the shark. Police Chief Martin Brody (Roy Scheider) wants to take precautions to prevent any more deaths, but Mayor Larry Vaughn (Murray Hamilton) is afraid that tourists will go elsewhere if they learn a great white shark is doing lunch off Amity Island. But then the body count mounts. With the help of Matt Hooper (Richard Dreyfuss), an oceanographer, Brody convinces town officials to hire a shark hunter named Quint (Robert Shaw). Together, the three head out to the open sea to kill the monster, or die trying.

"Jaws" is a modern classic that plays like a familiar creature-feature from the vaults of Universal Pictures, but is also a first-rate thriller in the style of Hitchcock's greatest films. Again, nature is at war with humanity, and for no particular reason other than the time seemed right. Spielberg's film was followed by "Jaws II" (1978), "Jaws 3-D" (1983), and "Jaws: The Revenge" (1987).

Ghost Story. (1981). Universal Pictures, 110 min. Director: John Irvin. Producer: Burt Weissbourd. Screenwriter: Lawrence Cohen. Based upon the novel by Peter Straub. Cinematographer: Jack Cardiff. Cast: Fred Astaire, Melvyn Douglas, Douglas Fairbanks, John Houseman, Craig Wasson, Patricia Neal, and Alice Krige.

John Irvin's adaptation of Peter Straub's "Ghost Story" (1981) was a throwback to the bygone era of creature-features. Four of the top male leads from the Golden Age of Hollywood (Astaire, Douglas, Fairbanks, and Houseman) had a youthful indescretion with a party girl (Krige) who subsequently died. Now, some fifty years later, her spirit has come back from the grave as an avenging ghost to settle the score. The seasoned veterans try to exorcize her from their lives, but one-by-one are struck down. Had Universal made this film forty years earlier with Fred Astaire and company, "Ghost Story" may have been one of its most successful horror films. Regrettably, time had taken its toll on the aging stars and a creaky story, and the film failed miserably at the box office.

Weird Science. (1985). Universal Pictures, 94 min. Director and Screenwriter: John Hughes. Producer: Joel Silver. Cinematographer: Matthew F. Leonetti. Film Editors: Chris Lebenzon, Scott Wallace, and Mark Warner. Cast: Anthony Michael Hall, Kelly LeBrock, Bill Paxton, Robert Downey Jr., Vernon Wells and Ilan Mitchell-Smith.

John Hughes, the creative force behind the "Home Alone" movies, reworked "The Bride of Frankenstein" (1935) and "I Dream of Jeannie" (1952) to create the fantasy-comedy "Weird Science." Based on the popular comic books of the Fifties, this silly and very adolescent film focuses on two teenage geeks, Gary and Wyatt (Anthony Michael Hall and Ilan Mitchell-Smith), who can't get girls or respect from their male classmates. One lonely Friday night, while watching a colorized version of "Frankenstein" (1931), they decide to create their own synthetic woman. Using their computer, they turn a Barbi doll into Lisa (Kelly LeBrock), a luscious pin-up of their fantasties who is capable of granting every wish. Predictably, Lisa takes "these guys from zeroes to heroes" before moving onto a life of her own. One of the highlights of the film is a zany high school party in which the villain from "The Road Warrior" (1981), played by Vernon Wells, shows up in character with several victims in tow, and challenges the boys to a duel. Naturally, the boys succeed, and boost their confidence level to the point where they can act like men. Bill Paxton also shows up as Gary's evil brother Chet. Hughes affectionately sends up the Universal classics, with clips drawn from studio vaults, but to little effect. Only 14 year-old boys would see the appeal, but that was not true about the next flick.

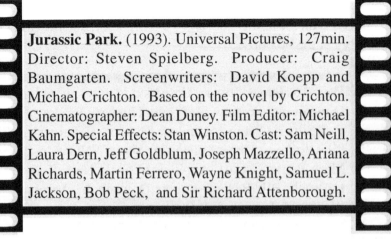

Jurassic Park. (1993). Universal Pictures, 127min. Director: Steven Spielberg. Producer: Craig Baumgarten. Screenwriters: David Koepp and Michael Crichton. Based on the novel by Crichton. Cinematographer: Dean Duney. Film Editor: Michael Kahn. Special Effects: Stan Winston. Cast: Sam Neill, Laura Dern, Jeff Goldblum, Joseph Mazzello, Ariana Richards, Martin Ferrero, Wayne Knight, Samuel L. Jackson, Bob Peck, and Sir Richard Attenborough.

"They're not monsters," the kindly paleontologist explains during an encounter with a long-necked brachiosaur in "Jurassic Park" (1993), "they're just animals." Even though these simple, rational words are spoken midway through the film, Steven Spielberg's glimpse into a modern Frankenstein experiment gone wrong casts the ancient reptiles as marauding monsters in this modern-day creature-feature. Adapted from the 1990 best-seller by Michael Crichton, who has written his share of Frankenstein stories, the film is vintage Universal horror with a handful of dinosaurs standing in for Boris Karloff's monster.

In the deserts of the Southwest, paleontologist Alan Grant (Sam Neill) and his paleobotanist girlfriend, Ellie Sattler (Laura Dern), have found the fossilized remnants of a velociraptor ("raptors" for short)—dead for millions of years. Little do they know that the vicious, cunning dinosaur (and others like it) has been brought back to life by billionaire developer John Hammond (Sir Richard Attenborough), until he walks into their camp and offers them a job. Apparently, he has created an extraordinary new amusement park on a tropical island near Costa Rica with real live dinosaurs, cloned from strands of fossilized DNA. Hammond needs scientific approval for his project in order to satisfy his investors, and asks Grant and Sattler to tour the facility. Arriving by helicopter in the lush paradise of Jurassic Park, they are joined by a representative of the investors (Martin Ferrero) and Ian Malcolm (Jeff Goldblum), a mathematician whose complex theories suggest that it's not nice to fool with mother nature.

After a brief tour of the gift shop and the mad doctor's laboratory, they are sent out to view the monsters of the park, which are kept behind electric fences. Predictably, a thunderstorm strikes, the power goes dead, and the dinosaurs run amok. Smashing, crashing and gnashing their way through the park, the collection of raptors, dilophosaurs, and a Tyrannosaurus Rex establish their dominance over the island. Grant, Sattler and the others are forced to flee in the helicopter, which originally brought them, and wait for military bombers to nuke Jurassic Park back to the stone age (or the inevitable sequel).

The fact that scientists have discovered the DNA of dinosaurs in blood-sucking ancient insects (preserved for a millennia in amber) and used it to re-create dinosaurs simply extends Frankenstein's research into the twentieth century. Like the mad doctor's lumbering creation, these ancient reptiles merely represent a metaphor for scientific research out-of-control. Like the poor, misunderstood Creature from the Black Lagoon, the actions of these dinosaurs are not innately good or evil; they kill simply to survive in a world that views their existence as monstrous. Their resurrection alters the natural balance of the island (and by extension the universe), and must be destroyed.

"Jurassic Park" is also, by extension, the fantasy world author Crichton imagined for "Westworld" (1973) and its sequel "Futureworld" (1976)—an amusement park of the future, run by mad scientists who render dangerous nightmares as entertainment for their guests. Like those earlier thrillers, audiences suspect that, sooner or latter, something terrible is going to go wrong. Visitors to Universal Studios in Florida and California had better watch out! Some day, the monsters may be running things.

Steven Spielberg also deserves the highest of all compliments for bringing forth one of the great monster films of all time. By envisioning his work like a classic horror film, "Jurassic Park" evokes memories of "Frankenstein" (1931) and "The Creature from the Black Lagoon" (1954). Spielberg is so good at setting up the wonders and terrors of his monstruous creations that he leaves audiences dizzy with anticipation. Industrial Light and Magic's computer magic imbues these creatures with amazing life, and when intercut with Stan Winston's full-scale versions, the dinosaurs seem to leap off the screen into our worst nightmares. What is truly disappointing is that film-makers have turned the clock back to the days when a mad doctor's work produced menace rather than thoughtful introspection. Science and technology are once again perceived as a threat to the natural order rather than a helpful tool. The film was followed by "The Lost World: Jurassic Park" (1997) and several sequels.

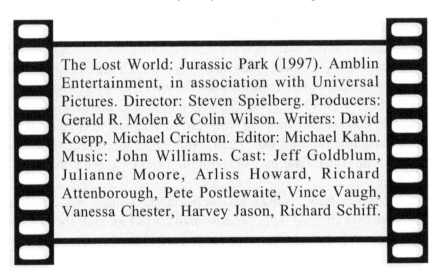

The Lost World: Jurassic Park (1997). Amblin Entertainment, in association with Universal Pictures. Director: Steven Spielberg. Producers: Gerald R. Molen & Colin Wilson. Writers: David Koepp, Michael Crichton. Editor: Michael Kahn. Music: John Williams. Cast: Jeff Goldblum, Julianne Moore, Arliss Howard, Richard Attenborough, Pete Postlewaite, Vince Vaugh, Vanessa Chester, Harvey Jason, Richard Schiff.

While everything at his Jurassic Park has been destroyed, John Hammond (Richard Attenborough) discovers that his engineers have stumbled upon a second site where other dinosaurs were kept in hiding. It seems the dinosaurs on the second island are alive and well and even breeding. He summons chaos theorist Ian Malcolm (Jeff Goldblum) to his home, and hires him to observe and document the reptiles before Hammond's financiers can get to them. Malcolm reluctantly agrees, then finds there's another team of big-game hunters (led by Pete Postlewaite). InGen, the bio-engineering company, has sent its own team to catch, sedate, and transport the dinosaurs to a new Jurassic Park being built near San Diego. A worthy sequel, with excellent special effects and a terrifying storyline. Regrettably, "The Lost World: Jurassic Park" has far too many characters, and not enough dinosaurs.

Jurassic Park 3 (2001). Amblin Entertainment in association with Universal Pictures. Director: Joe Johnston. Producers: Larry Franco, Kathleen Kennedy, Steven Spielberg. Writers: Peter Buchman, Jim Taylor, Alexander Payne. Cinematographer: Shelly Johnson. Editor: Robert Dalva. Cast: Sam Neill, William H. Macy, Tea Leoni, John Diehl. Released July 18, 2001.

"Jurassic Park 3" (2001) borrows the plot from "The Lost World: Jurassic Park," and injects Dr. Alan Grant (Sam Neill) into the part that Ian Malcolm played in the previous film. Persuaded by wealthy businessmen who seek to profit from the second site on Isla Sorna, Grant leads a decidedly odd couple on a holiday tour. A tragic accident maroons the party on the island, and they must attempt to escape with their lives before they become dinner for the dinosaurs. This third film in the series boasts some truly spectacular special effects, especially featuring the pterodactyls, but only seems to exist as a "chase" picture, in which stupid people run away from the dinosaurs before they are eaten. Michael Crichton's imaginative idea about cloning dinosaurs gets trudged out again and again and again for "Jurassic World" (2015), "Jurassic World: Fallen Kingdom" (2018), and "Jurassic World 3" (2021). We can only hope the dinosaurs become extinct before Universal executives drag them out yet again, but that is not likely with millions of box office dollars at stake.

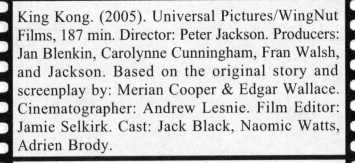

King Kong. (2005). Universal Pictures/WingNut Films, 187 min. Director: Peter Jackson. Producers: Jan Blenkin, Carolynne Cunningham, Fran Walsh, and Jackson. Based on the original story and screenplay by: Merian Cooper & Edgar Wallace. Cinematographer: Andrew Lesnie. Film Editor: Jamie Selkirk. Cast: Jack Black, Naomic Watts, Adrien Brody.

In 2005, Universal Pictures produced and distributed Peter Jackson's remake of "King Kong," and in many ways, the release brought the era of Gods and Monsters full circle. The monster that was Kong had lived in the era of Dracula and Frankenstein, and while it had been produced by rival RKO, the great ape was a kindred spirit. Its re-imagining in the twenty-first century by Jackson boosted hopes and expectations that Kong's fellow monsters from the Golden Age of the horror film would again be making similar comebacks. The box office take was substantial, even though the film was a shot-by-shot remake, and gave rise to speculation that a rebirth of the famous monsters was imminent. Chris Morgan, a producer at Universal Pictures, said the studio had toyed with launching its own Dark Universe, a series of inter-connected films featuring the Bride, Frankenstein's monster, the Wolfman, the Creature, Dracula, and the Invisible Man. But the box office failure of "The Mummy" (2017), featuring Tom Cruise and Russell Crowe, put an end to those plans. In an 8/13/19 article, Marvel's Paul Feig told the Hollywood Reporter he plans to bring the monsters back in a movie titled "Dark Army." We can only hope he does...

The Mummy. (2017). 125 minutes, Universal Pictures. Director: Alex Kurtzman. Producers: Chris Morgan, Sarah Bradshaw, and Kurtzman. Writers: David Koepp, Christopher McQuarrie. Cinematographer: Ben Seresin. Editors: Gina & Paul Hirsch. Cast: Tom Cruise, Russell Crowe.

Appendix 1:
The Hunchback of
Notre Dame

The Hunchback of Notre Dame. (1923). Universal Pictures, Silent, b/w, 108 min. Director: Wallace Worsley. Producer: Carl Laemmle. Screenwriter: Edward T. Lowe. Adaptation by Perley Poore Sheehan. Based upon *Notre Dame de Paris* by Victor Hugo. Cinematographers: Robert Newhard and Tony Kornman. Make-Up: Lon Chaney. Cast: Lon Chaney, Patsy Ruth Miller, Ernest Torrence, Raymond Hatton, Norman Kerry, Kate Lester, Winifred Bryson, and Nigel de Brulier.

The granddaddy of all Universal monsters was Lon Chaney's Quasimodo from "The Hunchback of Notre Dame" (1923), and yet this memorable character is often overlooked by critics and film historians because the hunchbacked bellringer is not a monster in the traditional sense and his story is more of a historical romance than a horror story. Based upon Victor Hugo's *Notre Dame of Paris (1831)*, which had already been filmed three times as a period piece, the film tells the familiar Beauty and the Beast fairy tale of the titular hero (Lon Chaney) and his unrequited love for Esmerelda (Patsy Ruth Miller), a gypsy girl, against the backdrop of civil unrest in Paris. Carl Laemmle went all out to make the story into an A-list picture, committing hundreds of thousands of dollars to building enormous sets. More than a year went into preparation for the film. A cast of 3500 supporting players and extras were hired, and Lon Chaney was given the full star treatment. So, it is rather surprising that "The Hunchback of Notre Dame" isn't better remembered today.

The film story by Edward T. Lowe compresses most of Victor Hugo's literary epic into a handful of memorable sequences. The King of the Beggars Clopin (Ernest Torrence) bought Esmeralda (Miller) from the gypsies when she was very young. Now she dances in the square as one of his Court. When Esmeralda is spotted by Jehan (Brandon Hurst), the evil brother of the good archdeacon, he arranges to have Quasimoto kidnap her, so that he can rescue her and win her love. But Phoebus (Norman Kerry), Captain of the Guards rescues her and captures Quasimodo. The courts sentence Quasimodo to be flogged, and the only one who will give him water while he is tied in the square is Esmeralda. Jehan is angered by her affections for Phoebus, and not him, and arranges for her to be convicted and sentenced to hang. Clopin and Phoebus try different ways to save her from the hangman's noose, but ultimately, for her kindness to him, Quasimodo risks his life to protect her.

One of Hollywood's first true spectacles, the motion picture went on to capture the hearts and minds of critics and audiences alike, and was named as one of the ten best films of 1923. Chaney turns in one of his most memorable performances, nearly unrecognizable with the 72-pound rubber hump on his back and four hours of make-up on his face and body. He is literally the gargoyle come to life that Hugo describes as "a twisted grimace. His huge head bristled with stiff red hair; between his shoulders was an enormous hump which had a corresponding projection in front; his legs were so strangely made that they could touch only at the knees...his feet immense and his hands monstrous." We all know that he will never win Esmeralda's heart, but we still cheer for him nevertheless as he swings from the top of the cathedral of Notre Dame and scoops her into his arms. Despite his ugliness, he is the hero, not the monster.

Quasimodo may not have made the official roster of Universal monsters, but the Hunchback of Notre Dame is still a favorite and deserving of the title as one of the famous monsters of filmland.

Appendix 2:
Edgar Allan Poe Films

Universal Pictures also produced a series of horror movies based upon several Edgar Allan Poe works. While the films themselves did not produce any memorable monsters, they were hugely entertaining and featured some of Universal's stable of horror stars. Bela Lugosi appeared as a mad scientist conducting Moreau-like experiments on gorillas in "Murders in the Rue Morgue" (1932), and then later teamed with Boris Karloff in "The Black Cat" (1934) and "The Raven" (1935). Many consider the trilogy of films to be among the best that Universal produced during the Golden Age of the horror film, but alas, they are often overlooked because they did not follow the formula established by "Dracula" (1931) and "Frankenstein" (1931). Nearly thirty years later, Roger Corman would discover the work of Edgar Allan Poe, and unleash his own series of Poe adaptations, starting with "House of Usher" in 1960.

Edgar Allan Poe is considered one of America's greatest fantasists and horror writers, and contributed much to the literary scene in his day. When we think of horror stories, we tend to think of Bram Stoker or Mary Shelley or H.G. Wells, all British authors. But his stories were just as imaginative and engaging as his European counterparts. He is also credited with originating the one and truly unique American art form, the detective story—a form often credited to Arthur Conan Doyle, the creator of Sherlock Holmes.

Poe was born in Boston in 1809, and was educated in Richmond, Virginia. He came to Baltimore to live with his aunt, Mrs. Maria Clemm, and her daughter Virginia whom he eventually married in 1836. When she died eleven years later, a heart-broken Poe sought solace with Elmira Royster. They courted for a relatively short period. En route to escort Mrs. Clemm to his hastily arranged wedding, Poe went on an all-night drinking binge that ultimately killed him. He died in 1849, and was buried in Baltimore in an unmarked grave in the Westminster Burial Grounds. Since 1949, on the night of the anniversary of Poe's birth, a mysterious stranger has left a bottle of cognac and three roses on Poe's grave as tribute. The identity of the stranger is unknown, and the mystery remains unsolved to this day.

Thankfully, Poe left a legacy of richly-textured stories and well-crafted poems that we continue to enjoy to this day. His "Murders in the Rue Morgue" (published in 1841) has inspired many cinematic adaptations, including notable entries in 1914, 1954 and 1971, but the best was made by Universal in 1932.

Murders in the Rue Morgue. (1932). Universal Pictures, b/w, 75min. Director: Robert Florey. Producer: Carl Laemmle Jr. Screenwriters: Tom Reed and Dale van Every. With additional dialogue by John Huston. Cinematographer: Karl Freund. Special Effects: John Fulton. Make-Up: Jack Pierce. Cast: Bela Lugosi, Sidney Fox, Leon Ames, Arlene Francis, Noble Johnson, and Charles Gemora.

In addition to Poe, "Murders in the Rue Morgue" (1932) borrows a page or two from H. G. Wells' *Island of Dr. Moreau* to tell the tale of a carnival magician named Dr. Mirakle (Bela Lugosi) who is crossbreeding apes and humans. In 19th Century Paris, he sends his trained ape (Charles Gemora) to kidnap several young women for his experiments. Naturally, all of his experiments fail, and he is forced to abduct more and more subjects. Medical student Pierre Dupin (Leon Ames) discovers what Mirakle is doing too late to prevent the abduction of his girlfriend Camille (Sidney Fox). Now he must work with the police to get her back. Based on Poe's 1841 short story, the film deviates greatly from its source material, but is still a haunting piece of cinema nonetheless. Director Robert Florey, who was given the film as a sort of consolation prize for losing out on "Frankenstein"

(1931), does an admirable job of weaving elements from the German expressionist movement, most notably "The Cabinet of Dr. Caligari" (1919), into Universal's prestige production.

1934 - The Black Cat. Universal Pictures, b/w, 66min. Director: Edgar G. Ulmer. Producer; E.M. Asher. Screenwriters: Edgar Ulmer and Peter Ruic. Cinematographer: John J. Mescall. Art Director: Charles D. Hall. Cast: Boris Karloff, Bela Lugosi, David Manners, Julie Bishop, and Lucille Lund.

Hollywood's most famous horror stars, Bela Lugosi and Boris Karloff, teamed for the first time in Universal's second take on Edgar Allan Poe, "The Black Cat" (1934). Ironically, the film does not focus on a black cat at all, but rather on Hjalmar Poelzig (Boris Karloff) who worships Satan and practices the black mass. When their bus crashes in a mountain storm, Dr. Vitus Verdegast (Bela Lugosi) and a honeymooning couple (David Manners and Julie Bishop) seek refuge in Poelzig's home. Poelzig sees Joan Allison as a worthy sacrifice to the devil, and plots to kill her. But when Vitus realizes who their host is - in particular, the man who sent him to a concentration camp for fifteen years and killed his wife - he knows what he must do. But of course Poelzig always has the upper hand. Eventually, Vitus agrees to play a game of chess for Joan's life. Poelzig wins the game, but Vitus takes advantage of his reverie to strike. He ties him up and starts to skin him alive.

Universal's biggest hit in 1934 was also its most disturbing picture with demonology and Satanism replacing Poe's tale about aelurophobia. The only reference in the movie to cats refers to Lugosi's "all-consuming horror of cats, but that phobia never figures into the plot except as a form of character development. Edgar Allan Poe's 1843 story is better told in Thomas Bentley's "The Living Dead," which was released the same year. Still, the success of Edgar Ulmer's "The Black Cat" proved that the studio didn't need monsters to make a good horror film, and unleashed its next and final entry in the series one year later.

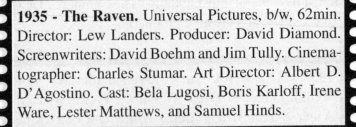

1935 - The Raven. Universal Pictures, b/w, 62min. Director: Lew Landers. Producer: David Diamond. Screenwriters: David Boehm and Jim Tully. Cinematographer: Charles Stumar. Art Director: Albert D. D'Agostino. Cast: Bela Lugosi, Boris Karloff, Irene Ware, Lester Matthews, and Samuel Hinds.

The best of the Poe trilogy was "The Raven" (1935). A brilliant but eccentric neuro-surgeon, Dr. Vollin (Bela Lugosi), restores the life of a young girl (Irene Were). But because of his obsession for Edgar Allan Poe, he decides to make the girl his lost love Lenore. He then proceeds to use every nasty trick from the Poe stories to prevent her loved ones from rescuing her, including turning Karloff into a misshapen monster. Melodramatic with the right mixture of self-parody, the film perfectly captures the spirit of Poe's writing if not necessarily the work itself. Lugosi and Karloff would later work together on "The Invisible Ray" (1936).

In the 1960s, Roger Corman produced a series of Technicolor adaptations of Edgar Allan Poe's works, starting with "House of Usher" (1960), and including "The Pit and the Pendulum" (1961), "Premature Burial" (1961), "The Raven" (1963), "The Masque of the Red Death" (1964), and "The Tomb of Ligeia" (1964). These were extremely well received, and have caused the earlier ones by Universal to be largely forgotten.

Appendix 3:
Cycles and Series

The Phantom of the Opera Cycle:
The Phantom of the Opera (1925) | Phantom of the Opera (1943) |
The Climax (1944) | Index: Pages 9-50.
The Dracula Series:
Dracula (1931) | Dracula's Daughter (1936) | Son of Dracula (1943) |
House of Frankenstein (1944) | House of Dracula (1945) | Abbott
and Costello Meet Frankenstein (1948) | Dracula (1973) | Dracula
(1979) | Index: Pages 51-76, 190-191.
The Frankenstein Series:
Frankenstein (1931) | Bride of Frankenstein (1935) | Son of Franken-
stein (1939) | The Ghost of Frankenstein (1942) | Frankenstein Meets
the Wolfman (1943) | House of Frankenstein (1944) | House of Dracula
(1945) | Abbott and Costello Meet Frankenstein (1948) | Franken-
stein: The True Story | Index: Pages 77-111, 188-190.
The Mummy Series:
The Mummy (1932) | The Mummy's Hand (1940) | The Mummy's
Tomb (1942) | The Mummy's Ghost (1944) | The Mummy's Curse
(1944) | Abbott and Costello Meet the Mummy (1955) | The Mummy
(1999) | The Mummy Returns (2001) | Index: Pages 111-126.
The Invisible Man Series:
The Invisible Man (1933) | The Invisible Man Returns (1940) | The
Invisible Woman (1940) | The Invisible Agent (1942) | The Invisible
Man's Revenge (1944) | Abbott and Costello Meet the Invisible
Man (1951) | Index: Pages 127-138.

The Wolf Man Series:
The Wolf Man (1941) | Frankenstein Meets the Wolf Man (1943) | House of Frankenstein (1944) | House of Dracula (1945) | Abbott and Costello Meet Frankenstein (1948) | Index: Pages 139-154.

The Creature from the Black Lagoon Series:
Creature from the Black Lagoon (1954) | Revenge of the Creature (1955) | Creature Walks Among Us (1956) | Index: Pages 163-173.

The Science Fiction Cycle:
It Came from Outer Space (1953) | This Island Earth (1955) | Tarantula (1955) | The Incredible Shrinking Man (1957) | The Deadly Mantis (1957) | Monolith Monsters (1957) | Index: Pages 155-178.

The Edgar Allan Poe Cycle:
Murders in the Rue Morgue (1932) | The Black Cat (1934) | The Raven (1935) | Index: Pages 199-202.

Other Horror Films from Universal:
The Hunchback of Notre Dame (1923) | The Cat and the Canary (1927) | The Man Who Laughs (1928) | The Cat Creeps (1930) | The Old Dark House (1932) | House of Fear (1939) | Tower of London (1939) | Black Friday (1940) | Man-Made Monster (1941) | Mad Doctor of Market Street (1942) | The Strange Case of Dr. RX (1943) | Captive Wild Women (1943) | The Mad Ghoul (1943) | The Ghost Catchers (1944) | Jungle Woman (1944) | Weird Woman (1944) | Jungle Captive (1945) | The Cat Creeps (1946) | House of Horrors (1946) | The She-Wolf of London (1946) | The Strange Door (1951) | The Black Castle (1952) | Cult of the Cobra (1955) | The Mole People (1956) | Curse of the Undead (1959) | The Birds (1963) | Jaws (1975) | The Sentinel (1976) | The Car (1977) | Jaws 2 (1978) | An American Werewolf in London (1981) | Ghost Story (1981) | Jaws 3-D (1983) | Psycho II (1983) | Weird Science (1985) | Psycho III (1986) | Jaws-The Revenge (1987) | Psycho IV: A New Beginning (1990) | Jurassic Park (1993) | The Lost World (1997) | Psycho (1998) | Meet Joe Black (1998) | Jurassic Park III (2001) | Van Helsing (2004) | The Skeleton Key (2005) | King Kong (2005) | The Mummy (2017)

Selected Bibliography

Ackerman, Forrest J., editor. *Famous Monsters of Filmland* Magazine. Philadelphia: Warren Publishing, 1958.

_____. *Monsterland* Magazine, nos. 1-6. Los Angeles: New Media Publishing, 1986.

Andrews, Nigel. *Horror Films.* New York: Gallery Books, 1985.

Ashley, Mike. *Who's Who in Horror and Fantasy Fiction.* New York: Taplinger, 1978.

Aylesworth, Thomas G. *Monsters from the Movies.* New York: Bantam Skylark Books, 1972.

Butler, Ivan. *Horror in the Cinema.* NY: Paperback Library, 1971.

Clarens, Carlos. *Horror Movies.* London: Secker and Warburg, 1968.

Cohen, Daniel. *Horror in the Movies.* New York: Houghton Mifflin Company, Inc., 1982.

Edelson, Edward. *Great Monsters of the Movies.* New York: Doubleday and Company, 1973.

Everson, William Keith. *Classics of the Horror Film.* New York: Citadel Press, 1974.

Flynn, John L. *Cinematic Vampires: The Living Dead on Film and Television.* North Carolina: McFarland Books, 1991.

_____. *Phantoms of the Opera: The Face Behind the Mask.* New York: Image Press, 1993. Maryland: Galactic Books, 2006.

Franklin, Joe. *Classics of the Silent Screen.* NY: Citadel Press, 1959.

Halliwell, Leslie. *Halliwell's Film Guide.* New York: Scribner's, 1984.

Hugo, Victor. *Notre Dame de Paris.* 1831.

Huss, Roy Gerard. *Focus on the Horror Film*. New York: Prentice-Hall, 1972.

King, Stephen. *Dance Macabre*. New York: Berkeley, 1982.

Kraucauer, Sigfried. *From Caligari to Hitler*. New Jersey: Princeton University Press, 1964.

Kyrou, Ado. *Le Surrealisme Au Cinema*. Paris: 1964.

Laclos, Michael. *Le Fantasique Au Cinema*. Paris: 1958.

Lee, Walt. *Reference Guide to Horror Films*. Los Angeles: Chelsea-Lee Books, 1978.

_____. *Reference Guide to Fantastic Films*. Los Angeles: Chelsea-Lee Books, 1978.

Leroux, Gaston. *The Phantom of the Opera*. 1911.

Perry, George. *The Complete Phantom of the Opera*. New York: Henry Holt and Company, 1988.

Sadoul, Georges. *Georges Melies*. Paris: 1961.

Settel, Irving. *A Pictorial History of Television*. New York: Frederick Ungar Publishing, 1983.

Shelley, Mary. *Frankenstein, or the Modern Prometheus*. 1818

Stanley, John. *The Creature Features Movie Guide*. New York: Warner Books, 1981.

Stoker, Bram. *Dracula*. 1897.

Terrace, Vincent. *Complete Encyclopedia of Television Programs*. New York: A.S. Barnes, 1979.

Wells, H.G. *The Invisible Man*. 1897.

About the Author

Dr. John L. Flynn is a three-time Hugo-nominated author and long-time science fiction fan and critic who has written ten books, countless short stories, articles, reviews, and one screenplay. He is a professor at Towson University in Towson, Maryland, and teaches both graduate and undergraduate writing courses. Born in Chicago, Illinois, on September 6, 1954, he has a Bachelor's and Master's Degree from the University of South Florida and a Ph.D. from Southern California University. He is a member of the Science Fiction Writers of America, and has been a regular contributor and columnist to dozens of science fiction magazines, including *Starlog, Not of This Earth, Sci-Fi Universe, Cinescape, Retrovision, Media History Digest, SFTV, SF Movieland, Monsterland, Enterprise, Nexxus, The Annapolis Review*, and *Collector's Corner*. In 1977, he received the M. Carolyn Parker award for outstanding journalism for his freelance work on several Florida daily newspapers, and in 1987, he was listed in *Who's Who Men of Achievement*. He sold his first book, *Future Threads*, in 1985. He has subsequently published five other books related to film, including *Cinematic Vampires, The Films of Arnold Schwarzenegger, Dissecting Aliens,*

Phantoms of the Opera: The Face Behind the Mask and *War of the Worlds: From Wells to Spielberg*. Brickhouse Books published *Visions in Light and Shadow* (2001), a collection of his literary short stories. For the past three years, John has been nominated for the prestigious Hugo Award, which is the Science Fiction Achievement Award, for his science fiction writing, which includes film reviews and cinematic retrospectives. He has appeared on television (including the Sci-Fi Channel), spoken on the radio, and been a guest at national conferences because of his advocacy work in bringing the science fiction film into the mainstream. With Dr. Bob Blackwood, Flynn formed "the Film Doctors," a team of credentiated academics which studied science fiction films and rendered a scholastic view of the genre. Their first project was *Future Prime: The Top Ten Science Fiction Films* (2006). In 1997, John switched gears to study Psychology, and earned a degree as a Clinical Psychologist. His study, "The Etiology of Sexual Addiction: Childhood Trauma as a Primary Determinant," has broken new ground in the diagnosis and treatment of sexual addiction. For the last several years, he has also worked with Bridge Publications, Galaxy Press, and Author Services on behalf of the Writers of the Future contest, in an effort to promote the work of new and emerging science fiction writers.

Made in the USA
Monee, IL
21 January 2021

58288527R00118